Amazing Win, Amazing Loss
Miss America Living Happily, EVEN After

Angela Perez Baraquio

Amazing Win, Amazing Loss
Miss America Living Happily, EVEN After
APB Publishing
c/o Isle Entertainment, Inc.
9852 W Katella Ave. #282
Anaheim, CA 92804

Cover Design by Howard John Design
Cover Photo by Naomi Masina

Printed in the United States of America
2014—First Trade Paperback Edition

ISBN-10: 0990359409
ISBN-13: 978-0-9903594-0-1

FROM THE AUTHOR

For years, people have asked me to write a book or a memoir about my experience as the first Asian Miss America. While I kept decades of journals and considered writing a book fourteen years ago, only now, do I feel compelled to put my life's most defining moments and reflections on paper.

With suitcases of memories, the process of unpacking the flurry of emotions has been all at once eye-opening, cathartic, and sometimes painful—but it was necessary. Perhaps I was placed in this notable position for a time such as this; to share my story and how it has unfolded. My reasons for writing are to touch and inspire others. To change lives for the better. Whether or not you agree with certain things in this book, it's *my* truth, with all the raw emotions that come with it. I bare my soul in this book for you, in hopes that you will gain some insight, solace, or comfort in the fact that you are not alone. Please take what helps you, and leave the rest.

Though my story is hardly over, my past is worth telling. As my roles have evolved, so has my outlook and the way I live my life. Today I am a wife, a mother of four, a motivational speaker, television host, a business professional, teacher and school administrator. As I approach forty, I view things with a different perspective than in my youth. Some incidents that seemed so important back then are so trivial now, but were still defining.

My story has a universal message but my focus is mainly young adults, especially women, seeking their place in this world and learning how to live their life with faith and purpose.

In addition to three sons, I have one daughter, my youngest, Keilah. I write with her in mind, as one day she will grow up to be a young lady. This book chronicles my journey before, during and after my time as Miss America, and depicts my evolution from childhood through motherhood.

Some of you might ask, *Who becomes Miss America and what happens after she's crowned?* I thought the same thing when I was competing. I devoured books and articles about former titleholders to "get in their head" and achieve their winning mindset. Many see Miss America as a polished woman, but no one sees the doubts, fears, and pageant losses she endures before her victory.

I will take you through the roller coaster of emotions and self-talk with which I coached myself. I wish I knew then what I know now! The tips and thought processes in this book are helpful to anyone who wants to win at

Life. Winning is never easy. In fact, it's losing that helps one appreciate success. While every winner is different, I can only share my own personal experience to lend insight to these questions.

Depending on which life stage you are in, maybe, you'll find answers right away for parallels in your life, or perhaps you will read the following words now in bewilderment and detachment, but stumble across them later in life when you really need the insight from someone who's been where you have yet to go. As a teacher in the classroom, I've heard that fourth graders are "rock stars" to third graders. I may not be a rock star, but I've already gone down that rocky path, and have acquired hard-earned wisdom to share so you can become your best self and shatter self-inflicted limitations.

Like yours, my journey also contains the highest of highs and the lowest of lows. Just as a trained athlete endures victories and defeats, I tackled the preparation for my biggest win—and biggest loss—in the public eye, with relentless perseverance. I hope my story helps you tackle life and persevere as well, no matter what you are going through. Remember that even in your darkest hours, you are *never* alone. Faith is what kept me going when I felt like I couldn't go on. When it seemed like everyone abandoned me, God was always beside me, loving me unconditionally. I was given the strength to move on even when I had fallen repeatedly.

Even Jesus cried, died, and still rose again. And so it is with me and all my fellow ladies out there: Women have so much inner strength, wisdom, beauty, and power, but many of us are unaware of or are afraid to embrace our God-given graces. Because women are the backbone of society, we must stand together, respect our sisters, and support one another.

Many coaches and mentors have taught me invaluable lessons. I've learned that a great coach brings out the best in you to reach heights you never thought possible. A mentor has already achieved the success you are trying to attain. I have had great coaches and mentors. Both are beneficial. To each of them, I am forever grateful.

Because I always hoped it *could* be, my life has been a fairy tale in many ways, with all the excitement, beauty, glamour, and dreams that have come true. However, like any fairy tale, my story is not without twists, turns, terror, and demons. I have been blessed with incredible moments, but I've also experienced unspeakable tragedies. Yet, I emerged with greater compassion and empathy for others in despair.

I understand now that I was able to rise above extreme circumstances by relying on my faith, family, and friends—the basis and foundation of my character. Each setback and loss has been a jewel in my crown. My struggles have helped shape the person I am today and I am thankful for those hard times—they did not weaken me, they made me strong.

If you've ever felt like you wanted to stand out, if you felt like you weren't being heard; if you wished you had a stronger voice; if you've lived with unfulfilled dreams, if you've lost a loved one, questioned your life and faith; or daydreamed about how different things might be if you won a national and internationally recognized title, this book is especially for you. The road ahead won't be easy, but it's worth traveling.

In many ways, I am just like you. I grew up an ordinary girl and came from humble beginnings, but somehow, by the grace of God, I've been fortunate to live an *extraordinary* life, which is a continuous work in progress.

Even as a child, I had an inexplicable, burning desire to succeed, make a difference in my community, and leave a grand legacy. I wanted to stop struggling and spend my time creating a brighter future for my family and me. Perhaps you feel the same way.

Please don't take my willingness to go public with my story for the first time as boasting in any way because I only boast in the Lord, and attribute every success I have in Him. With God, all things are possible.

Recent events have been a striking reminder that time is one's greatest commodity. I have lost many loved ones in a few short months and have come to the painful realization that time waits for no one. I remember being a high school senior like it was yesterday, and in the blink of an eye, my class is celebrating its twenty-year reunion.

It's hard to believe that it has already been more than a decade since I was crowned Miss Hawai'i, and then, Miss America, an honor that less than one hundred women in the history of the world have achieved. To say I have been a former titleholder who made history is pretty cool, and I am deeply humbled. Where has the time gone?

It has taken me years to process the whirlwind that was Miss America. Now that I am out of the eye of the storm, I'm ready to share my story with all the beauty, tragedy, and raw intensity of a traditional fairy tale. Even in fairy tales, the plot often twists unexpectedly, but there's always a glimmer of hope. After experiencing great adversity and loss, I now see that my mother was right. By following God's will, I can still live happily, EVEN after. I wish the same for you. And hopefully, you and I will have many more years ahead of us.

Life is a journey, not a destination, and it certainly won't slow down for anyone. So let's make the best of today—the first day of the rest of our lives. Today, my imperfect life works for me. I continue to thrive day by day, moment by moment.

By the time you finish this book, may you have a heightened sense of self-discovery and awareness, a realization of your unlimited potential, and an inspiration to share your talents with the world.

All my Love,
Angela

INTRODUCTION

I believe that deep inside every successful person, every accomplished entrepreneur and every celebrated professional, there is a child. A child who believes that dreams, like fairy tales, can come true—not adult goals, but innocent, *childhood* dreams. The thing is, most do not know how to go after their dreams or have the courage to pursue them. My dreams were innocent. I never wanted to be Miss America because I never thought it was possible and no winner ever looked like me. Instead, I felt the best way I knew I could make a difference every day was to be a teacher.

I don't know many women who hold to the fact that their life will resemble anything close to a fairy tale. I sure didn't, but I hoped for love and happiness, despite dire circumstances, with all my heart. I came from a family of strong women (with seven girls and three boys in my nuclear family). I grew up watching Disney movies and reading fairy tales. While I didn't really buy into the whole "getting rescued by a prince" thing, I definitely longed for true love. And of course, I loved when everyone lived happily ever after. I learned from a very young age that if I wanted something done, I had to do it myself. I wasn't about to wait for some guy to save me. Girl power, all the way!

Mama was strict and exacting, but she had a lighter side, too. She passed down her love of Disney movies to me at a young age. I never understood why she held them so close to her heart until much later. As a little girl, I too, fell in love with those tales because there was always a happy ending. But in real life, mine was not always easy or happy. I needed something to keep me positive, and those stories helped me believe that no matter your circumstances, dreams can come true.

In college, I had an entertainment center decked out with Disney characters and figurines. One day, my mom surveyed my fairy tale paraphernalia and smiled. "Angie, I love all those stories about Cinderella and Snow White. But you know, if you obey God and follow His Will, your life will be better than any fairy tale." She left the room with those words dangling in midair. I pondered that statement, but just couldn't imagine my life actually surpassing Disney's "happily ever after."

Five years later, I was crowned Miss America 2001, and became the first Asian and first teacher to receive the coveted title in the pageant's then eighty-year history. My mother's words had proven prophetic. And the blessings that followed exceeded my wildest imagination.

This will always be *my* story, a story of race, of identity, faith, character, and ambition. It's a tale of American girlhood, of dieting and mirror gazing, of false eyelashes, high heels and inside-out beauty. It's about recognizing the limitations and advantages you were born into and then moving past them, breaking free from stereotypes and an old version of beauty, refusing to let anyone or anything define you. That's *your* job.

DEDICATION

This book is dedicated in loving memory to my younger brother, Albert, and all of our relatives and friends who have crossed over to the eternal. To Ma and Pa, thank you for the gift of life. Your countless sacrifices, prayers, and undying love have not gone unnoticed. I am proud to be your daughter and love you both very much. You were my first teachers that modeled positive character traits and lived by example. You believed that all your children were extraordinary and invested everything you had in us. I only hope to give back to you even a fraction of what you have given me. To my Grey and Baraquio Families, we are all connected and I love each and every one of you. To Tini and our children, you have my heart and are my greatest achievements. Thank you for giving me the most immense joy that I have ever known. I'm living for you for the rest of my life.

To God, without Him I am nothing,
but with Him, I can do all things.

CONTENTS

CHAPTER 1

MY AMAZING WIN

"Someone's life is about to change forever," said Donny Osmond. He and his sister Marie, co-hosts of the Miss America Pageant on October 14, 2000, nodded in agreement. We all heard the drum roll, and everyone held their breath. Donny read from his notecard, "The First . . . Runner-up . . . is Miss Louisiana, Faith Jenkins and Miss America 2001 is Miss Hawai'i Angela Perez Baraquio! Congratulations!" The crowd went wild, and just like that, my life changed forever.

The statement could not have been more accurate. In a split second, I transformed from an elementary schoolteacher in Hawai'i to the first Filipina/Asian Miss America in the pageant's history since it began in 1921 on the shores of Atlantic City. It was the eightieth year of the pageant, and I was the seventy-fourth woman to hold the title.

I had no idea that I would be crowned that night, even though I hoped for it with all my heart. It was the single most humbling recognition I had ever received. I had mentally prepared and visualized it repeatedly for months, and finally, the dream of representing my state and country was coming true!

~ Days Earlier ~

Meeting the other contestants during pageant week was a humbling experience. We were all vying for the title and job of Miss America, and we were all qualified to win. I remember during the week of preliminary competition, Miss Texas, who made the Top Ten, told me, "Hawai'i, I have a really good feeling about you." Then Miss Louisiana, who later became First Runner-up, said to me after the preliminary interviews, "I think you'll

1

do very well on Saturday." These offstage and candid comments helped to boost my confidence before the final night. Winning the Swimsuit Competition allowed me to come out of the shadows, and people started to see me as a top contender.

Most people think that all pageants have cat fights between contestants. Not in this case. I came to Miss America with the intent to make friends and have fun. During rehearsals and in our downtime, I hung out a lot with Miss Maryland, Miss D.C., Miss Michigan, and Miss Connecticut, all of whom I enjoyed being around very much. Halfway through the week, we stopped calling each other by first name and affectionately referred to women by their state, mostly because it was easy to remember. I also spent a lot of time singing well-known church songs and hymns with the Christian contestants. It was a pleasant surprise to witness how well all the ladies seemed to get along.

~ Pageant Nears ~

The days leading up to pageant week were spent mostly in rehearsals in Boardwalk Convention Hall. The contestants ate at a gathering place called "The Galley" where many volunteer hostesses from the New Jersey area helped us with whatever we needed. They were our angels who selflessly gave their time to shuttle us to and from hotels and take care of us during our stay.

Former Miss Americas walked around freely and state contestants like me were thrilled to have photo opportunities with them. Aside from meeting the popular boy band O-Town at Walt Disney World and Donny and Marie during rehearsals, it was one of the highlights of my week getting to know these women I considered real-life heroes. I had read about them, but to meet them in person was bliss. Heather Whitestone, Shawntel Smith, Kate Shindle and Nicole Johnson were all winners, whose stories I had read about in the program books at home, and I got to speak to them in person! They seemed untouchable in competition magazines, but here they were so friendly and approachable. They candidly answered our questions about the title and it was enlightening. I aspired to be like them. Later, Heather French, Miss America 2000, spoke to us about what the new titleholder could expect when she crowned one of us. She shared with us the highlights of her year surrounding her work with Homeless Veterans. We listened intently, with wide-eyes and anticipation, perusing our group to see who among us might be the next Miss America.

Then Heather's booking manager took the microphone and laid it all out for us. She advised us to take notes because she was about to inform us what to expect when one of us became Miss America on Saturday. *This was what I was waiting for.* Her manager broke the itinerary down moment by moment.

She explained how it would be the first year that cameras followed the new winner *after* she was crowned and would continue to follow her while getting interviewed by Joan Lunden, for the first forty-eight hours of her reign. I ingested all the exciting details and studied my notes intently when I got back to my hotel room.

In the Boardwalk Convention Hall, where the pageant takes place, there is a quiet area reserved for the contestants to use in their downtime, which was referred to as "Sleepy Hollow." There were fifty-one cots in the room (one for each state contestant, including Miss District of Columbia). Contestants found repose there between rehearsals and took catnaps when necessary.

Carrie Ann Inaba, known now as a judge for *Dancing with the Stars*, was our choreographer and the contestants kept saying she reminded them of me. The day before the finals, she was the "stand-in" on the monitor and it helped me visualize what I could expect to happen to me if I were to win. I took mental notes of her as she showed the contestants the blocking onstage for where the Top Five and winner would stand, and what she would do and where she'd walk after she was crowned. Then she walked over to an area off stage where the first official press conference would be held. I held tight to that visual the morning of the competition. Only instead of *her* standing behind the podium at the after-show press conference, in my mind, it was *me*.

~ October 14, 2000 ~

On the afternoon of the televised pageant, I remember being the only one in Sleepy Hollow. I could hear contestants vocalizing, practicing their talent, and socializing with one another, but I blocked out any distraction. It was my ritual to bring my headphones with me and listen to my Reign CD (my boyfriend Tini Grey's musical group) wherever I went. The Christian track on the album "Draw Me Nearer" was on repeat. The song helped me meditate, focus, and find my center on demand. Plus, I could hear Tini's vocals loud and clear and feeling him close calmed my nerves.

I recited positive affirmations in this space, and told myself not to become attached to any outcome that night. I had to be prepared either way for what was to come. I packed my bags to go home to Hawai'i—just in case. My visualizations became clearer of me walking confidently in Swimsuit, dancing hula with the most aloha I could give, walking regally during Evening Gown, talking to Marie Osmond casually in the Top Five, and finally, imagining what I'd do *if and when* Heather crowned me.

Of course, my visions were a long shot. My chances seemed slim to none, but I dared to dream big. I knew that someone's life could change

3

forever, and because I was a state finalist, I believed I had just as much a chance as anyone.

I thanked God for the opportunity to be a part of Former Miss America, Kellye Cash's prayer circle before the telecast, which gave me an outlet to get my nerves *and* tears out.

As the countdown began toward the start of the telecast, nerves escalated backstage and the excitement reached a crescendo. In order to stay calm backstage, I prayed to the Holy Spirit asking Him to be with me, the new panel of celebrity judges, and with all those watching in the audience. I asked God to give me the peace in my heart to accept any outcome, and the grace to be used as an instrument the entire night. I was merely a vessel to be used according to His Will. At this point, I gave it all up to Him.

I felt like I had cleared any spiritual blockages through prayer. Backstage, they proved powerful and I literally felt like I had a direct pipeline to God. I remembered the Scriptures saying, *Ask and you shall receive*. So I asked to be in the Top Ten, but specifically, to be Contestant No. Five, and I was called fifth. As the night went on, and I was still standing, I hoped to be in the Top Five, but specifically asked to be in the middle as Contestant No. Three, and I was called third.

In the process I made some incredible friends in the pageant "Class of 2000." Miss Minnesota, prayed with me and kept me calm before the Talent portion. She even helped me with my flower headpiece for hula when I was fumbling with it, seconds before competing in Talent. (Later, as I traveled the country I would call her when I visited Minnesota and got in touch with many other state contestants so we could meet up in their respective state.) Miss New Hampshire and Miss Maine both gave me the encouragement I needed in the final phases of competition as the time was dwindling down, and the winner was about to be announced. (Eventually, those two east coast contestants would fly over to attend my wedding in Hawai'i.)

At the end of the day, I realized that we were all really in the same boat. Yet on that night, there would only be one person named Miss America 2001.

On the evening of the final night, I found myself standing onstage as one of the Top Five finalists out of the twelve thousand young women who compete for this title annually. It was extremely humbling. Faith Jenkins, Miss Louisiana, had an incredible voice, a commanding presence, and was studying to be a lawyer. She had won not only the Swimsuit and Talent Awards during preliminary week, but also the coveted "Quality of Life" national community service award. Rita Ng, Miss California, a Stanford valedictorian, was a concert pianist who won the Preliminary Talent Award, and was a pre-med student aspiring to become a pediatrician. I stood five-foot-four-inches tall, was a Hawai'i-born Filipina physical education teacher and athletic director, Swimsuit Preliminary Winner, and graduate of the University of Hawai'i at Manoa—not the most obvious stats for a Miss America finalist but, hey, I made it into the Top Three! Whitney Boyles, Miss Kentucky, and Christy May, Miss Mississippi, rounded out the Top Five.

I felt so honored to be among the fifty-one contestants. I wondered how in the world the judges could choose *just one person* from among all the beautiful, talented, and intelligent women onstage. Then I looked at the last five standing. I remember thinking, *No matter what happens, I'm a winner. If I walk away now as Fourth Runner-up, I will earn at least ten thousand dollars in scholarship assistance. Awesome!* I was already paying down my student loans in my head!

When I didn't hear the first syllable of my state, I took a sigh of relief and thought, *Whew, I'm still standing. Now I can earn at least twenty-five thousand dollars!* Preparing for the escort to come get me as the Third Runner-up, I readied myself to walk away with grace and hold my head high, being grateful for the experience and proud of my best effort. And yet, I was confused when my state *still* wasn't called. For sure, I'd be Second Runner-up, looking at the competition still standing.

It was Miss California, Miss Louisiana, and Miss Hawai'i. I thought, *Obviously, I'm next.* So I awaited to be called and escorted offstage. After a pause, the host said, "Miss California, Rita Ng!" *What!?* I thought. *How am I still here?* And even if I got that far, I knew for sure that I was the next to be eliminated. I pulled Faith close to me, in a tight embrace, and said to her amidst the deafening noise in the Boardwalk Hall filled with twenty-five thousand spectators and fans, "How do you feel? We're the top two in the NATION!" I was basking in the moment. She replied, "I'm in shock, I'm just in shock!"

I believe at that moment, it hit her that she was going to be the next Miss America. Honestly, *I* was more than certain that she *WAS* going to be crowned. So I was not stressed at all. In that instant (which lasted an eternity), I wondered why she was so nervous. She had this thing in the bag. I smiled contentedly, thinking that I could go home happy. I was at peace, enjoying this moment, knowing that I'd be able to experience it all over again someday, when I was old and gray watching the video with my own children.

I had reached my personal goal of making the Top Ten at Nationals, I got into the Top Five, and I could still be Miss Hawai'i when I went home. Plus, in my head, I just earned forty thousand dollars in scholarship grants as the First Runner-up. I was on cloud nine and had nothing to lose. Yes, all this went through my head. Time was outstretched, as if in slow motion—long enough for me to collect my thoughts and process all that was happening.

5

Then a different thought flashed in my head, *Wait a second, I might just have a chance at winning! I'm still here, too. Could it be possible that I might be the new Miss America?* I said a quick prayer in my mind: *God, I know what it takes to win. I have done all I can to get here. The rest is up to you. If you don't think I can handle this job, and I know it's not easy, then please DON'T let me win, but if you think I can handle it, then please give me the courage, strength and wisdom to do the best job I possibly can to represent all these phenomenal women.* The moment seemed like forever, even though only seconds had passed. Faith and I waited in suspense for the moment of truth.

Finally, Donny Osmond announced *me* as the winner! In relief AND disbelief I exclaimed, "Oh my gosh!" and emphatically hugged Faith. Then I turned around to point to the contestants and told each girl I loved them. They were all winners in my eyes, and I was completely humbled to be chosen from among that group of women. I truly believe that on any given night, with a different set of judges, the outcome might have been different. But that night was *my* night. I was beyond elated, and I was going to celebrate!

As Heather French, Miss America 2000 crowned me, I joined my hands in prayer to give thanks to my Heavenly Father. It was exhilarating and unbelievable! To hear my name called onstage was an affirmation that He had faith in me and my ability to do this job. If I had any lingering thoughts of self-doubt, they had temporarily vanished in that glorious moment. All the dreams that I once secretly wished in my heart for so long were finally destined to come true.

It was a surreal experience, but unlike past winners I didn't cry onstage. Because I attended Kellye Cash's prayer circle before the show, there were no tears when I was crowned. I got it all out beforehand. Earlier, I prayed for the woman who was going to win that night, asking the Lord to bless her and help her on her journey. How gratifying it was to find that on that night, the chosen girl from all those lovely women was me.

Walking down the famed runway to the iconic song that Bert Parks made famous, "There She Is, Miss America," wearing the coveted crown and carrying a Waterford Crystal scepter, I felt like a queen. I swung the scepter like a bat, signaling to my students back home watching the pageant that I was still Miss Baraquio, their PE teacher, who, just a few months earlier, taught first-graders how to play T-ball. I was still me, just in a gown, heels, and makeup.

Filled with hopes and dreams of my own and of all the people I was representing, I wasn't about to let anyone change me. I was really on a mission to change the world. Being Miss Hawai'i was an honor. Becoming an American icon in front of millions, was beyond comprehension. And so began my exciting yearlong tour of duty as America's goodwill ambassador.

I flashed the "hang loose" shaka sign to represent my island roots, and it hit me how far I had come. From the shores of Honolulu, Hawai'i, thousands of miles away, this Filipina girl—born American from immigrant parents was gliding down the runway as Miss America. I was living an American Dream.

After I was crowned I went backstage for a photo shoot where I met with all the "Forever Miss Americas" in attendance at the eightieth anniversary pageant. I was floored to see so many legendary women in one place, and it was a tremendous honor to be among them. We took our photo and afterward, each woman hugged and greeted me with a warm, "Welcome to the Sisterhood!" In a matter of four months, I had joined the Miss Hawai'i and Miss America sororities! Lee Meriwether (the original Catwoman in the film *Batman*) and the late Jean Bartel told me to enjoy every moment of my year and keep a journal. That was a valuable piece of advice, which I took to heart. I made it a point to write in it every day.

Journalist Joan Lunden followed me for the first forty-eight hours of my year of service for an A&E TV special called, *Behind Closed Doors with Miss America*. We went from one press conference to another. Finally we arrived at my own room in Caesar's Penthouse suite, where all my luggage was delivered from my previous room, one I shared with my Miss Hawai'i Traveling Companion (a.k.a. TC), Leilani Keough during pageant week. Leilani laughed at me for packing all my bags before I left our room on final night because I was ready to catch a flight home afterwards, if I didn't win. I figured, *Hey, no matter what happens, you always have to be prepared for any outcome!*

I would always have someone near me, whether it was the officials, a guard, or a TC. A female security guard slept in my living room suite, keeping watch over me. At least two other male security guards were placed outside my door throughout the night. I could hardly sleep that evening—I was in dreamland! I remember sitting in my oversized bathtub just laughing and thanking God for such an amazing and beautiful experience. I waited for someone to pinch me so I would wake up, but it never happened. In fact, reality would sink in immediately at dawn. It was time to begin my reign.

At sun-up, I arose to a morning wake-up call for the traditional day-after Miss America romp in the Atlantic Ocean. That photo shoot would be seen all over the world. At the beach, a young, seventeen-year-old Filipina girl broke through security and ran up to give me a hug. She held my hands and said, "Angela, I'm Filipina. I have always wanted to be Miss America but never thought I could win, but after you won last night, I know I can do it, too. Thank you!" She hugged me tightly and Joan Lunden asked if we were sisters. I said, "No, we just met!"

Little did I know that this young lady would be the first of hundreds, if not thousands, of Asian-American sisters I would inspire across the nation.

For the first time, I realized that my Filipino heritage was one of my greatest assets. It made me stand out among the crowd, and it felt magnificent.

In the midst of the whirlwind, I asked for a drink of water and my manager half-jokingly said to me, "Honey, you're Miss America. You can have whatever you want!" I thought, *Wow, as one of ten kids, I can assure you I have never heard THAT before!* After the string of press conferences, I asked the Miss America officials if I was able to attend Mass. As a Catholic, weekly church service was a priority in my life, and I knew that I would definitely not want to miss it while I was on the road, traveling an average of twenty thousand miles a month. I needed it for my sanity, my spiritual grounding, and daily strength.

When I brought up church, the staff informed me that Miss America typically gets only one day off a month. I said that I needed to take Sundays off. They agreed, but said that I would earn less money due to unscheduled appearances. That didn't matter to me. It was important that I stayed grounded in my faith. I needed spiritual fuel to be able to handle my year ahead and was unwavering in my request. They granted it, casually reminding me once again, "You're Miss America, you can do whatever you want!" We laughed. Although I wasn't about to abuse that privilege, I was thankful for the approval.

Just then, I heard whispers from my security guards who quietly admitted that they, too, were Catholic. One guard told me, "I'm studying to become a deacon." Another said, "I am a lector and Eucharistic minister at my church." Still another said, "I was an altar boy growing up." *It was so cute!* It was also refreshing to be in the company of believers. Yet again I felt God was looking out for me. Then my Traveling Companions (TCs), the two women who served as chaperones/road managers throughout my year and alternated months of service, both admitted their Catholic faith. They were thrilled to be able to travel with me and not miss Mass on Sundays because of my personal request. That choice proved to yield countless blessings throughout my year.

I left New Jersey the following morning, in a stretch limo en route to New York. I was scheduled to do TV interviews with *Good Morning America, Live with Regis* with guest host Whoopi Goldberg, CNN, Fox Studios, among many other radio and newspaper media outlets. I embarked on a thirteen-city "5 Minutes with Miss America" tour with major pageant sponsors and news media outlets before beginning my travels of twenty thousand miles a month. Literally, I was in a different city every eighteen to thirty-six hours, nothing close to what I was used to. My exposure to other cultures was mainly through my friends and visitors to Hawai'i before this. I had never left the islands for more than ten days, never lived outside of Hawai'i, or did any extensive travel before winning. I only visited California and Washington states, so my travels were eye-opening and I was eager to begin this new adventure.

Realizing the tremendous honor and responsibility that comes with the title of being the first Asian-American Miss America, I learned quickly that I had many people's hopes and dreams resting on my shoulders. I was so grateful to all my predecessors for paving the way for me, and I saw firsthand just why the Miss America crown, my Hawaiian culture, my Filipino heritage, and Catholic values were important to so many people.

CHAPTER 2

COMING TO AMERICA

My story as the First Asian Miss America doesn't begin with my birth in the states but traces back to my roots in the Philippines. (When I was younger, my parents told me we also had Spanish and Chinese blood). As a child, I never gave it a second thought about the sacrifices my parents made to bring our family to America—what specifically attracted them to the land of the free, and who and what they left behind to get here. Over the years, I learned that Claudio and Rigolette "Letty" Baraquio, my immigrant parents who stared into the face of war and scarcity, clung to faith, hope, and love when it mattered most. Today, I have a greater appreciation and more admiration for them than they will ever know.

My family came to the United States through a sequence of dramatic events. We might have remained in the Philippines if it weren't for my Grandma Teresita's strength and determination to bring us stateside. My mother's mom always loved America and knew she'd get here someday. So when she married an American citizen who brought her to Hawai'i in 1965, her plan was to bring all her children over so they could all be together in the land of opportunity. My parents intended to come to America at some point, but they left it up to God's Will.

At that time, according to my mother, U.S. visas for Philippine citizens were first prioritized: unmarried children of U.S. citizens, and second, for married couples. But for married couples with children, like my parents, it was a bit more complicated to enter the country. My parents had three children and another on the way. Mama was resolute about not leaving her family behind or splitting any of us up. Unlike others before her who would set out for America and work in the states to bring over each family member one by one, she decided to stay in Manila until the family-based

10

immigrant visa was open, which could, quite possibly, have been indefinitely.

A lot of immigrants had come to Hawai'i in waves from various countries including Japan, China, Korea, and the Philippines. Many came in the early 1900s as plantation laborers. By the 1970s more than twenty thousand Filipinos had entered the U.S. through the U.S. Navy. While there was an influx of immigrants from the Philippines, Ma and Pa were not among the plantation workers that came over to Hawai'i in a bulk group. They arrived as educated professionals with teaching certificates. Pa even taught as a professor at the college level in Manila for a short time. Some immigrants entered the U.S. without visas, but our family came at an extremely high price, and not just monetarily.

Grandma wanted to abide by the law to earn the privilege for her family to come to America. She worked hard as a seamstress in Hawai'i to help bring everyone over one by one. It seemed like this feat would take years. The fees for citizenship were not cheap. In 1966, Grandma's youngest daughter, my Tita Emy, arrived in the islands as the first of Grandma's children. She was eighteen and single. Tita (a Tagalog term for "aunt") Emy soon married a young, handsome American marine from Maine, named Normand Deschaine. He was deployed to Vietnam and planned to return by June 3 to celebrate their one-year anniversary. My grandma began to file papers requesting that my family come over to Hawai'i, but it was taking longer than expected. My parents were ready to leave Manila at a moment's notice because they wanted the chance to live and work here. They were just waiting for a call from the Philippine Embassy.

On June 7, 1968, military officials came knocking on Tita Emy's door in Hawai'i to regretfully announce the devastating news of her husband's untimely passing. My twenty-year-old Uncle Normand died while serving in active duty in the Vietnam War. He never made it home for their anniversary, and my Tita Emy found herself a widow at twenty-two years old.

Tita Emy's role, as the wife of a veteran who died in the line of active duty, enabled the petition (for our family's entry into the U.S) to be moved to the top of the list, making it high priority. Grandma's petition for our whole family to come, all at the same time, was not only granted, but expedited! Consequently, my parents and older siblings, and eventually the rest of my siblings and I, were able to gain U.S. Citizenship. Because of Uncle Normand's life, we came to America as a family unit. My uncle, a respected marine, made the ultimate sacrifice for our country, and showed extreme courage at such a young age. The thought is sobering.

Without my parents making the choice to create a better life for our family, without Grandma Teresita, her husband, Tita Emy and Uncle

Normand, I might not be an American today. I reflect on how my family almost stayed back in the Philippines. Mama's unwillingness to separate her family, was commendable. In a few months, Papa and Mama worked hard to pay back Grandma every cent they borrowed from her, and our new life in the states was about to begin.

As an adult, I have the utmost respect for Mama and Papa. They left their families and everything they held dear, to give us the things they never had as children.

Had events not transpired in the way they did, and had we not left in that window of time, we might still be in the Philippines, and my life would be completely different. My parents arrived in America in 1970. I truly believe it was also God's constant guiding hand that carried our family across a vast ocean at that time in history. Two years later, in 1972, then-Philippine President Ferdinand Marcos declared martial law, and no one was allowed to leave the country for eight years.

~ Growing up Filipino-American in Hawai'i ~

Because my parents were teachers in the Philippines, they were accustomed to a comfortable lifestyle. But in 1970, they took the plunge, leaving all they knew behind and moved to the island of O'ahu, with three kids in tow, a baby in utero, and a suitcase full of hopes.

When my parents first moved to Hawai'i, they spoke Tagalog to my older siblings, but when my oldest sister, Ceci first attended school in Hawai'i in 1970, the teacher didn't understand her and asked my parents to speak only in English to her. For a child growing up in the 70s, it was a widely held belief that teaching a second language to a child would lead to confusion and result in the child becoming a "late talker." From then on, my parents spoke Tagalog to each other and only English to their children.

Since my parents didn't want any of us to be impeded in school, they did as the teacher advised. They felt that to really excel in this country, we had to have a strong command of the English language, and speaking two languages in the home might confuse us. Research today, however, tells us quite the opposite. I read recently that learning a second language boosts your brain power. As Oprah Winfrey says, "When we know better, we do better . . ."

Mama and Papa knew it would take time to establish themselves, so they initially found housekeeping jobs at a Hilton hotel in Honolulu. My dad also worked as a waiter to earn extra income and eventually found work as a pest control operator. They worked long days and did what they had to do for our family, but being "employees" was short lived. Their determination, work ethic, and entrepreneurial drive led them to start their own business in termite control just a few years later.

12

I was born on June 1, 1976 as the eighth of my parents' ten children. I grew up in a four-bedroom, two-bathroom house in Palolo Valley, with my parents and nine siblings. We lived there for seven years. Just think, my mom had ten kids in a span of fourteen years, with a pair of twins sandwiched in the middle of the bunch!

The walls of our house were saturated in the aroma of a Filipino kitchen: garlic, onion, vinegar, bagoong (fermented fish, shrimp, and salt) and foods like lumpia, longganisa (Filipino pork sausage) and bangus (milkfish). They pulsated with the steady rumble of ukulele, guitar, piano, singing, Papa's records playing, yelling, constant chattering, chaos and laughter. Even throughout the noise and movement, I could still hear a faint whisper in my heart: *God loves you and has a special plan for you.*

I had ample evidence to believe this. My parents raised us watching Disney classics. Pinocchio became a boy, Gretel escaped from the witch, and Little Red Riding Hood defeated the wolf. Happy endings happened. Good triumphed over evil. I vowed to tread the path of good. Besides, it elicited praise from my parents, and I devoured any attention I could get.

My parents' deep Catholic faith spurred me. They taught us parables and Bible stories that seemed cut from the same fairy tale fabric. David conquered Goliath, Daniel survived the lion's den, Lazarus rose from the dead, and the little boy's meager offering of bread was multiplied. I loved a story with a hero overcoming obstacles and a happy ending. At age six, I recognized a clear-cut division between good and evil and I had the irrepressible urge to instill that in my only two younger siblings (the ninth and tenth children), Albert and Gloria, who were two and four years younger than me respectively.

Armed with colorful children's books, I happily assumed the teacher role. In our playroom, Albert and Gloria gathered around me on a queen-sized bed, propping their heads in their hands, wide-eyed. I pointed to the books' graphic depictions of the Ascension, Heaven, and Hell. "See," I told my four-year-old brother and two-year-old sister, "This is why you want to be a good person. You want to get to Heaven someday." They acquiesced earnestly: "OK, we'll be good!" Mama reinforced that message. She was always dispensing proverbs like, "An idle mind is the workshop of the devil." Some were her own creations, including the succinct rhyme, "Pray and obey!"

I thought Papa was the strongest man in the world. He wore a white tank top and climbed mango trees barefoot. He told stories about walking around without shoes in the Philippines and effortlessly breaking thorns with his calloused feet. "Flex your muscles, Papa," we'd insist. We three youngest were always dazzled by his bulging biceps. Then we'd beg for rides, and he'd swing three of us back and forth on one arm at the same time. He was our real-life Superman. To this day, he still is.

13

While Papa was the quiet provider with a humble confidence, an infectious laugh, and a smile that could soften any heart, Mama served as the vocal disciplinarian. She was always pushing us to make sure we were on the right track. An English teacher, Mama taught us phonics shortly after we were potty-trained. I remember crying when I just couldn't get it. I was afraid to take too long sounding out the words, so I'd guess at them. "Don't guess!" Mama would reprimand.

By age three, I felt pressured to be right, to nail it the first time. It marked the beginning of a lifelong battle against the weighty expectations of others and myself, something that would take years to overcome before I realized I was good enough just as I was.

Mama kept a close watch over us. We did roll call before each outing. And when she needed our attention, she'd call out in her Filipino accent: "Maricel, Jerome, Lucy, John, Tess, Berna, Rose, Angie, Albert, Gloria!" It rolled off her lips like a Hail Mary.

Most of my siblings were named after Catholic saints whose feast days fell on or near their birth dates. Maricel (Marce) was an abbreviation of Maria Cecilia. Today we call her Ceci. Jerome, Lucy, and John were all named after saints as well. Tess was a nickname for Therese; Berna was short for Bernadette. Rose is her actual name, but she was really named after the Rosary, which my mom profusely prayed during twenty hours of labor. Mama says that as soon as she prayed, Rose was born!

them, I cried for I Then came me. I arrived on June 1, the day before the Feast of the Angels, hence the name Angela. My parents nicknamed me "Angie Bebe" because I was the baby for two years before my younger brother Albert was born. According to them, I cried for months after his arrival because I felt he was replacing me. They called me the nickname to reassure me that I was still their baby girl and to remind me that no child of theirs could ever be replaced.

My little brother Albert was named after St. Albert the Great. He certainly seemed anxious to enter the world. No joke—he was born in a station wagon! As the famous family story goes, my oldest brother Jerome (who was eleven years old at the time) helped my mother deliver him right before the car pulled up to the emergency room at Kapi'olani Children's Hospital. Like all the children that came before, this birth was truly a miracle! But Albert had pneumonia, so he almost died in infancy. Mama requested the prayers of all our friends, priests, and nuns at our school, Maryknoll, and Albert survived.

Gloria Marie was their last child, born on August 15, on the Catholic Feast of the Assumption, so she was named after the song the angels possibly sang when Mother Mary was assumed body and soul into Heaven. When she was born, I didn't feel I was being replaced. I was so happy to have a baby sister, and she was the cutest one of all! I had a playmate, and she would be my "Baby Cindy" every time we played House. For some reason, I just loved that name Cindy!

In 1981 we moved from Palolo Valley to Waialua, but still attended school at Maryknoll in Honolulu, which elongated our trips to school at least two hours each way, in heavy traffic! Our most frequent nearby trip was to church at St. Michael's in Waialua, on the North Shore of O'ahu, where we literally *were* the church choir. We'd all pile into our yellow Dodge family van (a.k.a the minibus) which read in bold letters on the interior "CAPACITY 15."

There weren't frequent stops on our two-hour drive to and from school each day. On weekdays we would all wake up at four a.m. and return home around six p.m. It was a long drive! For lack of space, or to fill a need for privacy, I often burrowed under the back seat of our van, where I sometimes slept during road trips.

Once, I was left behind at my parents' office because my siblings thought I was under the seat sleeping. They called my name for me during roll call but I was in the bathroom upstairs at the office. One of my sisters forgot to tell Ma I was still in there. I walked downstairs to find an empty parking lot and no van. I cried, "Mama! Papa! Where is everybody?" Thankfully, minutes later, my dad's coworker, Felicia (my angel!), found me covered in tears and called my dad's pager to return for me. This was before cell phones, so Papa pulled over to call Felicia back from a payphone. Mama overheard and frantically screamed, "Turn around! Let's go! Angie Bebe is by herself!" Felicia comforted me until my family got me. Being only five years old, that was a traumatic experience for me and my first feeling of abandonment.

Upon arrival to our destinations in the minibus, (usually church functions or family parties), we'd emerge from the van with our musical instruments in hand. People called us the Baraquio Bunch. "Someday, we'll beat the Osmonds!" Mama proclaimed in her excited Tagalog accent, and we'd all cheer. It was a lofty goal to aspire toward, but it kept hope alive for us. How ironic that one day I'd share the Miss America stage with the Osmonds, and that they would be announcing me as the winner.

Our family made up the church choir so we practiced together every Thursday and played for two or three Masses a week. I debuted at age five. I was so excited to be part of the band. Finally, I felt I was a full-fledged family member. I belonged! I loved harmonizing with my older siblings, and admired how well they played their ukeleles, guitars, and drums. To my pleasure, I was eventually entrusted with the tambourine, and in later years, graduated to playing piano during Mass and leading the Tongan youth choir with my husband at our parish in Waikiki.

At family functions and parties, my parents arranged the four oldest, "The Big Ones," in the back row. The rest of us, "The Small Ones," stood in the front, poised and ready to perform on demand.

"You have God-given talents," Mama told us. "Our purpose is to bring you up in the faith so you can give those talents back to God." And in the process, she always made us look our best. "Don't touch your face! Put your hand down. Eye contact. Smile!" Those were my first lessons in stage presence. I never thought of Mama as a "stage mom" but I guess she taught me the importance of poise and grace and that whether we like it or not, people are watching, and we have a responsibility to behave well because in truth we are all *always* on display.

The sixty minutes of weekly Mass marked a fraction of our time at church. It became our second home. After Mass, we'd collect the music books and compress the microphone stands, stack up the transparency sheets that had song lyrics handwritten by my sisters with erasable pens.

Scripture seeped into my mind through a sort of musical osmosis. And prayer seemed very accessible. I casually conversed with God as if I were talking to a buddy. *Oh, thanks for my toys and my family, God. And thanks for my second grade teacher, Miss Rudeen.* Gradually, the faith took root in me as a teenager. Even now, as a mother, I try to instill that same attitude of gratitude in my own children during daily prayer.

By junior high, since Mama was head of the cleaning committee, we set to work each Saturday wiping the pews, refilling the holy water, cleaning bathrooms, and mopping the floors. Since our lives were centered around the church, I didn't realize that God, prayer, and service played a lesser role in others' lives.

While most kids our age were at the beach, hanging out at the mall, attending summer fun or swimming lessons, we were in the basement of the Daughters of St. Paul Bookstore in downtown Honolulu, helping the nuns take inventory on their items and stock bookshelves. Our parents would drop us off around seven a.m. and we wouldn't get picked up until six p.m.

Oddly enough, I actually enjoyed my time there with my siblings, listening to music, pushing books around in shopping carts, organizing faith-based materials and spending our snack and lunchtime together with the kind nuns who ran the store.

Subconsciously, we heard Christian music and were surrounded by uplifting, inspiring, spiritual literature that became part of our vernacular. It's no wonder that I am still heavily involved in Catholic education and consistently gravitate towards being surrounded by a faith community, even as an adult. Those early experiences shaped me, giving me a sense of grounding, belonging, and meaning.

I took the sacraments seriously. I made First Reconciliation at Maryknoll Grade School in Honolulu. However mild my eight-year-old sins were, their absolution brought tremendous relief. After my very first confession in second grade , I skipped back to class in my navy blue pleated skirt and white collared blouse. And when I was chosen to be a student lector for my First Communion Mass, held on Easter Sunday, I was so proud to be chosen. I even memorized my Reading from the prophet Ezekiel and proclaimed the Word without any notes.

After Mass, Mama typically made a glorious brunch, indicative of Sunday mornings together as a family—eggs, Portuguese sausage, Spam (yes, a Hawaiian staple) and garlic fried rice. Family meals weren't just about food. It was a sacred time that was reserved for fellowship and community with each other. Then we'd read the Sunday paper cartoons, nap and head to Ala Moana Beach Park, where we would swim or play Keep Away.

Swimming and playing in the sand fueled a frantic scramble for the shower at home. The sisters would pair up and call dibs on who was ultimately first, second and third. Hot water was in limited supply, and *dibs* carried a lot of weight. If Tess and Berna yelled "First in the shower!" even before getting out of the car, that was final, and you accepted your standing. And the lucky boys, there were only three of them sharing the other shower, instead of seven of us girls fighting over one. I thought, *They have it so easy.*

To speed along a school morning, all seven of us girls squeezed into the bathtub together. We played Red Light, Green Light to take turns under the showerhead. The older ones normally claimed their authority. The younger ones would grumble: "Is it green yet? Hurry up—I'm freezing!" On those chaotic mornings, I daydreamed about one day having my own private space, let alone my own shower.

We didn't have much, but it was enough, and Ma and Pa made sure we never lacked the necessities. I found simple ways to make daily life beautiful and enjoyable. When I was at home during summers, I'd turn on our fan in the living room, lay a sheet on the ground, get a glass of ice water with a straw, and rest my head on a pillow while watching TV. My sisters would sarcastically remark, "Look at Angie. She's such a queen." That term did not sound like something I would ever aspire to be. And certainly not after the way *they* said it.

In public, all our personas were different. We never ceased to perform. I began ballet in kindergarten, piano in second grade and ukulele in fourth. Mama and Papa hosted Marriage Encounter meetings in our home with other Catholic couples, and they called on us to entertain on cue.

The Baraquio Bunch snapped into action, a burst of melody and movement. A staple in our repertoire was Kermit the Frog's "The Rainbow Connection." The lyrics reinforced my belief in the ideal: *Someday we'll find it, the rainbow connection . . .*

On Saturday mornings, the Small Ones took the bus to our piano lessons in downtown Honolulu. It was a long ride, and we transferred at several points. But there was a sweet incentive. While one sibling attended her lesson, the rest of us went to what we called "The Small Store," a mom-and-pop candy shop that sold a wide array of one-cent candy. "Holy smokes!" I exclaimed. We each had a *dollar* to spend; we could get one hundred pieces of candy. It was like winning the lottery! I deliberated over each selection and carefully protected my little brown sack of sugar (from any sibling who tried to snatch some) on the bus ride home.

I loved music and infused it into school projects whenever I could. For one science assignment in fifth grade, my classmates and I wrote an original rap about the wonders of the urinary system. "The urinary system is pretty rad, 'cause it filters out your waste and that's why it's bad, uh huh, uh huh, we sang. It might be gross to you, but only if you knew, that it filters out the uric acid and urea, too. Uh huh, uh huh." When my teacher heard our rap, she took us to the principal. We cowered in fear. It turned out that she was so impressed she wanted us to perform it for him.

At home, I loved to play teacher. I would give timed math tests to Gloria and Albert and found pleasure in marking their errors with a red pen. I used old textbooks as my guide, looking up the answers in the back. I dreamed of being a Catholic elementary school teacher someday, following in the footsteps of my parents and my second-grade teacher, Miss Rudeen.

Despite my yearning to be studious I needed an escape once in a while. The only TV we were allowed to watch was *Sesame Street* and the six o'clock evening news, but only after praying our nightly rosary. And yet, the soap opera, *Santa Barbara* held forbidden appeal to my older sisters. They'd turn it on when they thought Albert, Gloria and I were napping in our rooms. We'd sneak out and scale the walls of our hallway to catch a glimpse of the elevated TV in the living room. Our big sisters' backs were to us, yet invariably one of us made noise. Then we'd dart back to bed and pretend to be sleeping, trying to slow our accelerated breathing. Those were fun times.

On every birthday, we labored over hand-made cards. This was a family tradition, which we continue with our own families to this day. We presented them in lieu of gifts to the recipient, one by one, gathered 'round the circular kitchen table or the living room couch. It was an early lesson in communication skills, writing a speech, reading in front of a group, and listening attentively. Even today, the sentimental cards mean so much more than a store-bought gift.

Ultimately, we took mom's exhortation to heart; we were never idle. Finding pleasure in simple things, we constantly invented our own fun. My siblings and I made games using slippers and tennis balls as props. We designed our own Scrabble board. And I held my own swap meets, selling hot commodities to my siblings like gently used hairbrushes, stuffed animals, barrettes, and chewing gum. We owned one Betamax tape, *Breakin' 2: Electric Boogaloo*, and we memorized every word and dance routine on it.

We were never bored, *that* was for sure!

Some mornings at the break of dawn, the six youngest kids devoted ourselves to the pointless task of dumping loose rocks from our dirt-covered front yard into the empty neighboring lot. Our sense of solidarity kept us from questioning our purpose. Once we turned a bookshelf into a Flintstone-style, foot-powered car. There was never a lack of action, creativity, or a shortage of playmates.

But even in a loud, busy, crowded household, there were times I felt lonely.

At seven years old, I turned a plastic Easter egg into an imaginary friend, which I never really named. I stored it in a drawer and pulled it out when I was in need of intimate conversation. I occasionally hid in a corner of my closet to escape the noise and chaos and find peace of mind. Once my sisters caught me talking to the egg. "You're such a baby," they teased. And I would protest, "I am not!" Then I whispered to the egg, "Don't worry, I know you're really there."

Looking back, I think I was seeking a tangible representation of God in that egg. As a child, I truly believed in Him. I leaned on His unconditional love. And I craved His companionship.

As No. Eight, the oldest of the youngest batch, I became the convenient babysitter when my older sisters went out. They also expected me to do their chores on demand. I willingly accepted that lot in life and did it joyfully. Every so often they'd joke to their friends about my servitude because they knew they could take advantage of it. "That's Angie—she's our Cinderella. She'll get you what you want."

Being the oldest of the "Really Small Ones" and the youngest of the "Big Ones," I felt like somewhat of a middle child. I wanted so badly to hang out with my big sisters, but when I did get to join Tess, Berna, and Rose, I often felt like a tag-along.

By the time the twins left for college it seemed like we got much closer. They'd write letters home to Rose and me, telling us of their college life. I finally felt included in their group. When I was sixteen, Tess and Berna returned from college to surprise Rose on her birthday. The four of us kids left at home were so excited to see them! When Rose opened their present in front of the family, it was a framed print called *The Three Sisters*. I was devastated! Despite my best efforts, I just wasn't part of their inner circle. Maybe I never would be. I slipped into the bathroom to cry and then wiped my tears. I returned with dry eyes and my chin up, a ritual I would eventually learn to do instinctively at defining moments in my life. That spirit of acceptance and resilience would serve me well in the future.

Sometimes I felt invisible, like just another number in the family. It was hard to stand out in the Baraquio Bunch. Everywhere I went at school—the cafeteria, the bathroom, the playground—kids were constantly saying, Are you a Baraquio? Which one are you?" Even Mama confused our names once in a while. I felt like a broken record, straining for recognition: "I'm *Angie!*"

Teachers asked the same repetitive question. Then they'd launch into a story about a smart older sibling. The implicit comparison was daunting. *What does it mean to be a Baraquio?* I wondered. *Will I ever measure up?* It took all I had to try to stand out or make a name for myself, but there were days I was too tired to keep up.

Then I would lean on God. As long as I can remember, I've always felt close to Him. In kindergarten, I drew a picture with the caption "ALTAR" and it resembled the one we had in our living room. I brought it home to show Mama, telling her, "I want to be a nun when I grow up." Mama beamed with pride. Likely, she was having memories of the times she spent studying in a convent in the Philippines, surrounded by holy sisters.

All my idols were saints. Not a typical upbringing, but it definitely colored my future. As I grew older, I realized that marriage and motherhood were my vocations, in addition to being a teacher. But I never stopped loving God and He never stopped loving and watching over me. That was crystal clear.

My dreams versus my reality were very different. Sometimes I felt like I was straddling two opposite camps. Being too old for the babies or too young for the Big Ones . . . Being athletic versus being feminine. Being Filipino-American but raised in Hawai'i. Neither side, it seemed, fully embraced me. They each highlighted the reasons I *didn't* fit.

I felt like God kept telling me, *Just wait, I have a special plan for you.* I needed to find a niche, my place in the world. The process of exploring and creating my identity was just beginning.

CHAPTER 3

THE EARLY YEARS

While in second grade, our class was discussing "What's in a name?" Our assignment was to go home and ask our parents why they gave us our particular name. It was an intriguing topic, and all the students were buzzing about what theirs meant. I was particularly interested because my parents had ten kids, and I wondered about the reasoning behind *mine*.

During recess I asked my teacher, Miss Rudeen, "What does 'Angela' mean?" She smiled, bent down to meet me at eye-level and said, "Angela means 'messenger.' My eyes got big. "What's my message?" I asked. She gently touched my shoulder and continued, "I can't tell you *that*. It's *your* job to find out what your message will be to the world." She smiled, and I went out to play.

Huh, that was something to mull over, I thought.

Miss Rudeen was a tall, young, novice Caucasian teacher with light eyes and blonde hair. She was my favorite teacher because she always made me feel special. After that day, I couldn't get our conversation off my mind.

That Sunday, after playing Baraquio Ball (our version of Keep Away) at Ala Moana, I wandered off along the beach. I wriggled my toes deep into the sand and felt the steady, salty splash of the water on my ankles and stared into the ocean. Vastness, as far as the eye could see. Suddenly, I felt so tiny. I was one miniscule speck on the shore of an island in the middle of the Pacific Ocean.

That sensation stirred my soul. *How do I fit into the grand scheme, God? Why am I from a large family? Why do I live on an island so far from the mainland? Why am I Filipina? And what is my message to the world?*

Yes, I really asked this at that age. I was a small girl with big questions.

I wrestled with my yearning to be pretty. My rice-bowl hair and hand-

21

me-down clothes didn't exactly scream femininity. Once, a cashier at the local store asked me, "Will that be all, Sir?" I was so mortified that I answered, "Yes," in the lowest voice I could muster and bolted out of the store in my thick navy blue windbreaker and blue jeans, red-faced.

When I looked in the mirror, I didn't see a pretty reflection. And when I turned on the television, I didn't see any short Asian Filipina girls like me. Some kids called me the derogatory nickname, "flip." Although it was supposedly all in fun, it was hard to not develop an inferiority complex. I looked Filipina but didn't speak the language. I wished that I had learned to speak my mother tongue. I have been told hurtful things like, "You're not Filipino because you don't speak the language." I thought, *I may not speak Tagalog, but I understand some and I'm a Filipina (pinay) at heart.*

I loved going to the beach and getting browned by the Hawaiian sun, but my ten-year-old Filipino friend cautioned me: "My mom said dark people are poor. The lighter skinned you are, the more rich you are." I fired back, "I don't buy that!" Yet that message was hard to erase from my young mind.

My biggest hang-up was my nose. Once while performing at a family function, I turned around to the second row to wiggle my itchy nose, without using my hands, so Mama wouldn't scold me for touching my face while onstage. My older brother John, took the liberty of making fun of me in front of all my siblings, whispering that my nostrils were huge. He called me "Two Worlds," and my brothers and sisters tried hard to restrain their laughter in front of the crowd before we sang. *Grow up*, I thought. We were just kids and he meant no harm, but the harsh nickname stuck, and unbeknownst to him, it scarred me for years until I finally forgave him.

Most girls become conscious of their bodies at a young age. I was no different. Aside from dealing with my nose issues and dark skin, I was concerned about my size. I always felt chubbier than my sisters. Mama insisted I was the healthiest, saying it was because she breastfed me the longest—until I was two years old, but my sisters would joke about my thick legs. When they saw me eating my candies they cautioned that I would become overweight if I kept eating the way I did. *Ouch, that hurt.*

It's funny how different you view things as a child. After reprocessing certain experiences as an adult, I have learned to forgive and heal those parts of me that were hurt, and I'm better off because of it. Those tough times made me who I am.

I realize now that self-image boils down to the way someone feels *inside*—not by their clothing size or the numbers on a scale. Looking back at old pictures, I was not a chubby girl. But I felt like one in comparison to my stick-thin sisters. I grew to understand that we are all created differently and began to see the danger of comparing myself to others. When I did, I always fell short.

Still, I saw flashes of beauty. When I was ten, I caught my reflection in the rearview mirror on the way home from Kailua Beach. The wind was blowing just right and I thought, *Well, I'm not the prettiest girl, but I'm kinda cute. And I look better when I smile. I think I'm gonna smile more.* I did. And it worked. People complimented my smile and called me "Rainbow Eyes" because of the shape they took. I felt like I had something going for me!

My best accessory became my smile. I started focusing on my strengths, and downplaying my weaknesses. I had to be my own best friend and biggest cheerleader, even in times when I seemed to be my own worst critic.

Mama always told us kids, "Act as if you love each other." I hung onto the idea: "act as if…" I started self-coaching as a girl, reciting a positive inner monologue until I believed it. After that rearview-mirror moment, my monologue was, *I'm OK and I like myself.* Not a TV star or model, but good enough for me.

I knew that inner beauty would be harder to develop than outer beauty. The cosmetic stuff would be easy. I could eventually maneuver a mascara wand and master a curling iron. Anyone could. But when it came to confidence, grace, patience, poise, and character—those were virtues that would take time. I needed years of life experience to master those essential behaviors, and that's exactly what God had in store for me.

I admired the island girls on the covers of tourism magazines, with their feminine curves, flowing hair, and lovely faces. They conveyed the Hawaiian ideal to the rest of the world. The girls in the posters seemed to possess everything I seemed to lack. I never saw myself growing into one of them. And Miss America, let alone Miss Hawai'i—seemed untouchable. As much as I admired the winners, at the time, I didn't dare dream of walking in their steps.

Before my parents left the Philippines, my mom said she used to watch the Miss America pageant when she could, in the rare homes that had TV sets in Manila. If anything, she heard about the pageant whenever a new winner made headlines there.

When our family moved to Hawai'i, Mama tried to catch it every year, if she remembered to turn on the TV, on that particular night in September. I didn't realize until I got older how popular pageants are in the Philippines. I've heard they are followed like the Super Bowl is in America. What's funny is that people say: "You have more of a chance of your son playing in the Super Bowl than you do of your daughter competing in Miss America." With those odds, and my background, I thought I had *no* chance!

In 1991, our family watched the first Miss Hawai'i get crowned Miss America. I remember Mama calling us to the TV when Carolyn Sapp made the Top Ten. She was gorgeous: a tall, sleek, polished beauty. And she was Caucasian. *I could never do that,* I thought, as she took her victory walk down the runaway. And yet, I imagined how incredible she must have felt being bestowed such an honor. Watching her win was like watching a real fairy tale come true.

Unlike most pageant winners I never fantasized of being Miss America as a little girl. Pageants got my attention when I was younger, but just like fairy tales, I never thought either could happen to me. I couldn't relate, but I *could* imagine what it might be like.

My dreams were more conservative, more realistic. I wanted to be a Catholic elementary school teacher—second grade to be exact, like Miss Rudeen. And then when I had kids, I wanted them to attend that same school so we could be together. Oh, and yes, I wanted to have a loving and supportive husband. *Was that too much to ask?* It was what I wanted most in life.

For a young girl craving any bit of attention from her parents, Miss Rudeen was just the female figure I needed in my life. I also admired the fact that she was a published author and was working on writing a children's book about *menehune*. (The Menehune are said to be a people, sometimes described as dwarfs in size. They live in the deep forests and hidden valleys of the Hawaiian Isles, and normal humans are unable to see them.)

Miss Rudeen used to leave me cute notes and holiday surprises in my desk so *I* considered her my best friend. Yet, when I tried to brag about the special treatment to my classmate, she laughed and said, "Miss Rudeen does that for everyone in class!" My bubble was burst thinking that I wasn't a standout, but I still loved coming to school every day. Miss Rudeen made learning fun and she was pretty, too.

The last day of second grade was sad and I missed her after a few days of summer. I wrote her a letter from home and my sister helped me mail it out. In it, I included whatever I could find around the house that would show my appreciation for all she had done and what she meant to me: a single stick of spearmint gum, a marble, and a pen that had sadly, already run out of ink. I mailed it off with a heartfelt letter in an envelope. My sister laughed at me for sending my teacher such ridiculous gifts, but it was all I could give.

In any case, I got the last laugh when, a few days later, Miss Rudeen wrote me a gushing thank you note back for the thoughtful letter and gifts. I tore open the envelope and her words made my day. She had a way of making all her students feel special. It was a quality she had towards everyone she met. With the profound impact she made on me at a young age, I wanted to do the same. I told myself, *One day, I'll be a teacher just like her.*

Carving a niche in my large family was the difficult part of solidifying my identity. With seven older siblings, no roles remained to be claimed.

They had covered every one I could think of: talented musician, skilled athlete, yearbook editor, class president, valedictorian, even homecoming queen. I had to find my own calling and define my role in the family, and in the world.

Above all, it seemed that I was a people pleaser, a "yes girl." I was always straining to earn Mama's and my siblings' praise and approval. But in my young mind, Mama always seemed to point out what was wrong and neglect what I did right. She had such high expectations that weren't always easy to reach.

When I helped my team win a basketball game, she questioned me about the basket I missed. If I got a ninety-nine percent on a test, she asked, "Couldn't you have done extra credit for an A-plus-plus? Aim for 110 percent!" I know now she was just using tough love to challenge me to be my best self, but it was a hard pill to swallow during those formative and precarious years.

Some of those insecurities transferred into the classroom. In first grade, I remember hopping onstage during our class talent show, assuming "The Rainbow Connection" would come naturally to me. I had never performed without the support of my family. My trembling voice was barely audible. Soon I was sweating and shaking. I reflexively sang the echo part my older sisters usually did and I felt so foolish. *That didn't play out as well as it was supposed to,* I thought, *I'm never doing that again!*

When I had to present book reports the following year, I was deathly afraid. I had developed a bad case of stage fright. And yet, my primary school classmates saw a tough girl, protector and defender of the underdog. If someone was bullied on the playground, they turned to me. "Who did that?" I'd bellow in indignation. "Let's go get 'em!" I'd grab their hand and we'd go confront the enemy, and they would back down because I was intimidating.

All the tag-team wrestling matches I did in the living room with my older siblings at home made me fearless. Once, in fifth grade, I got sent to the nurse for fighting a boy who was picking on my friend. I didn't get in trouble. I did however, get a few cuts and a newfound respect from the boys in my class.

Many classmates treated me like an older sister. The role came naturally because I had so many older siblings as guides, and I had two younger siblings to watch over. To them, I was a leader. In my own mind, I struggled with high expectations for myself, which were impressed upon me by Mama and the other teachers and coaches who compared me to my high-achieving siblings who had come before me.

In eighth grade, I followed in my sisters' footsteps and ran for class president. Campaigning was fun. I made huge posters with catchy slogans and handed out lollipops. When I won, I was honored and relieved. I had successfully maintained the *Baraquio standards*. After all, my older sister, Lucy, had just been named her high school class valedictorian and was accepted to the University of Notre Dame on scholarship. It was a lot to live up to, but it inspired me to *be* more. Once in a while Mama would tell us kids, "You are *not* ordinary." I guess some of us believed it. As class president, I helped organize a food and toiletry drive for the homeless and volunteered at the shelter. My sister Lucy told me she was impressed by my commitment to community service. That meant a lot to me.

As much as I had done, it still never felt like I was accomplishing as much as my siblings. I was driven to do more because we were held to such high standards. There was a time when Mama worked as a realtor and she used to come home and practice her positive affirmations on us, which she learned from work. She'd drill us in the van on the way to school, "Who are you?" To which we'd all reply in unison, "I am the best!" There were days we were tired and did not say it emphatically, and Mama would repeat her question until she was satisfied with our response. We all laughed because we felt silly. Then Mama would play Pattie LaBelle's song, "New Attitude" on the radio so it would seep into our subconscious. Apparently, it worked.

At school, I strove to be No. One in everything—to do the most sit-ups, run the most laps, and clock the fastest time on the fifty-yard dash. The little girls in PE class would squeal in delight, "Ooh, you beat a boy!" I relished in overcoming the odds. I also played on the volleyball and basketball junior high teams and was named team captain. I figured if I always aimed for the moon, even if I missed, I'd still be among the stars.

In the spring of 1990, I was chosen as the eighth grade May Day Queen. May Day is Lei Day in Hawai'i, and our school was celebrating this event. Being given the title was an honor, especially in Hawai'i, where some would argue it's a bigger deal than being named homecoming queen. In any case, I was proud to accept the role. Every May, schools across Hawai'i choose members of a royal court with eight princesses and escorts, each one representing one of the Hawaiian islands. While all the other girls wore the different colors for each island, I wore white, and got to dance hula on stage with my court.

In the eighth grade yearbook poll, I was voted "Most All Around" and was pictured carrying textbooks and athletic equipment. These votes of confidence struck me as ironic. *It's funny how people see me, but I don't feel that way,* I thought. All the accomplishments were just *things I did*, but I wasn't really passionate about any *one* thing. I was only trying to make the most of my junior high school years. It marked another occasion to "act as if … "

I longed to integrate all the pieces of me, but there was no assembly manual to guide me. Instead, I focused my energies on excelling. Any type of competition afforded me a healthy channel toward helping me unravel my lofty ambitions.

My imagination ran wild creating a storyline for the script of my life that would be *my* story alone. I knew that I could manifest my reality, and that God was guiding me along the way. There were times when I wasn't sure of where I was going, but my inner compass never steered me wrong. Somehow I always knew I was on the right path. And deep down, I never stopped searching to find the messages that I was meant to deliver to the world.

~ "Becoming" Miss America ~

When I first began competing in pageants after high school, I used to wonder what type of woman becomes Miss America. Is she really the girl next door and could I possibly have anything remotely in common with her? Although no winner ever looked like me, I was still curious to find out what it took to capture the prestigious title. I devoured all the reading materials I could get my hands on about former titleholders. Quickly, I realized that their backgrounds and upbringings were not that much different from mine.

The common denominator for most winners is that they possess a positive attitude, persistence, a winning mindset, and an unwavering focus. They have a mental toughness and a drive to succeed that catapulted them to the top. They also seem to innately self-coach and had *consciously* been preparing themselves for something greater from a very young age. Winners create experiences for themselves that allow them to increase their self-esteem, develop their strengths, and give them the necessary confidence, character, and poise to be victorious at the highest level, under extreme pressure. I wondered, though, *How much of their success was of their own doing, and how much of it was predestined by a Higher Power? Maybe it was a combination of both.*

After winning Miss America, people, especially little girls and their mothers, often asked me what prepared *me* to win the title. I suppose the short answer to that is the compilation of *all* my experiences that came before, which prepared me for that moment. All the *losses*, no matter how painful, that led up to that win were also valuable. I have always worked hard and tried to bloom where I was planted, tackling any challenges that came my way, and I believe that—plus the experience of being raised in a family of twelve—gave me a competitive edge. I would tell them that by knowing where I was going, I was able to weed out the things that I was willing *and* unwilling to do. Once that was clear, it made my path easier to follow.

As a little girl I daydreamed about falling in love, having a family, and finding my place in the world. I blended in so well with my siblings, which made me determined to stand out. Having six other sisters made it easy for people, especially teachers, to constantly mistaken us Baraquio girls for one another. I never stopped imagining a better life ahead and wondered what God had in store for me.

Then I discovered that those daydreams—my sometimes obsessive thoughts—were actually my passions, which led to my vocations. By following those passions, I found my purpose. The seed sown in me at a young age was the desire to teach young people about life, to make a difference on a large scale, and to change the world for the better, which drove me to be a teacher, and eventually, Miss Hawai'i and Miss America. It's what drives me today as a mother.

Like me, your passions will determine *your* destiny.

I wonder now, if God was molding me into a Miss America, long before I ever had the desire to *be* her. Here are some of the biggest milestones and moments in my life, that prepared me and defined who I was destined to become.

In second grade at Maryknoll Grade School, my teacher, Miss Rudeen, inspired me to become an elementary Catholic School teacher. She was one of the most influential women in my young life. I'd often play "school" with my little brother and sister, Albert and Gloria. I adored teaching from a young age, and had wonderful role models to emulate. So, in college, I chose to major in Elementary Education because it I knew I could make a positive difference in the field.

My teen years were predictable and unchanging. Every day was filled with sports practices and games (for basketball, volleyball, and cross country). It seemed I was always "in season" for some sport. There was no rest for this active teen, but I liked staying busy. Plus, it kept me out of trouble! I began to get exposed to things I never saw before. I could hardly believe some of the things that were happening at my school among kids my age. I had really lived a sheltered life up until then, and in many ways I was grateful. I made it a point to steer clear of anything unhealthy.

Even as a teen, I still wanted to be a "good girl." Being the eighth child, I had the luxury of learning from my older siblings' successes, and mistakes. If I wasn't studying hard to get on the Honor Roll in school, I was with my family cleaning our house and our church, or crying over the "drama of the day" having to do with my parents, siblings, coaches, boys, and friends. Then it was *rinse and repeat,* day in and day out.

What stands out to me now about my high school years is how I got stronger in my faith, mostly out of necessity. I was facing the challenge of transitioning from a K-8 Catholic education into a 9-12 public school education, *with three* of my older sisters—all during adolescence. And I had lots of questions. There were moments of doubt, but after a lot of reading, praying, researching, and soul-searching, I found my truth and fell in love with the Catholic church all over again.

By the time I graduated high school, I got interested in media and entertainment. After declaring my major in elementary education, I also declared an emphasis in speech, which would eventually aid in developing my public speaking skills and would lead to future on-camera work.

Meanwhile, I worked part-time as a bookkeeper and administrative assistant with Ma in the office of our family business, Able Termite Control. This was my first real job. In college, I got certified as a pest control operator like my dad, and many of us siblings would earn extra cash in the summers by helping Papa out in the field. It was humbling to be at the front lines of our business and see what my dad did for us all those years.

He worked happily each day because after a hard day's work, he always knew how to celebrate! My best memories, after hours of working in the hot sun, included eating local food like kal-bi (Korean barbecue) and rice or poke (seasoned raw fish) and lomi salmon with my dad and siblings. It was a time to eat, laugh, and bond. Those experiences allowed me to see firsthand how hard my parents worked, and I learned to appreciate what Ma and Pa did on a daily basis, to sustain our family.

Another key period in my life was being part of an all-girl rock group with my sisters in college. "High Tide" was the name of our band. Tess, Berna, Rose, and I, the four girls closest in age, all attended high school together. After years of playing basketball and running cross country simultaneously, we all attended college at the same time. We took the talents that we utilized and developed in church and turned them into our pastime. At first it was for fun, then we began to book gigs and get paid for our performances.

We even tried out for the Hawai'i Music Awards and created a music video for an original song Rose wrote called *Fade*. I was a full-fledged member of the group. My long-held insecurities were diminishing. At this point in time, I was beginning to come into my own.

Rose was our powerful and fearless lead singer and bassist, Berna was our up-tempo drummer, Tess was our nimble guitar player, and I was the lively keyboardist and smiling percussionist. We all sang backup vocals to Rose. While most of our days were spent in college courses, our nights were filled with long rehearsals, live performances, or all-nighters studying for exams in the library. It was a busy, but exciting time.

Eventually, though, family issues and old drama got caught up in the mix. With that, came hurt feelings among sisters. After a few years of making music together, High Tide broke up. It was a difficult time. We tried to pick up the pieces, but our group would never go back to what it once was. Plus, we were all moving on with our own lives and interests. It would take some time before the four of us would collectively reconcile our differences. Working with family was hard, but we gave it a try. We decided

29

to take a breather and just enjoy each other as sisters and friends first. And that would be necessary, if we ever wanted to work together professionally on anything again. The fact was, we *loved* each other but we had to learn how to move through our childhood roles and grow into our roles as adult sisters. At least we were aware of that.

Eager to put the past behind, and still make the most of my college years, I took electives that made me well rounded like ballet, hula, history of rock and roll, and storytelling, in addition to core classes and courses for my education major. School was opening up fascinating new worlds for me.

Meanwhile, Tini was always in the picture, encouraging, supporting, and loving me unconditionally, even though he was three thousand miles away from me in Southern California.

At one point, Rose and I worked at the University of Hawai'i Stan Sheriff Arena when it first opened. As ushers, we got to watch all the college basketball and volleyball games. After work, I'd stay back to shoot hoops with the players.

I actually contemplated playing college ball for a minute, but then realized that I had my heart set on being a teacher. With all the traveling the athletes did, my counselor said I wouldn't be able to fulfill my Student Teaching requirements if I tried out for the team. I conceded that my days of playing organized basketball had come and gone, and I was fine with my decision. *Off to new challenges!* The world was my oyster and I was bursting with optimism and possibilities.

Once I became college age, Mama said I should experience dorm life, since I was the first child who never got a chance to attend school in another state. Happily, I prepared to live away from my home, with my parents' consent. I spent one semester rooming at UH, all the while competing in pageants.

When I turned twenty, I was given the opportunity by a producer to host a local television show called *Hit-TV* on the 'Olelo Channel. What started out as an observation to learn the ropes of interviewing live guests from a veteran host, quickly turned into my *first* experience as an on-camera host. The hip-hop group, 2 Live Crew, was in Honolulu for a concert, and one of our roving reporters was supposed to interview them.

At the last minute, she couldn't make it. Since she was a no-show, I was thrown into the fire and asked to do the interview in her place. As uncomfortable as I was, I got through it, and afterward, the producer asked me to come on board as a regular TV reporter. Eventually, I became the show's main host. It was my secret dream to be a broadcast personality or a video jockey (VJ) at the time, and I was about to get that chance.

The time I invested in pageants had paid off and I learned poise, stage presence, and communication skills, which easily translated into the world of television. For several years, I was known as "Angie from *Hit-TV*," a local-style version of MTV. It was an entertainment spotlight that allowed me to speak off-the-cuff on camera. I interviewed celebrities that came to Hawai'i for concerts, and introduced music videos on a half-hour show that was pre-taped, edited, and shown on statewide television.

I met celebrities like No Doubt, Cypress Hill, Hall and Oates, Dishwalla, Shaggy, Ice-T, Babyface, After 7, and many others. I even got invited to be at the private welcoming (with only the press present) when Michael Jackson landed in Honolulu for his HIStory Tour in 1997, a moment I will never forget!

I was a big fan, and when I saw Michael up close, descending from the steps of his private airplane, (I had planned to greet him with some words of aloha), I was *completely* speechless in his presence. I only mustered up enough courage to *touch his jeans*. Yes, it's pathetic, I know, but he was the King of Pop and he had that effect on me! In any case, his concert at the Aloha Stadium was epic! I still can't believe I met him. Tini, my siblings, and I all got to see him live in concert—definitely a highlight, and one thing I could cross off my secret bucket list.

My younger brother, Albert, whose stage name was "Big Al," started working as a co-host with me on *Hit-TV*. At the time, he and I were roommates downstairs in our parents' house. He would host the live dance parties for *Hit-TV* and was always the guy who stood out, with his slick dance moves and his spiky hair, which he dyed every few weeks. I remember he and his friends colored their hair fiery orange once, and nicknamed themselves, the Lightning Brothers. *Oh boy*.

Not only were we roommates and co-hosts, but Albert and I also coached basketball together at Holy Family Catholic Academy, our former elementary and junior high school. We spent a lot of time together in those days, and we created some of our favorite memories.

Albert was a jokester, even in our college years. He liked to jolt me at the most inopportune times. Once he waited for a whole hour at the bottom of our stairwell just to jump out and scare me before I walked into our house. Luckily, I saw him hiding and so I took my time descending the stairs. When he heard my approach he readied himself for his best scream, but before he could jump out to frighten me, *I* scared *him*, and he began to shriek like a little girl! It was one of the most hilarious moments I can recall about my little bro—the same kid I used to ignore in high school when we passed each other in the halls.

Because I had weekly exposure on the state public access channel with *Hit-TV* I was starting to get recognized around town. I was called by a producer to host an Emmy-nominated TV show called, *Hawai'i Winter Baseball's Road to the Show*. For a college student, the pay was excellent, and it sounded exciting! My persona on the show was "Angie Baseball," and I got to travel to games in Honolulu and on the neighbor islands to interview these baseball giants in the major and minor leagues, who came to Hawai'i for the Winter Baseball season. I was supposed to draw in the female audience, who didn't necessarily like to watch baseball but might tune in if they saw someone just like them asking basic questions like, "What's a bullpen?" or "How many innings are in a game?" The show was fun and well-received.

Once I got to dress up as a mascot and even wear the umpire's gear to see what it was like to be *him* during a game. The ump gave me a sample demonstration of how to say, "You're outta here!" to a player. He couldn't contain his laughter when I then tried to do his job and shouted, "You are SO outta here!" *Not quite, but good effort, Angie Baseball.* I was on the show for a whole season, and it gave me more TV exposure and media experience to add to my resume.

All of these experiences helped develop my strengths in different fields, gave me exposure to people of all walks of life, and taught me how to be in front of the camera with poise and confidence. Through the people I've met and worked with (including my friends, and family) I learned compassion, hard work, interview skills, the importance of goal-setting, having a positive attitude, and how to develop a winning mindset.

Like other winners, I knew that whatever I wanted out of life, it would require persistence, focus, mental toughness, and a drive to succeed. I continued to self-coach throughout the whole process, as I knew I was being prepared for something greater, even at a young age.

By the time I turned twenty-four, I had a better understanding of the world around me. All these real-world life experiences would help me become a better teacher, Miss Hawai'i, Miss America, wife, and mother.

The experiences I created for myself increased my self-esteem and helped me to win the biggest competition of my life, under enormous pressure. Through it all, God, my family, and closest friends were right beside me.

How much of my success was my own doing, and how much was predestined? Was my fate written in the stars long before I was born? I don't know. What I do know is that everything aligned for me in the cosmos the night I won, but I still had to do my part to get there. And no matter what your goals and dreams are, you will have to do yours.

CHAPTER 4

SOMEDAY MY PRINCE WILL COME

After graduating eighth grade, I knew I would soon leave behind the comfort and safe cocoon of the Catholic education I had grown to love by attending public high school like my sisters. The Big Ones were in college at private Catholic universities, and the expenses were mounting for my parents. Financial aid and student loans helped, but it wasn't enough.

Ceci was at Loyola Marymount University, Jerome at Dominican College, Lucy at the University of Notre Dame, and John at Portland University. The tuition, frequent trips home for the holidays, books, dorm rooms, and travels abroad had proven to be too expensive to add private school tuition for the six of us still in grades six through twelve.

My freshman year at Moanalua High School was slightly intimidating. The twins, Tess and Berna, were seniors, my sister Rose was a junior, and I was the newcomer. Think about it: my parents had FOUR teenage girls in high school at the same time . . . *Whoa! 'Nuff said.* People loved my sisters and they were outstanding student athletes. I knew I had to find a way to make myself stand out somehow.

Overall, I was thankful that I had my three older sisters, Tess, Berna, and Rose to lean on. We all made the varsity basketball team and ran varsity cross country together my freshman year. There was a sense of freedom in not wearing uniforms, not having to abide by such strict rules, and being engulfed in a more diverse environment with people of various faiths and upbringing. I felt pressured to dress like the other girls in the latest fads, I discovered makeup, and found that boys were interested in me, which was a completely new concept. I was warned by my older sisters about what to expect in high school—like which boys to steer clear from. I felt that I had a good head on my shoulders and strong foundation to rely on.

While I was not looking for a boyfriend at all, at fourteen, I met a guy who liked me, and we started dating. I never intended to "play the field" like older friends advised. "You're young, have fun!" they said. That wasn't my style. Crazy as it may sound, I was looking for a prospective husband at that young age. With all my extra-curricular activities, I didn't have time to date, but it was a new experience for me. After spending time together for over a year, we broke up at the beginning of my junior year.

I had always dreamed of finding my future husband in high school and we'd be faithful to each other forever. You know, the cliché of boy meets girl, they fall in love, get married and live happily ever after. I guess the joke was on me. *Fairy tales are fun to read, but they don't come true.* The perfect ending for us was inevitably not the case because he easily moved on with another girl, and we weren't as serious as I thought we were. Understandably, he wasn't looking for a wife back then.

Since I was resolute about saving myself for my husband, I kept my purity intact. Still, after the breakup, I felt I had lost a part of me. Although I was young and naïve, I believed then that I knew what love was. That's how I experienced my first heartbreak. For the first time I felt like someone *saw* me and loved me for *me*. I realized later that I didn't miss *him* as much as the *idea* of having a boyfriend. I wanted to find true love.

After the breakup, I had a pathetic moment when I found myself wondering how I would move forward alone. It was so unlike me. *Who was I becoming? I was stronger than this.* I didn't need a boy in my life to show me my worth. Thankfully, I still had my pride and my purity. I did not want to get hurt again.

Amidst normal teen pressures and expectations from family, friends, teachers, and coaches, I did what I knew best. I fell back on my faith, did some soul searching, and started asking some big questions. Few of my friends at my public high school were Christians, so I began to critically examine my own Catholic faith. *Was I living in a dream world with my head in the clouds?* I began to experience doubt in my religion and wondered what this life was all about. After much reading and research, I found the answers.

That year, I started preparing for the Catholic sacrament of Confirmation, which deepens all of the graces granted at Baptism. My questions and doubt eventually solidified that there *was* a God who loved me unconditionally and would be near me at times I felt most alone and broken. That was a turning point for me, in terms of confirming my beliefs and strengthening my faith. There was no turning back.

~ Finding True Love ~

It's been said that love appears when you least expect it. At fifteen, I met a boy named Tini (pronounced Tee-nee as in martini, short for

Tinifuloa) Grey, who was four months older than me, and we were both sophomores. He was my brother Albert's friend and fellow altar boy at our church in Waikiki. Although he entered the scene when I was still with my first high school boyfriend, I didn't really get to know Tini until our senior year.

Tini was six-foot-four and weighed 220 pounds. He was an athletic and handsome Samoan, yet quite shy and nonverbal. At first sight I thought, *Cute for other girls, but not my type.* At the time I never considered him a love interest. He attended a prestigious all-boy Catholic high school in Honolulu—he was a St. Louis Crusader.

Our first conversation went like this: "What's your name?" "Tini." "What grade are you?" "Tenth." "Do you play sports?" "Football." "Anything else?" "Basketball." And that was the extent of it. *OK, that was fun . . .*

Ironically, Tini and I never really saw each other except on Sundays at church. Our paths crossed when he, Albert, and the altar boys would come over to our house and play cards, or we'd see each other at the park during Sunday barbecues, randomly at Fastop near Ice Palace, or at beach volleyball games with the family.

Apparently, all this time he had admired me from afar and told his cousins in secret that he loved me from the moment he saw me. *What!* They would tease him but he said to them with unshakeable confidence, "I'm gonna marry that girl one day." (I still don't believe this claim, but he says it's completely true and his cousins attest to it.) During my junior year, I was watching my brother Albert's JV basketball game and Tini came up to me afterward to say goodbye to our family. I looked up from reading a book when he asked me, "Can I call you sometime?" I was taken aback, but in the spur of the moment I said, "Yes." I turned to my little sister Gloria and said, "Did the tall altar boy from church just ask if he could call me? Weird!" I could not fathom that the quiet Samoan was interested in me. On the surface, it seemed we had nothing in common.

My senior year, I needed a date to my school's Winter Fantasy, and I told my mom I didn't know whom to take. She told me to go with my brother, Albert. *Yuck!* He was just as repulsed and told me to ask our friend, Preston, another altar boy. Preston knew Tini liked me, and in an attempt to match us up he said, "I don't want to go with you. Go with Tini." I was fine with his rejection because I knew Preston would never be dating material; he was hoping to be a priest someday. That week at the beach, I asked Tini if he might want to be my date. He later told me he was so excited that I asked him. However, his cool and immediate response to me was, "Let me ask my mom." I was a bit peeved to say the least. Time was running out.

Meanwhile, another boy at school asked me to the dance, and since I had asked Tini to be my date, and he never responded, I was about to say yes to this other guy, who was two years my junior and the new kid at school.

When I got home, I was getting ready to call Tini to cancel with him. Albert learned what I was about to do and he yelled at me, "You better not do that to Tini! Don't you know he *likes* you?!" (I was clueless about the fact that Albert, Gloria, and Preston were plotting our matchmaking all along.) I was in complete shock and denial. His actions surely didn't give away any feelings he had for me. I felt bad for not giving him a chance to officially reply to my request, so I gave a courtesy call to check in with the poor guy. After asking his mom, he said yes. And that was it. We talked about what colors we'd wear to match and ironed out all the details of when and where we'd meet.

So on December 20, 1993, Tini and I went on our first date—to my high school's winter ball, the first of three senior formals we would attend together. After that, Tini asked me to his St. Louis High School senior prom, an all-boy Catholic high school in Honolulu. I eventually asked him to my senior prom as well, since I was still flying solo. Who knew that he would be the man I'd marry nine years later? We still have pictures to prove how we started our friendship and it's pretty amazing to show our kids that their parents have been best friends since they were teenagers.

Tini and I were not exclusively dating in high school, but we had developed a really good friendship. When I found out that one of his all-time favorite movies was *Breakin' 2: Electric Boogaloo*, I could not believe it. It was mine, too! We'd talk for hours about life and death, Heaven and Hell, deep issues that no other boy my age showed interest in or could converse about.

Then we'd see each other at church and practically ignore one another. *It was so high school—literally!* But somehow, Tini transformed into my only solid friend and confidant when I was trying to overcome heartbreak at sixteen and answer heavy questions about my faith at age seventeen and eighteen. I never regarded him as anything more than a friend . . . until the day he left for college.

After my high school graduation ceremony, Tini was right by my side. Even surrounded by all the people who greeted me with lei afterward, we ended up walking home alone together to my graduation party, which was only a few blocks away. I wasn't fully aware that I was developing feelings for him, and I certainly wasn't ready to admit it, nor did I want to hear he had feelings for me because we were such great friends. I knew I'd miss him when he left for college in Burbank, California.

Even though he had been offered a football scholarship to a school in Oregon, he chose to study Architecture at Woodbury University. We both had just turned eighteen and we were getting ready for college and a new phase in our lives. We didn't know what the future had in store for us, but we knew we'd miss each other terribly. I had dreams of going to Notre Dame like my sister Lucy, but I knew there was no way that I would ask my parents to pay the high tuition for a second child. I was happy to stay in Hawai'i to attend a local college and save my folks some money by getting in-state tuition. I also knew I didn't want to have a pile of debt in student loans.

As summer went on, Tini and I hung out almost every day. One day, I met a pageant director who told me I could earn scholarship money to pay for my college education. Tini was the one who drove me to my first meeting with Tino Montero, one of the directors of the Miss Asian Universal Pageant. He waited in the car while I went to the meeting. Tini was there every step of the way as I started my career in pageants.

The last day of summer was approaching and Tini was about to leave for college. He kept telling me, "I have to tell you something." Deep inside, I knew he wanted to tell me how he felt about me, but I wasn't so sure I was ready to hear it. Up until then, I had guy friends who had told me they had feelings for me, and I was the "all or nothing" type. If I knew a guy liked me, I stopped being friends with him so that I wouldn't lead him on. I didn't know if I was ready for a more serious relationship with Tini, especially if he was leaving! *Couldn't we just stay friends?*

The day came for him to leave for California, and I was invited to his farewell dinner with his family at Duke's, Waikiki. When I got there, I was surprised when he gave me a gift and told me not to open it or read the card until I got in my car on the way to the airport.

Once dinner was over, I jumped in my car and nervously ripped open both of them. He had given me an angel book of daily inspirations and reflections, a precious angel music box that played "Ave Maria," and a card confessing his love for me. *It was happening!* He was telling me for the first time that he was in love with me and, as long as it took, he was willing to wait for me. He encouraged me to stop looking for the right one because that special someone was right under my nose. I never thought in a million years that he and I would be compatible or that we would even be remotely interested in each other. We seemed to be polar opposites. Discovering that he was deeply in love with me from the moment we met was shocking.

By the time I got to his flight gate (remember the days we could do that?), I didn't know what to expect or how to act when I saw him. Right away, he asked if I read his card. I nodded and smiled. My heart was racing.

He went on to greet his friends and family, rehashing memories and listening to how much he'd be missed. They all hugged him and said their goodbyes. I was overcome with anxiety and apprehension because I didn't know how to deal with this news of his undying love for me. I thought we were just friends. Did I feel the same? Was I ready to lose him? Was I prepared to say goodbye? How was our relationship going to change moving forward?

The hours passed quickly and soon the flight attendant announced his boarding time. Everyone gave him embraces and their final farewells. I felt insignificant amongst his family and friends. So many people loved Tini. I was just one of many. Hiding in a corner until everyone had a moment with him, I waited patiently for my turn. He told me he was looking out for me, waiting to say goodbye to me last.

Then the time came for final boarding. His sisters, parents, and brother were weeping and being comforted by friends and family. Miraculously, we had a moment alone together, and no one seemed to pay attention to us. The gentle giant looked down at me, and I looked up at him with watery eyes. He said, "I'm gonna miss you." I said, "I'll miss you, too." Then he smiled and leaned in toward me, kissed me gently on the lips. It was perfect. Not realizing what just happened, I stood there in tears. Filled with newfound confidence, Tini walked toward the gate standing tall, with a huge grin on his face, raised his hand up and flashed a big shaka sign, saying, "Kay den, boys!" to all his friends, and he walked away down the corridor until he disappeared. I was left in complete shock. I knew then that we could no longer go back to being just friends. I loved him.

Tini and I stayed in touch by mail and phone from the moment he left on that September evening in 1994 until December 15 that year when he returned to Honolulu for Christmas break. Those were the days before Skype and Facetime. Email, cell phones, and the Internet were just making their way into the mainstream!

By Christmas 1994, our courtship began. In college, we endured a challenging five-year, long-distance relationship. I was studying elementary education at the University of Hawai'i at Manoa, while he was earning his architecture degree from Woodbury University. He said he'd wait for me.

I waited for him too, and we became closer with each passing year. There were times I wanted to quit because the distance was too hard, but Tini was always reassuring me that we could stick it out and beat the odds. I believed him.

Up to this point, the majority of our relationship was spent apart—we learned to readjust each time we experienced being in the same place at the same time, let alone in the same state! I was no damsel in distress, but he was turning out to be a Prince Charming.

After our college graduations in 1999, he left his Grey family in California, where they had moved, and came back to Hawai'i to be closer to me.

We volunteered to start a Tongan youth choir together at our church that would remain intact for seven years. As music ministers, we served about twenty youth. Tini played the guitar, I played the piano and percussion instruments, and we were both cantors who led the choir in three-part harmony. The raw talent the youth had was incredible. We disbanded the choir when we moved to California, but recently it has been resurrected. It was heartwarming to learn that our former members, who are now college graduates, have taken over as the new choir directors, infusing new energy and excitement into the ministry.

It was a tremendously gratifying experience for Tini and me to be able to work with these students, ranging from ages eight to twenty-one, and create a music ministry. The choir became our second family and it was a glimpse into what Tini and I could do as a couple, and what our life would look like when we started our own family.

In 2000, when I decided to run for Miss Hawai'i, Tini told me that if I didn't win, he wanted to start planning for our wedding. When I ended up winning, we put our engagement plans on hold. Then when I won Miss America in October of that year, he realized that he'd have to make a bold move.

~ The Power of Yes ~

On June 15, 2001, I came back to the Miss Hawai'i stage at the Hilton Hawaiian Village as the new Miss America. Eight months into my reign, I was honored to be back home to see my successor, Billie Takaki, crown our new Miss Hawai'i, Denby Dung.

Dancing hula onstage to the song, "Blue Hawai'i," I was thrilled to be accompanied by Tini's all-male Polynesian singing group, Reign. The same group had shared the stage with me the year before, when I was crowned Miss Hawai'i. Moments before we went live on camera, Tini whispered, "I'm so excited to be on the same stage as you. I can't wait for tonight." I thought, *Weren't we on the same stage together last year?* Then another thought rushed into my mind: *He might propose to me tonight on a quiet beach somewhere!* I was so excited. I thought, *Let me just get through this performance, and we can have a quiet moment together!*

As I got onstage, I enjoyed this moment home as the current Miss America. Unlike other times I stood on this pageant stage, there was no pressure—it was just a fun and quick performance. Reign started singing the song behind me, and I went through the hula motions to the words, *Night and you, in blue Hawai'i, the night is heavenly, and you are Heaven to me . . .* The song seamlessly moved into the second verse, *Lovely you, in blue Hawai'i, with all this loveliness, there should be love.* Then I waited for the chorus, *Come with me . . .* but the words never came and the music suddenly changed. Obviously confused, I stopped dancing. This was unrehearsed. Puzzled, I turned to Tini and saw him grab the mic to start serenading me. I mouthed to him through a forced smile, "What are you doing?"

39

I didn't know how to react but I was little upset that he interrupted my hula dance. I stood there uncomfortably on live television with my hands behind my back. I thought to myself, *How sweet, he's decided to surprise me and sing to me in the middle of my hula. Ok, go with it. And keep smiling no matter how uncomfortable you are, the cameras are still rolling.*

Then the accompaniment played the background music to Stevie Wonder's song, "You and I." Tini sang, *Here we are, on earth together, just you and I. God has made us fall in love it's true. I've finally found someone like you.* I kept smiling. I was touched. He then inserted his own lyrics, *So now I pray that you would be . . . MY BRIDE someday, 'cause it's your love that I'm living for, you see. You can trust in me. 'Cause in my mind we can conquer the world, in love you and I, you and I, you and I.* Those words, *my bride* actually sounded as if they were sung in slow motion. That was only the second instance in my life that had happened. The first time was when Donny Osmond announced me as Miss America. That's when I realized what was going on . . .

Then, Tini put the mic aside, got down on one knee and asked me to marry him! Shocked, amazed, and crying tears of joy, I said yes, while the audience wondered if this was part of the scripted show. Tini put the ring on my finger. He was shaking because he was so nervous! He got up and wiped the beads of sweat on his forehead. Then he hugged me, and we kissed before he whispered, "Keep dancing. They're about to cut to commercial." I quickly fell back into step as the music to "Blue Hawai'i" continued. At the end of the song, I showed my ring to the audience and had a huge grin on my face. Flashing two shaka signs, I jumped into my new fiancé's arms, hugging him again and telling him how much I loved him. I was floating!

The audience began to applaud before cutting to commercial. Then the host, Howard Dashefsky, announced that this was not in the script, and had to tell the viewers at home that I had said yes. The entire moment was incredibly romantic and so unexpected—like a scene out of a movie! This was completely out of character for shy, quiet Tini, but I knew he did it to catch me off guard. He knew I wanted a surprise proposal and he wanted to give me an unforgettable one. He definitely succeeded!

The next day, my friend called me and said she was flying home from her honeymoon in Belize and read about my engagement to Tini in *People* magazine on the plane ride back. Others called me and said they read about it in the paper and online. I had waited so long for this moment, and now I was going to marry the man of my dreams!

Tini and I try not to take it for granted that we have seen each other grow up and have witnessed the transformations we have both undergone from childhood to parenthood. Through it all, Tini and I had jumped through hoops and overcame obstacles to be together and we continue to fight for our love so it grows stronger with each passing day.

We are happy to be each other's sounding boards, support systems, and biggest cheerleaders when it comes to reaching our goals individually, as a couple, and as a family. He has always supported me in everything I've done, quietly taking a backseat when I was in the spotlight. Now, it's so gratifying for me to support him in his successful solo music career. We have co-written songs together, filmed music videos as a family, and have worked on releasing several albums as a couple. I have even used his own sage advice on him when *he* gets onstage at big concerts and performances (like the time he auditioned for Season 7 of *The Voice* on NBC). I am so proud of my husband. We've been through so much together, and I am continuously convinced that we were made for each other.

The year 2014 marked twelve years of marriage and twenty-one years since that first date together at my high school's Winter Fantasy. Love truly is exciting and brand new when you marry your best friend. And while no one is perfect, we are well aware that we are perfect for each other. I know God exists because He sent me my husband to show me that He loves me. In my youth, I needed an imaginary friend to remind me of God's love. Today, Tini is a representation of that undying, unconditional love for me on earth—and I will love him till the day I die.

CHAPTER 5

WINNERS ARE THE MINORITY

No matter how hard we try, there are some days that can never be erased from our memory. One such day occurred during my junior year at Moanalua High School, when I was just seventeen. The instant replay in my head haunts me every so often, with shocking clarity, but I'd like to say that I see the situation anew with clearer focus, now that I'm an adult. The events leading up to that day started when I was only fourteen.

Three of my sisters and I participated in sports beginning in the fifth grade. I was proud to have made the varsity basketball and cross country team as a freshman and the varsity volleyball team as a junior at Moanalua High. Serving as a team captain on my basketball and cross country teams was an honor, and I learned quickly that character counts both on and off the court. My involvement in athletics has taught me about life, and those experiences have colored my outlook and approach in all things, to this day.

Coach Dana Takahara was a rookie Moanalua Menehune girls' basketball head coach in 1991. As a former University High point guard, state championship Most Valuable Player, and a University of Hawai'i Wahine standout, she arrived on our high school campus and brought along with her an impressive track record. We knew she meant business. Under her leadership and guidance, our girls' varsity squad made it to the semifinals in the state championship four years in a row. We broke the team's twelve-year streak of not making it to the state tournament since 1979. Coach Dana understood us because she had been in our shoes once before and had the credentials to prove it.

As a freshman in 1991 at Moanalua, I played on the same basketball team as my sisters Tess, Berna, and Rose. Some games, Coach Dana would put the four of us in at once, all in the same lineup. I finally felt like I was "part of the team" when I got to be on the court with my sisters. We had natural synergy on the court. Our team had a strong season and placed fourth in the state. That year, the twins graduated.

In 1992, Rose was now a senior, while I was a sophomore. We played Kamehameha School for the girls' high school basketball state championship title, but fell short in the last quarter of the game, placing second overall in the state. That year, Rose was named Female Athlete of the Year for our entire school and made the statewide All-Star team. Once again, I felt like I was living in my sisters' shadows. There was a lot of pressure for me to continue the "Baraquio basketball legacy" after she graduated, but I had to push through and make a name for myself.

I was a junior in 1993, and by then, all my older sisters were gone to college. Only Albert and I were in high school together. He was a freshman. Our team had a good handful of returning veterans, and finishing second place at the state championship a year before, gave us valuable tournament experience, which alone proved to be a deciding factor in our "winning" regular season. There's no question that basketball is a game of precision, finesse, and discipline, and our team was polished and driven that year.

We focused on fundamentals during our grueling four-hour practices, and there were days we never even touched the ball. We only worked on defensive drills and did squats against the gym walls to build our physical and mental toughness. Coach reminded us that we needed to be in peak physical condition in order to beat the competition.

Cardiovascular endurance and speed training were crucial if we wanted to be on top of our game. One of our sprint workouts was commonly known as the "suicide." Beginning at the baseline, we sprinted to the free throw line closest to us. Then we returned to the baseline and immediately sprinted to the half court line. Again, we returned to the baseline and turned to sprint toward the free throw line farthest from us, then we sprinted back to the baseline. Finally, we ran the full length of the court at full speed and returned to the starting point on the baseline. That was *one*. Some days we would do twelve to fifteen suicides in a single practice.

I dreaded hearing Coach say the words, "Baseline," "Suicide," "On the line"—each term meaning the same thing, and she usually said it when she was angry with our performance or behavior. Coach used it to condition and to reprimand us. In order to improve our speed and stamina, we were timed, and each girl had to come in at a certain time. The guards were expected to be faster than the forwards, but everyone on the team had to come in before a certain time or beat the last record. If we didn't beat the clock, it was back "on the line." Training was relentless. We dripped with sweat after each practice and gulped down gallons of water to replenish our lost energy. I couldn't stand "suicides," but I lived through them.

Our team knew that not being conditioned physically and mentally would make us tired during games and that would lead to mental mistakes and breakdowns, which could lead to multiple losses. With a collaborative determination to win, we won every single game in both the preseason and regular season. All our hard work was paying off!

~ May 1, 1993 ~
Moanalua vs. Kailua, OIA Championship Game

Despite several key players being sidelined by knee injuries that season, my teammates and I managed to defend our coveted title of O'ahu Interscholastic Association (OIA) Champs from the previous year (when my sister Rose was our team captain), but—I *almost* didn't attend that game at all.

My sister Lucy (eight years my senior) got married on the same night of the OIA Championship game. Because the game time conflicted with the time of the wedding reception, I was not planning on even going to the game, out of respect for my sister.

Coach was disappointed, but she understood. I felt guilty because I felt like I was letting my team down by not even showing up. But this was a big day for my sister and I couldn't leave the reception early. My team was on edge because our starting guard got injured in a game just days before, and would have to sit out during this championship game. Coach always said we were only as strong as our weakest link. So our whole bench knew that each of us would have to step up.

I was torn. My sisters and I had been preparing a hula for Lucy's reception for months. We were supposed to perform in the evening, but how could anyone have predicted that our team would be undefeated and make it to the divisional championships that fell on the exact same day? Although I wanted to be there for Lucy, I wished I could be in two places at once.

As the afternoon turned into evening, I kept staring at the clock nervously, wondering what my teammates were doing: possibly changing for the game in our locker room, doing warm-ups, shooting baskets, visualizing, and doing our normal rituals like we always did before game time. As the sun began to set in Manoa, (where the reception was held), I whispered to Mama and Papa to ask if there were any way I could still attend the 7:30 p.m. game, if only just to watch and support my team with my *physical* presence. I thought, *Please, Ma, I don't even have to play!* After all, I had packed my gym bag with my team uniform, basketball shoes, and my warm-up outfit . . . just in case.

My parents, who had been loyal fans of our team all season, knew how big this game was. At the last minute, after more prodding from me, they decided to let me go. *I was so happy!*

Ceci got the keys from Ma and Pa and drove me to Moanalua gym, just minutes before the pre-game warm up began. I walked into the locker room and Coach Dana was in the middle of giving our pep talk and was about to announce the starting lineup. I snuck in quietly. When the team saw me, their eyes lit up. They weren't expecting me, but I could tell it was a pleasant surprise.

Coach looked up and said, "Hi Angie—I thought you were at your sister's wedding!" I said, "I couldn't miss this game. I'm just here to support." Coach said, "Do you have your uniform?" I said, yes. Then she said, "Suit up. You're starting." I was honored. This was so unexpected, but I was thrilled to prove to Coach that I could do it! She made me starting point guard, taking Pohai Frank's place, because she was out due to her knee injury. I wanted to make Pohai proud. Seeing her in her cast made me want to work harder.

That night, we beat Kailua High School and won the OIA Championship title for a second year in a row. Coach said that although Pohai's presence was hard to replace, she felt confident that I had the ability to step in as the new starting point guard, if necessary. I scored eight points that night and had some assists, which helped our team garner another win. I was proud to have contributed in some small way to our victory that night and was overjoyed to celebrate with my team!

My parents and siblings came to the gym after the reception was over (all dressed in formal wedding attire), just in time to see us play in the last quarter. Tess, Berna, and Rose walked into the gym wearing their dresses and heels, and caught the last seconds of the game. When we were announced the winners in a formal ceremony afterward, my three sisters came up to congratulate me and my teammates. It felt good to win, independent of my sisters, and to see them being so supportive. I was stepping up my game and finally earning my position on the team. On top of that, I was starting to feel like I was coming out of the shadows.

~ The Playoffs ~

A few days later, the playoffs began, and we were on our way to the girls' high school basketball state championship tournament once again. The adversities we faced, as we lost starting players to knee injuries, gave way to early inspiration for our team. Coach rallied us by telling us to concentrate on who *was* here, and not on who *wasn't* here. There was also more incentive to win, since no Moanalua girls' basketball team had ever won a state championship and here, we actually had a fighting chance!

Unlike the prestigious private schools, like Kamehameha, our public school team was made up of ordinary girls that had a lot of heart. Nothing came easy for us. We had to work twice as hard to earn our wins. I thought,

No problem, I'm used to working twice as hard.

Coach Dana always said during tryouts that she looked for three main things in a player: Attitude, Talent, and Potential (in that particular order). She stressed that we play with class and reminded us that we were ladies *first.* We were proud scholar athletes, and many of us made the Honor Roll each semester. Even though we didn't have handpicked players like other private schools in the state, who recruited only the best of the best to make their teams powerhouses, we were confident in our abilities and shared a special bond with one another.

My friend and All-Star point guard, Jodi Benson, was the only other freshman besides me who played for Coach Dana starting in 1991. By then, we both had two prior years of experience at the state level in the Final Four and knew the kind of hard work, commitment, and mindset it took to get there. There were other strong players: Samara, Amber, and Tanya, all offensive and defensive threats. Pohai (recovering from her torn ACL) would round out the starting lineup. I would be interchangeable with her.

Coach built the capacity of our thirteen-player team. Every girl on our squad, whether we played during the game or not, was an integral part. No matter the role, each person mattered and our chemistry was strong.

Our record was 17-0 and we were the top-seeded team in the 17th Hawai'i High School Athletic Association Girls' Basketball Tournament because we were the only undefeated team in the state.

As fate would have it, with only four teams still vying for the state title, we were slated for a rematch (in the semifinals), with the defending champions Kamehameha (who had three consecutive state titles). But this time, we both had *very* different teams. Both teams had starters out for the remainder of the season. But we still had our key players and a well-rounded bench, and we felt ready to steal that title. The pressure was mounting for both sides.

~ May 7, 1993 ~
Kamehameha vs. Moanalua, Semifinals

On the evening of May 7, 1993 the, Moanalua Menehune and the Kamehameha Warriors faced off again in a much-anticipated rematch at their home court. Regardless of how we were ranked, we knew that Kamehameha would put up a good fight. They were the team to beat in the state. I didn't know it back then, but this particular game would turn out to be one of my most defining moments, shaping me into the person I was destined to become.

I started the game as a guard, but got into early foul trouble. The refs kept blowing the whistle on us. It was frustrating because I played the same tough defense I always played, but I racked up fouls in a matter of minutes.

I was so disappointed at myself *and* with the officials' calls. I thought, *Why can't they just let us play our game?*

Coach was not happy. She yanked me from the lineup. It was hard to sit on the bench, because I felt helpless there, but I kept supporting my teammates. Coach didn't put me back in until the fourth quarter, when we were trailing the Warriors.

In the fourth quarter, as time was winding down, we suffered a major blow when we lost Samara, our key player (and starting forward) to a left knee injury with less than three minutes left in the final quarter. The drama continued to unfold with each second.

Our team had closed the point spread and was down by two points. The score was Kamehameha, 40; Moanalua, 38. We felt like we were in a pressure cooker as time was about to expire in the fourth quarter. Everyone on our team sensed the possibility that we might not make a comeback.

But, as always, the clutch player that she was, our point guard, Jodi, who was fighting a bad cold and could hardly breathe, brought our team back from near extinction after sinking a three-pointer, with only thirteen seconds left on the clock. That *huge* move put us ahead by one point! It was literally a game changer. The score was now 40-41, Moanalua leading in the final moments of the fourth quarter.

Our school's cheering section went wild! More than a thousand fans in the gym were on the edge of their seats, and we could almost taste victory. It seemed that we were about to seal the deal—to win the state championship title, and make Hawai'i girls basketball history. This was our chance.

We were known for our defense, so we felt confident and anticipated the win, like we had so many times before. The injured starters hugged each other and the other teammates on our bench. Every one of us, including our whole coaching staff, was wide-eyed and filled with renewed hope. We were not only still in the game, but *we could win this whole thing!* The excitement was building.

With 5.5 seconds left on the clock, the Warriors' point guard nervously rushed the ball down the court and suddenly made a bad pass to her teammate. The ball had obviously bounced off the girl's leg, and dribbled out of bounds. The crowd erupted because it was clear to everyone that possession would go to Moanalua. The roar of the crowd was deafening.

The Warriors' fans near the sidelines who witnessed it all, and the coaches on the opposite sideline were screaming at the girls for their costly mistake. It was loud, but I blocked out the distractions. We'd been down this familiar road before. In practice, we had gone over this particular situation and had executed it in many games that season. Since we were up, all we needed to do was inbound the ball and hold on to it until the clock ran out. *YES!* Amidst the noise and chaos, I made a hand target for the referee to pass me the ball so I could inbound it to my teammate and finish the game. But—to my shock—and everyone else's surprise, after the ball rolled out of bounds, not one, but ALL THREE referees looked at each other as if no one had seen the play. They didn't know what to call. *No way! You gotta be kidding me!* I said in my head.

By now, Coach was livid and called a timeout. *This was NOT happening!* My heart started to race even faster. She tried to calm down and keep us relaxed, even though we were encountering a situation that was beyond our control. After ten minutes of the referees' deliberation, which seemed like an eternity, the officials called a jump ball. *WHAT!? That's impossible! NO! God, please change the refs' call* . . . In that critical moment, the Warriors gained possession and the chance to take it all. With 1.4 seconds left, the Warriors inbounded the ball under their basket to a sophomore point guard, who sank a ten-foot soft jumper at the buzzer for the winning basket.

GAME OVER.

That singular moment changed me forever.

It was a game that boiled down to a fraction of a minute. The ultimate score would be Kamehameha, 42; Moanalua, 41. In front of a crowd of more than fourteen hundred fans, the Warriors gave us our ONLY loss that year in a heart-stopping finale. Kamehameha went on to beat I'olani, 55-49, in overtime the next day, giving the Warrior dynasty their fourth consecutive girls' basketball state championship. On hearing the news, I was in a daze and never felt more heartbroken in all my life. It just wasn't fair. As a teen, that was by far the biggest defeat I had ever experienced.

While I'd like to say that I wasn't bitter for many years, I would be lying if I did. However, what doesn't make us *bitter* makes us *better.* This truth wasn't really grasped until much later. I've come to terms with the loss, understanding that it was a necessary event in my personal growth.

I spoke with some of the girls from the Warriors team after the game. They acknowledged that the refs made a bad call (which happens in games), and there were no hard feelings toward them. It wasn't their fault. We had to learn to just accept it and move on.

Looking back, I felt cheated out of a championship that, by all indications, seemed to be ours, even for just a moment. Despite the unfair circumstances, the Warriors fought hard and they deserved that game as much as we did. They simply took advantage of the opportunity before them and ran with it. Perhaps we would have done the same if the tables were turned.

I remember crying so hard in the locker room with my teammates. I was learning that life wasn't fair, *even* when you give it your all. We left everything out on that court, *but still, it wasn't enough.* Coach Dana was emotional, too, but through her tears, she expressed her overall philosophy, "You have nothing to be ashamed of. You all played a hell of a game. Walk out of this locker room with your head up high. Show good sportsmanship and shake everyone's hand. Your opponents, the coaches, even the refs. All season, we have won with grace. Tonight, we need to lean on each other and show everyone that we know how to lose with grace. Let's come back strong tomorrow, and prove what this team is made of."

A painful moment turned into an opportunity of grace. It was humbling.

After the sobbing subsided and we regained our composure, we walked out in solidarity and were greeted by throngs of people, applauding us with a standing ovation—even people from the opposing side. My teammates and I walked with our arms around each other, and held our heads up high. We were gracious and thanked the fans, the coaches, and the refs, and congratulated the Warriors as they celebrated their victory. We may not have won on the scoreboard, but we left that locker room as winners.

~ Losing with Grace ~

This game was a milestone, a character building lesson, that revealed the importance of showing class both on and off the basketball court, whether you win or lose. We went on to win the next and last game of our season against Waiakea, with a win-loss record of 18-1. After all that, our team finished third overall in the state. It was hard to get super excited about that accomplishment. The sting of defeat would linger for years.

That one loss against Kamehameha—that *single* day in my life—changed me, and affected my entire outlook on life. I viewed every competition through the eyes of an athlete first, and came into each pageant with the same strategies and coping mechanisms I used in sports. In any competition, I learned that the winner is actually a minority.

The winner gets the most focus and attention, but *losers are the overwhelming majority*. So what's important to remember as teachers, coaches, and parents, is that we must teach our students how to win with grace *and* how to lose with grace, just like Coach Dana embodied and reinforced in us that day. My coach's voice still rings in my ears, "The game of basketball is like the game of life. When you lose, don't lose the lesson, because the worst mistake you can make is the one from which you don't learn." As a high school junior, I was given tools to deal with adversity. I learned later that losing that game was a blessing in disguise.

Without a doubt, Coach Dana remains one of the most influential women in my life. She was not just a coach who pushed me beyond my limits and forced me out of my comfort zone, but also a mentor who attained what I had hoped to one day capture—a state championship title.

~ Playing the Pageant Game ~

Pageants can be a fun pastime, but what most people don't realize is that winning a national pageant takes a healthy amount of desire, dedication, and discipline—all traits I learned through playing high school sports. Because I was an athlete and later a coach, I used that "game" mentality when competing in pageants.

The first time I stepped onstage to compete in Swimsuit, I was a little nervous, but I told myself that I needed to "play the game" in order to win. My prize was not a medal or ribbon, but scholarship money for college. If I wanted to alleviate any financial burden on my parents to help offset my tuition, this was my way to help out and grow in the process. I realized the need to "play by the rules," "wear the uniform," and accept any outcome because it was ultimately up to the seven judges in the panel if I place or not, and I didn't know what they might be looking for.

It took years to learn, but I know now that no referee or judge can tell me who I am. They can make a judgment, but they don't define me, only I can. So when I tell girls my best piece of advice, it's this: *Be Yourself.* But you can't do that unless you know who you are, where you are from, and where you're going.

I've had countless people, legislators, executives, students, and athletes ask me, "Did you win Miss America on your first try?" I always had to laugh at that question because there is no such thing as overnight success, and there's certainly no substitute for hard work.

People are surprised to learn I actually lost five pageants in my career. My pageant win-loss record currently stands at 5-5. However, the five wins were the ones that counted the most. It included the titles of Miss Island Paradise 1995, Miss Island 'Ilima 1996, Miss Leeward 2000, Miss Hawai'i 2000, and Miss America 2001.

But the losses in between were just as necessary for the process to unfold. Just like in any sport, it's crucial to know your competition, recognize your strengths, improve on your weaknesses, and stay focused on the opportunities that you could gain from winning. Preparation is everything. Visualization is imperative because what you see in your mind's eye and believe in your heart will inevitably manifest into reality. I know this to be true because I've lived it.

Had I not lost that game when I was seventeen, I probably would not appreciate any subsequent wins. If we won, I wouldn't have learned that milestone character building lesson. The bottom line is that you win some, you lose some, but it's your response that determines your character. That experience made me work harder to achieve what I wanted in life. When you don't feel loss, there is no joy in the victory—success is sweet and more meaningful when you have to earn it.

My husband and I now see the benefits of sports during childhood and adolescence, and are excited about getting our own children involved in athletics. Sports provide you with a playing field to deal with victory, anxiety, pressure, and unfortunate setbacks, which ultimately prepare you for the game of life.

Winning Miss Hawai'i in 2000, after three years of attempts on the same stage, meant so much to me. I learned from many losses along the way, but improved with each competition. God was by my side through it all, and my friends and family were in the audience cheering me on and lifting me up.

Following seven years of angst from the game against Kamehameha, life came full circle, and there was finally redemption. That fateful basketball game drove me to work hard to win, and I might not have become Miss Hawai'i if it weren't for that loss. I had gained a new appreciation for competing only against myself, and being the best ME I could possibly be. The lessons I learned in sports helped me win the biggest competition of my life. Being crowned Miss Hawai'i 2000 was like winning my own state championship title, and I was on my way to the nationals.

~ Traits of a Winner ~

Young pageant contestants often ask me what it takes to win. Here are my thoughts on some important traits of a winner, not just in pageants, but in *LIFE*. Winners possess confidence, character, and grace.

Confidence. You need to feel comfortable in your own skin. In this business, the reality is that some people *will* build you up before they break you down. It's important to grow thick skin and have the strongest belief in yourself that you can succeed.

Character. Character is who you really are when no one is looking. Someone once said that how you act is who you *want* to be and how you *react* is who you really are. No matter what is hurled at you in life, the way you handle obstacles and bear your crosses is what ultimately defines you.

Grace. Living with grace encompasses being a first-rate version of yourself at all times, behaving with elegance, class, and poise. Heavenly graces and blessings are always at your disposal if you ask for them. And whether you win or lose, grace comes with knowing you are a child and instrument of God.

Successful people surround themselves with people who are more accomplished than they are so they can be mentored. They also have a strong support system. And winners practice positive self-talk. If you take inventory of what you say to yourself in your head on a daily basis, you will be surprised at what you can learn and how easy it is to change negative habits.

51

When I played basketball, I learned the importance of desire, dedication, and discipline. This relates to anything you want in life. It's one thing to have the desire to attain something, but you'll never get it without putting in the hard work.

With a can-do attitude, perseverance, a mutual respect for self, others, and the world around you, you can achieve your goals and dreams. In the end, what *really* turns heads and evokes awe is someone who is kind and relatable. No one is perfect, but there's nothing wrong with striving for ideals.

~ Advice for Pageant Hopefuls ~

Some valuable advice for potential pageant contestants, and young women in general, is: Be careful about the choices you make now. They WILL affect you later, so be forward-thinking. Of course we all have our free will, but for every choice there is a consequence, good or bad, and we need to be prepared for the all the results of our decisions and we must learn to live with them.

Also, when signing contracts, especially pageant contracts, read the fine print carefully. You don't want to do anything you wouldn't want to be shown on TV or exposed over the Internet (this means anything you post on social media is also fair game)! When Miss America contestants run in pageants, even at the local level, they sign a clause which states that they have not done anything of "moral turpitude." Basically, the contestant is saying that there is nothing in her past that she is ashamed of. If something disreputable comes out in the future, she risks losing her crown.

This goes back to having good character. While we all fall sometimes, it's important to remember that we have to live with our choices in the end. Life is hard enough as it is, even when you make good choices. But what you do now will catch up with you later, so at every turn, try do the right thing to save yourself the extra heartache.

These are all the makings of a winner and were also fundamental to *me* in becoming Miss America.

CHAPTER 6

MY HAWAIIAN ROLLER COASTER RIDE

The path to Miss America is unique for every winner. There is a transformation that occurs the minute her first local pageant tiara is placed on her head. But what happens after she wins a local and state pageant? What happens after she passes her title on? And if she gets to the next level, how is her life affected as the new, the current, and later, former Miss America? Here's how my personal Miss America experience played out: My journey to the crown was spread out over a total of six years and ten pageants. Contrary to popular belief, there was no shortage of insecurities, self-doubt, close scrutiny, tears, and heartache. In fact, my road to Miss Hawai'i in itself was strewn with many highs and lows, where I experienced a roller coaster of emotions.

~ Summer 1994 ~

My pageant career didn't start early, so by no means was I a toddler in a tiara. In fact, I was a novice to pageantry as an adult, competing in my first one at eighteen, just months after I had graduated from high school. Being involved in pageants was the furthest thing from my mind until a chance meeting.

A young girl at the 50th State Farm Fair was passing out flyers for a free consultation at a modeling agency. I took it and thought, *What have I got to lose?* At my first meeting in that Kalihi office, where Tini waited in the car for me, I realized that I would have to dish out seven hundred dollars for modeling classes. I couldn't afford that, so I declined.

On my way out the door, the man interviewing me stopped me and said that he was a local pageant director. His name was Tino Montero. He

53

said if I was interested in running for his pageant I should give him a call. "So you are a scholar athlete, you seem pretty well rounded, and you have a good look. You should consider competing in pageants," he said. I never ever considered *that* option before. *Me in a beauty pageant? Ha!* This pageant had no fee for entry or for rehearsals. Already, it seemed like a better option than paying for classes to learn how to be a model.

He gave me his number, and I told him I'd think about it. After a long talk with my eldest sister, Ceci, she convinced me to compete. She said, "If you don't run in the pageant now, do you think you'd regret it when you are forty?" Without pause, I said yes, and she replied, "Well, there's your answer." I never wanted to live with regret, so I did it.

The biggest lures of the competition were the prize money I could use for school expenses, the experience of competing onstage in different phases of competition, and getting to work on different facets of myself. All of that was intriguing. Plus, now that I was living away from home I needed to find ways to pay for my college tuition and books. At the time, pageants weren't just a way for me to prove myself or stay busy that summer. I realized that I *needed* pageants to help me pay for higher education.

~ Fall 1994 ~

In November 1994, I competed in my very first pageant: Miss Asian Universal 1994. I was frugal and got what I needed, all within budget. For Evening Gown, I rented a friend's prom dress for twenty dollars. In Interview, I wore a skirt suit I already owned and sometimes wore to church on Sundays. Then I asked my friend, Tricia, to do my full stage makeup for competition. Tricia and I went to high school together and she competed in pageants before I ever did. When I told her I was running, she got so excited and offered to help me in any way. I was so grateful for her advice and guidance because this was all new to me. She generously lent me jewelry, shoes, and accessories, so that saved me a lot of money. I was named Second Runner-up, and earned four hundred dollars in that first pageant, which helped me purchase my college books that first semester in school. *Not bad—this was fun!* I thought.

Afterward, the pageant director, Tino, asked me to run in a separate and brand new pageant franchise where he was the executive director, giving away three titles. It was a preliminary pageant to Miss Hawai'i, which was part of the Miss America Organization. I was awestruck that the pageant was a feeder into the illustrious pageant we grew up watching (I even said to Tino, you mean the "There She Is, Miss America" Pageant)?

I was impressed by the program's mission to help women further their education through scholarships, its criteria to have a platform that promotes social change, the focus on community service, and its scoring system. Talent was weighted most heavily, followed by the Formal Interview, Evening Gown, and Swimsuit. This pageant attracted a certain type of woman—someone like me. I thought it would be a fun way to keep busy and productive while Tini was away at college. That was my introduction into the Miss America system.

~ Spring 1995 ~

To my surprise, I won my first Miss America preliminary, right off the bat! I was named Miss Island Paradise 1995 after dancing hula to Nalu's "In Your Hawaiian Way" for Talent. Tino's other two winners and I went on to compete at the state level that June. Every state has its own stipulations, but contestants in Hawai'i can only run in up to *two* preliminaries each year.

When I met the other contestants at the state level, I learned that many of the women there dreamed of becoming Miss Hawai'i and not necessarily Miss America. At the time, I was just happy to be competing in the prestigious system.

For my talent at Miss Hawai'i 1995, I performed hula to Loyal Garner's "Ku'u Lei Awapuhi." The competition was fierce, but I made the Top Ten and won Miss Congeniality. As a first-timer at State, I was definitely not ready to be crowned that year. I knew it wasn't my time. And I still walked away with about seven thousand dollars in scholarships!

Being that I was only eighteen, I had chosen a big Cinderella-type ball gown with lots of tulle under the skirt, designed by Gloria Burton. All my wardrobe at State was sponsored by my pageant director, Tino, which were all on loan to me.

In retrospect, I kind of felt like a puppet that first year, allowing people to tell me what to say, how to dress, how to act. But I didn't know any better. Everything was brand new to me. As a novice to the system, I was surrounded by veterans who I believed knew best how to style and primp me. Back then, I didn't fully believe in myself. It would take at least six years for me to build that inner confidence. The talented Traci Toguchi was destined to win that year. Traci was a twenty-year-old woman of Japanese descent, and she could sing! With her vocal rendition of "Natural Woman" she bested the other seventeen contestants that year, including me and Brook Lee, a future Miss Universe winner, who was twenty-four at the time.

To compete alongside such phenomenal women and "not win" that year at Miss Hawai'i, was nothing to pout over. Ironically, it boosted my confidence. I've always said I'd much rather be the "worst of the best" than the "best of the worst" any day. It was all about challenging myself, shattering limitations and aiming high.

On the way to the parking lot of the Hilton Hawaiian Village, after the

1995 state pageant, another Miss Hawai'i preliminary pageant director, Todd Oshiro, stopped me at the bottom of the escalator. Todd officially introduced himself to me and told me he had been involved with the pageant for many years as a volunteer. He hoped I would consider running in his preliminary, if I decided to compete again. I smiled at him and thanked him for his kind offer. That fateful day, he handed me his business card for Miss West O'ahu, and that moment would be the start of a beautiful lifelong friendship.

~ Spring 1996 ~

The following year, at nineteen, I entered Todd's preliminary, Miss West O'ahu 1996, but didn't place *at all!* I was devastated as a returning veteran to the program. My downfall was choosing to sing instead of dance hula for Talent. I rarely sang solo without the safety net of my sisters around me; singing solo was not my strongest suit. I wanted to challenge myself and do something I had never done before onstage. But my nerves got the best of me. Despite my extreme stage fright, I basically did a rerun of "The Rainbow Connection" at my first grade talent show. Neither event turned out as I had hoped.

While my shaky rendition of "On My Own" from *Les Miserables* was likely just as difficult to endure for the audience as it was for me, I knew it was just growing pains, and a necessary step to something bigger.

Tini was away at school and he called me that night with his friends on speaker. He sounded overly enthusiastic, ready to hear the good news, "So, what's your new title?" I broke down and could barely breathe. "I didn't win," I sobbed. Then I continued, "It was so embarrassing! I went to the state finals last year and couldn't even win a preliminary this time around!"

He immediately took me off speaker and walked to a quiet spot. "Honey, I'm so sorry. Hey, don't let seven judges tell you how good or bad you are at anything in life. They don't define you. You define yourself, nobody else does." Amazingly, that made a lot of sense and he calmed me down. Those words stayed with me in all my future competitions.

Sometimes reality fell short of my vision, shaped by the gilded narratives of the princesses and saints I often read about. But even when I didn't advance as I had intended, I was always moving. Each loss, made me want to quit. But I didn't. I just thought, *Pick yourself up and try again*. In the spring I decided to enter another pageant. My second preliminary was also my last chance for that competition year. I sang a jazz rendition of, "It Had to Be You" (which was a bit more in my vocal range). I was crowned Miss Island 'Ilima 1996. That qualified me to compete at Miss Hawai'i 1996 in June.

~ **Summer 1996** ~

Rumor had it that Carolyn Sapp, our first Miss Hawai'i to win Miss America in 1991, was returning home to emcee the pageant. It was an honor to meet her in person.

Carolyn had reached legendary status and was supreme to all Miss Hawai'i hopefuls. Putting our state on the map at Miss America was no small feat. The challenge by our state committee was, "Who will be the next woman to put Hawai'i back on the map?" When I first met Carolyn, I remember taking a picture with her with my Miss Island 'Ilima 1996 sash thinking, *I'm standing next to Miss America. Whoa!* Today we are good friends and I am still in awe of her as a human being, wife, and mother.

During pageant week at the Hilton Hawaiian Village, the contestants and I attended rehearsals and special events. I have such fond memories of those days, especially because *that* year I got to compete with my friend, Tricia Fujikawa (Miss Waikiki 1996), from high school, who had helped me in my very first pageant. She and I both won our preliminaries and were at Miss Hawai'i *together!* Tricia and I ended up as college roommates for that one semester I lived at UH and we are still great friends today.

One of my preliminary pageant sisters, Maxinne Anselmo Pacheco (Miss Island Paradise 1996) and I became close friends that year. She and I had both won two of the three preliminary titles our director Tino was sponsoring. We hit it off at Miss Hawai'i, and have remained friends since. Today she is my bestie, and I never would have met her, had I not entered pageants.

The week of Miss Hawai'i was filled with excitement, and after it was over, I ended up earning another seven thousand dollars in in-kind scholarships! Unfortunately, I didn't place at all, out of eleven contestants.

It was a stark difference from the year before, when I won my first preliminary, was voted Miss Congeniality, and made it into the Top Ten at Miss Hawai'i on my first try. It was a bit of a letdown to walk away without a placement, after all that hard work. I felt that I had disappointed all the friends and family who were watching in the audience and all those who helped me along the way. Trying to remember Tini's encouraging words from the last pageant I lost, I held my head up.

The new Miss Hawai'i 1996, Melissa Short was an obvious winner so I didn't feel too bad. She had a solid interview, looked stunning in Swimsuit and Evening Gown, and sounded like an angel with a big, operatic voice when she sang her playful aria for Talent. She deserved to win, and she represented our state well that fall in Atlantic City.

I was so impressed when she won Preliminary Talent and Swimsuit honors at Miss America, then went on to be a semi-finalist. I learned that things happen for a reason, and again, it simply was not my time to shine.

My confidence took a beating that year and I needed a break from competing. I didn't want my family to see me as a "career pageant girl" especially when I just couldn't cut it at Miss Hawai'i. *What was wrong with me? What was stopping me from winning it all?* Whether in sports or in my home life, it seemed as if I was involved in pageants because of the excitement and challenge of competition. I was running on the momentum that was set in motion a year earlier, striving to overcome any obstacles that lay before me. Like a hamster on a wheel, I seemed to be chasing all the expectations that chased me—and frankly, I was tired.

I took a few years off from pageantry, starting that summer, after I turned twenty. I wanted to gain more real-life experience, earn my bachelor's degree in elementary education, and pursue other interests.

In the meantime, our sisters' all-girl rock band, High Tide, was getting attention on the music scene, and we were earning money as professional performers. I was the host of my own TV show meeting celebrities and shooting stand-ups weekly with my camera crew on-location, around the state of Hawai'i; I interviewed out of town and local musicians; and traveled around the island covering concerts and hosting dance parties for *Hit-TV*. I cherished this time and I learned about confidence and stage presence on a whole new level.

Tini and I continued to keep in touch and see each other every year on spring break, over the summer, and during the winter break. In between, we kept in touch by email. We'd buy phone cards so we could talk over the phone every day, and would write and mail each other good old-fashioned love letters. We wouldn't see each other for months at a time, but when we were reunited, it was like no time had passed.

Pageants helped the time pass quickly when Tini and I were apart, and I earned a lot of money for school in the process. Because I had already gained so much from being involved in the system, I was ready to close that chapter.

After learning about my upcoming hiatus, one contestant's mom asked me, "How come you're not running again next year? Are you afraid of the competition?" I tried to ignore the offhand statement. I needed a break and I wanted to get off the crazy ride. I told myself if I *ever* returned, it would be for my last year of eligibility at age twenty-four . . . but I buried that thought DEEP in the recesses of my mind.

~ Summer 1997 ~

The Miss Hawai'i 1995 Pageant marked the first year I competed in the Miss America Organization, but it was also Brook Lee's fourth year competing at Miss Hawai'i. That year she "aged out" of the Miss America system at twenty-four. After that, she told me she was going to run for Miss

Hawai'i USA in 1997 (a preliminary within the Miss USA/Universe program), where the cutoff age was twenty-six. All of us who competed with her were very supportive.

The mind-blowing thing is that Brook never expected to win, but she went on to become not only Miss Hawai'i USA, but also Miss USA, and then Miss Universe 1997! Her victory turned her into an instant celebrity.

Watching from afar, it made me proud to know that Brook and I were on the same playing field at one point in time. I was completely inspired by her international success. A local girl went all the way to Miss Universe and she never gave up, even when the chips seemed down. In 1997, I didn't realize just how much of an impact her victory would make on me at the age of twenty-one. Brook did the "impossible" and so could I.

~ Fall 1997 ~

School was in full swing for me, once I declared my major as Elementary Education in 1997. Studying to become a prospective primary school teacher *sounded* easy, but nothing could have been further from the truth. The College of Education at the University of Hawai'i was demanding and time consuming—and I *loved* every minute of it!

College life was extremely enjoyable. Over the next two years, I immersed myself in all my classes and reveled in the beauty of our campus, nestled in Manoa Valley in the heart of Honolulu.

At the time, many of my siblings and friends were still single and/or college age, so we all spent a lot of time together at Ala Moana or Kailua Beach, pitching our volleyball nets on the grass and playing pickup beach volleyball games, going to Moanalua High school gym to play basketball at night, and going camping on the North Shore on weekends.

Sometimes we would fill our entire day with non-stop activities. We'd go hiking, then swim at the beach, play volleyball, go bowling, and end the day with midnight basketball. We were so young and carefree in those days, and we had lots of energy! At night, if my sisters and I weren't rehearsing or performing as High Tide, we'd hang out together watching new episodes of *Friends,* and then get ready to go dancing at the clubs afterward.

As for my career, I knew exactly what I was going to do in the future—earn my teaching certificate, get a job at a Catholic school, and teach there for at least thirty years, before I even *thought* about retiring. It was simple. I had a plan and I knew where I was going. I also intended to marry Tini and have kids with him, but only after graduating with a degree and starting my career.

It seems, however, that anytime I try to map out my life and plan for the future, something happens to throw me off the track I expected to be on. But then eventually, a better situation emerges that seems to work itself out for the highest good. When this happens, I know it's the Holy Spirit at work, planting things in my heart and putting people in my path, seamlessly orchestrating what has already been ordained. I know this, because that's exactly what happened to me.

~ May 1998 ~

Brook Lee, Miss Universe 1997, the same woman I competed with at Miss Hawai'i 1995, had crowned the new Miss Universe in May 1998 at the University of Hawai'i Stan Sheriff Arena, where I used to work as an usher. I had heard that Brook Lee and Al Masini (an entertainment giant and a future guest on my TV show), along with funding from the state of Hawai'i, were the forces behind the Miss Universe 1998 pageant, being held in Honolulu, for the first time. I loved that my friend was still representing her Hawaiian heritage and our home state, even after winning an international title.

Suddenly my daydreams about competing for Miss Hawai'i again began to surface. I toyed with the thought and imagined a life with greater outreach, but not winning the last two times I competed at the state level left a bitter taste in my mouth. I vaguely remembered saying that if ever went back, it would be when I turned twenty-four. That year was fast approaching, but I tried not to pay attention to the timeline or to those nagging feelings I had about the pageant. Instead, I focused all my efforts in teaching.

~ Summer 1999 ~

After spreading out my college experience over five years so I could graduate in the same year as Tini (he had committed to a five-year Architecture program), I graduated from college in May 1999. That fall I began teaching at my alma mater, Holy Family Catholic Academy in Honolulu, Hawai'i.

Armed with my newly obtained bachelor's degree from the University of Hawai'i at Manoa, I was ready to take on the world of education. It had been three years since I competed in pageants, and I was happy, doing what I loved. Not only was I about to teach at a Catholic elementary school, I was enjoying life as a TV personality, a member of a rock band, and a college graduate. Pageants seemed like a distant memory, because my life felt full.

My first choice was to teach second grade, but there were no openings, and I thought PE was a great way to begin my first year of teaching because I felt right at home with athletics. I was also credentialed, and qualified to teach all elementary school subjects. Plus, I had past experience at Holy

Family as a former graduate, an athlete, and a volunteer basketball coach. It was perfect.

That year, I was also named the athletic director and was in charge of coaching basketball, volleyball, and track for students in grades fifth through eighth. Being the PE teacher for two hundred students in grades kindergarten through third was enjoyable. I immersed myself in the job, and I did it well, but something kept nudging me in my heart. I felt the vague premonition that God had something bigger in store for me.

~ The Dare ~

In the fall of 1999, something happened that would change the entire course of my life. My students challenged me to run for Miss Hawai'i again. Rachael and Emerisa, two eighth graders I was coaching in volleyball at the time, approached me with fears of trying out for the basketball team. I told them that if they didn't try, they'd never know what they could achieve. I basically told them they had to be "in it to win it."

That's when they turned the tables on me and asked me if *I'd* ever done anything I was afraid of doing at first and later succeeded at it. I shared the story of how I competed twice before at Miss Hawai'i at eighteen and nineteen years old. Even though I was afraid of losing, I tried anyway, and in the process, I earned scholarship money, made friends, and improved myself.

They were both shocked and impressed, mostly because I didn't look like a typical beauty queen, arriving to school daily in my PE attire: a ponytail, no make up, shorts, a shirt, and tennis shoes.

But that's when they dared me to do it again. I tried to disregard their prompting. "This is not about *me*, it's about *you*!" I told them.

Inside, I was scared of making it about me because of the possibility of facing defeat a third time. All my family and friends had come out in years past to support me and I didn't want to disappoint them again. It was a lot of pressure. But the moment was finally here. I would be twenty-four years old in June, only months away.

I tried to block out the challenge I made to myself years ago when I was nineteen. My own words rang in my head, *If I ever run again, it'll be during my last year of eligibility.* The time snuck up on me. I was reminded that this was my last shot if I were to do it at all. I also thought that if I wanted to be a good teacher and role model, I needed to practice what I preached. The girls had to see me *walk the walk*, if I intended to *talk the talk*.

That night, I consulted with Tini, who was always a great listener and advice giver. I framed the situation, and in true male form, he immediately tried to solve my problem saying, "Then just tell them no, and don't run." I replied, "But I don't want to challenge *them* and not take *my own* advice about facing fears. I want them to try something that could possibly be a great experience, and if *I* don't do this, *I'll* be a hypocrite." Tini quipped back, "Then do it." I argued, "But I'm not ready to run in another pageant. My plate is already full!" He retorted, "Then don't do it." *Grrrr! This was frustrating!* This back-and-forth commentary went on for a bit before I finally broke down and got really passionate.

At this point, Tini challenged me, "Why would you want to do it? For the glory, the crown, the title, the prizes?" Through tears, I answered, "Of course not! I already have crowns and titles. I chose to be a teacher so I could *make a difference*, and I'm trying to prove a point to my students. Don't you realize that the Miss America Organization is the largest scholarship provider for women in the world? And Miss America gets to choose a platform that *means something* to her! She travels all over the country making a difference. If *I* did this and won, the *nation* could be my classroom! If I compete and *don't* win, at least I am showing my students that I'm taking my own advice."

Tini looked at me and said with sincerity, "Honey, it sounds like you already made up your mind. But I want you to realize that if you do this, you'll not only win Miss Hawai'i, but you'll go all the way and win Miss America." The mood lightened. I smiled at his sweet words and thought what a good friend he was to say that.

I just wanted to know he always had my back, and that, he did. He was there every step of the way from the moment I started my career in pageantry. When I needed him most, Tini believed in me more than I believed in myself. That's the mark of a true friend—*and* a faithful partner.

The next day I told the girls I had a deal for them. Because it was my absolute last chance to compete before I "aged out" at twenty-four, I agreed to accept their dare—but only if they would work with me everyday on basketball skills and promise to try out for the team, despite their fears.

I called my former pageant director, Todd Oshiro, and told him that I was back in the game. It was now or never. He was ecstatic! But he said, "Angie, you have two chances to win a preliminary before you age out. I want you to run in the next open pageant. If you win, awesome, you get to State, but if you don't win, you can compete in mine, and you'll have extra pageant experience, which will help you if you get to Miss Hawai'i." His strategic advice was on point.

~ Winter 1999 ~

In November 1999, I ran in the Miss O'ahu preliminary, directed by Miss Hawai'i 1991, Lani Stone Kaa'a. With only two months to prepare, I decided to sing for Talent. This time, I chose a Spanish love song, "Con Los Años Que Me Quedan," which means, "With the Years That I Have

Left." I gave a decent performance and was happy to choose a song from one of my favorite singers, Gloria Estefan.

Since I had two chances to run in a preliminary, I experimented with this first one. I seemed to be carrying out my secret fantasy of being a solo singer on the pageant stage. Having Talent as part of the scoring forced me to step up to the challenge of finding out what my unique gifts were. The Miss America Organization gave me the outlet I needed to creatively explore unseen sides of me and express myself in ways I would not otherwise have ever imagined—or possibly, even *bothered* to try.

Aside from singing the Spanish song, I wore a black one-piece swimsuit that I bought from a department store, a black evening gown I borrowed from my director Todd, and a red interview skirt suit that a friend loaned out to me. I was confident in Interview, even though I was critiqued that I talked a bit too fast. But the truth was, I had been out of the pageant scene for three years, so I was *not* at my peak, and I knew this.

Even though this pageant was a "practice run" to get out my jitters after being away from pageants for so long, I still wanted to do well.

During the announcement of winners, I heard my name called as First Runner-up. *Not bad, but not what I was hoping for.* As disappointed as I was to come in second, I stood there smiling, accepting my award, and looked out into the crowd where my students held signs that read, "GO COACH ANGIE!" I realized that I had just proven a point to them, and despite my short-lived embarrassment of the outcome, I also taught them a valuable lesson about facing fears and having the courage to be "in" the game if they wanted a chance to "win" the game.

Even though I was grateful for earning more scholarship money, my purpose for competing had evolved from just doing it for fun and earning money for school, to actually being a role model to my students who were looking up to me as their teacher, coach, and leader. My passion for competing was still there, but my *reasons* were changing—and so was I.

The winner of Miss O'ahu 2000 was Liane Mark, a Yale graduate, and Psychology and Theater major. She was a strong singer, competed in the Junior Miss system, and was a model on the TV show *Baywatch*, all impressive stats—ones that would be expected at Miss America. She had everything going for her, and she deserved to win that night. As her First Runner-up, I wondered how I would do if I won my next preliminary and was up against her again at State. It was a bit intimidating.

The next day, the school secretary announced on the loud speaker that I had won First Runner-up in a Miss Hawai'i Preliminary, and all the students greeted me at my PE office to congratulate me. Rachael and Emerisa told me how proud they were and went on to say, "You have to run again! You came in second this time, so next time you'll win for sure!"

Of course, there was no guarantee of this. I was through with pageants in my mind, but there was still a whisper in my head, *This is your last chance, just go for it.* So I signed up for Todd's pageant, just as he had advised me.

~ Valentine's Day 2000 ~

On February 14, 2000, just a month before my second pageant preliminary in my final year of eligibility, Mama had a *heart attack*—on Valentine's Day! I had never in my life seen my mother in a vulnerable state until I saw her that day in the hospital. The thought of losing her terrified me.

I almost didn't run in Todd's preliminary that March because of Mama's precarious condition. I told him I might sit out because, clearly, family was my first priority.

However, Mama's health miraculously improved. While in the hospital, her spirits were lifted whenever she'd watch my sister Berna anchor the evening news on *FOX2*. I realized then, that what fueled my mother was watching her children succeed and achieve great things in life. Armed with this revelation, I went on with my plans to compete in March, in quite possibly, my *last pageant ever.*

Knowing I was competing within the Miss Hawai'i pageant system again gave Mama some motivation to heal and remain healthy. For me, it gave me a reason to work harder and succeed. Mama recovered, and both she and my dad were able to attend Miss Hawai'i in June. Four months later, they were on a plane to Atlantic City to see their eighth-born child crowned at the national pageant. There, we experienced that unforgettable moment together.

~ March 2000 ~

Todd's pageant gave away three titles that year: Miss West O'ahu, Miss Honolulu, and Miss Leeward. I knew it was my final opportunity to get to State if I wanted to compete at Miss Hawai'i in my last year of eligibility.

As an employed educator with my first year of teaching almost over, I was confident in my abilities to speak in front of a crowd. This time, I was a completely different person in Interview, more polished than I had been in years past.

For Talent, I sang the Spanish song again by Gloria Estefan, since I already had the music from Lani's pageant just a few months before. Tini's friend helped me with my musical arrangement and cut it down to ninety seconds for competition. I practiced singing every day and loved it because it was one of my favorite songs.

For Swimsuit, I bought an orange one-piece suit off the rack at a specialty boutique on the North Shore of O'ahu. I knew my students would be coming to this pageant and I wanted to practice *some* modesty, despite being onstage in a swimsuit. The style was nice, but most of the contestants wore two-pieces. At the time I wasn't confident enough to do that, and even though I had been working out, my body wasn't in top form.

I borrowed a dress for Evening Gown from the pageant collection of dresses that Todd had in his flower shop. I chose a black long sleeved, pencil-fit gown with a slit. The front of the bodice was criss-crossed and the shape was flattering to my body. I had seen so many girls wear that same gown in different pageants before, but I didn't mind. I was thankful that Todd loaned it to me, and I ended up getting crowned Miss Leeward 2000 in that dress. Later, I would use the same dress for Evening Gown at Miss Hawai'i 2000.

My friend Juliet Lighter was crowned Miss West O'ahu that year (she later went on to become Miss Hawai'i USA 2001), and Alicia Lopes was Miss Honolulu. Because we became great friends during pageant rehearsals, we were all looking forward to experiencing Miss Hawai'i together as preliminary pageant sisters.

My joy was short-lived, though, because after the pageant, my judges told me that even though I had won a preliminary title, my lowest score was in Swimsuit. The fact was: I scored highest in my interview but I needed to score high in *all* phases across the board if I wanted to step up my game. The judges were under the impression that I was uncomfortable in that phase and that I lacked the confidence necessary in a Miss Hawai'i.

In addition, they questioned if I was insecure about my body. All this was true. Walking onstage in a swimsuit in front of judges and a live audience scrutinizing and scoring me was *not* the most comfortable or normal situation! Plus, I had not really dedicated the time to the strict physical training that was necessary to walk with great confidence onstage in a swimsuit. I knew I needed to step it up at Miss Hawai'i if I wanted to be a top contender.

The definition of insanity is doing the same thing over and over again and expecting different results. I knew that if I did the same thing I had always done at Miss Hawai'i and expected to win, I was out of my mind. I needed to do something different this time around.

But I was torn. That's when I talked to my parish priest, Father Mac, and brought up my concerns about possibly wearing a two-piece at Miss Hawai'i.

~ Guidance from Above ~

I'll never forget our talk. Father Mac (the pastor of our church and school) was of course, proud of me for winning Miss Leeward and qualifying for State. After all, he welcomed my family in 1988, saw me go through the school as class president, and allowed me to volunteer as a basketball coach at Holy Family when I was in college. Plus, he knew me and my family well from daily Mass, so he knew my heart. But as a teacher at the school, he was also my boss. I wanted his blessing to move forward and I needed spiritual advice.

We sat together in a pew at our church and I expressed my concerns about being a teacher at the school competing in a televised pageant. I brought up the dilemma about my low Swimsuit score, which affected my chances of winning, and how a two-piece might win the "game."

Silence.

Then he asked me how long I would have to be onstage wearing my swimsuit on TV. I told him it was only seconds. He asked me what I would get out of the experience if I won. I spoke of all the virtues of the pageant and the far-reaching effects I could have, if I were crowned.

That's when he paused and said slowly, "You can do this. You need to do this." He continued with sincerity, "Angie, we *need* more Catholics at the forefront to witness to Christ." I was shocked. Then he said, "And just so you know, you're not only going to win Miss Hawai'i. You're going to be Miss America. And when you win, remember that we will always be connected through the Eucharist . . ." I still remember how stunned I felt. His words were completely unexpected.

Still he went on, "And don't forget when you leave the position, to make it better than it was when you found it. Don't worry, you will always have a job at the school, as long as I'm here." I couldn't believe what he was saying. His support for my dreams and his words made my spirit soar. I felt comforted by his wisdom and advice. I felt like God was speaking to me through him, giving me greater clarity that this was *my* personal path, my calling. I thanked Father Mac as I left and was happy that I got the answers I was looking for.

However, my mother was someone else to consider . . . how would she feel seeing her daughter onstage in a bikini? She wouldn't even let us wear two-pieces at the beach, even though we sometimes did when she wasn't with us. *Come on, we lived in Hawai'i in tropical weather, we were in swimsuits every weekend! There were worse things we could do!* I didn't think it was such a big deal at the beach, but onstage in front of everyone on TV, with heels and makeup was a different story, *and* I was a teacher now. These were all important things to consider.

I didn't want to tell Ma about my decision. Because of her heart attack in February there was no need to upset her while she was recovering. Father Mac told me not to worry about it. He said he'd sit next to her at the pageant to help soften the blow. Then he joked, "I know you'll win. I have an 'in' with the guy upstairs."

Of all people, my parish priest, convinced me to give this last chance at Miss Hawai'i my *best effort*. Considering many issues, and being clear about my pure intentions for competing, I ultimately decided to wear a two-piece during Swimsuit. But preparation for it would not be easy.

~ Miss Hawai'i Prep ~

As I readied myself for the millennium Miss Hawai'i competition, I considered doing a vocal rendition of Ella Fitzgerald's "Too Marvelous for Words." I worked with "Uncle" Gordon Mark, who helped me with my jazz arrangement. Uncle Gordon worked with Carolyn Sapp for her talent at Miss America when she was competing as Miss Hawai'i 1991. Carolyn sang the jazz tune, "Ain't Misbehavin'" in Atlantic City before she was crowned Miss America 1992. I was well aware that I was in good hands and listened to everything Uncle Gordon advised.

After my first rehearsal during Miss Hawai'i week, however, I changed my song selection. Just as I tried to stand out within my family, I now needed to find a way to be noticed among the other contestants, especially the other singers in the competition. I approached the pageant like a basketball game and started to craft a strategic game plan.

I decided to stick with what I knew best and was most passionate about . . . the Spanish song I sang at my other two preliminaries, "Con Los Años Que Me Quedan," by Gloria Estefan. Uncle Gordon agreed with my decision and continued to work with me for a bit before insisting that I begin voice lessons with his friend Neva Rego, the renowned vocal coach for Miss Hawai'i contestants.

Being mostly Filipina, but also part Spanish, and Chinese, I was proud to represent the Spanish part of me onstage. Embracing my Spanish roots went along well with the trend of pop culture.

With Santana's song, "Maria Maria" being No. One on the Billboard charts for ten weeks in early 2000, and Hispanic sensation Jennifer Lopez (J.Lo) breaking into the mainstream with her first leading role in the 1997 movie *Selena* and successful 1999 debut album *On the 6*, it seemed appropriate, timely, and fresh to do something that celebrated a part of *my own* ethnicity.

Several people at that time even told me that I resembled J.Lo. After the movie, *Selena* movie came out, one of my friends called me from the mainland to congratulate me on being the lead actress in it. I had to really convince her that it wasn't me, but rather the actress Jennifer Lopez.

In all program books, I deliberately kept my full name and branded myself as, "Angela Perez Baraquio" instead of just "Angie Baraquio" to honor both sides of my family. Perez for my mom's side, and Baraquio for my dad's side.

Meanwhile, I met with my physical trainer at least three times a week to do cardio, lift weights, and tone my body for competition with hundreds of sit ups and leg lifts. At home, I worked out on my elliptical machine twice a day—morning and evening. After a detox, I resolved not to eat simple sugars, bad carbs, or drink anything but water.

Sadly, I had to give up my beloved white rice, but I didn't starve. If I wanted a scoop every so often, I didn't deprive myself. I felt a lot healthier this time around, as opposed to when I was training for pageants in prior years. I remember being so emotional about food and what I couldn't eat back then, that I was miserable to tears. This time I knew I could eat things in moderation, but I was more focused and disciplined now. I didn't *want* any junk food.

Mentally, I was getting stronger and so was my will to win. By now, I knew that finding a healthy balance was key.

I was in my best shape yet, as I prepared to compete for Miss Hawai'i 2000. Everyone wondered who this new contestant was. Even though it was my third time at State, some hardly recognized me. By then, I lost most of the "baby fat" I had when I was eighteen, and I definitely had better eating habits now that I was being more health-conscious.

The school year was coming to an end, and my students and co-workers were overjoyed that I would be representing them and our school at the Miss Hawai'i Scholarship Pageant. Many people from school said they'd tune in to watch the statewide telecast, but I also sold a lot of tickets to the live show.

For the first time, I was going to have a huge cheering section, beyond my immediate family, watching me compete at State! The pressure was on, and I was ready to for the challenge. I told my students to try for something or they'd never know, and I was doing just that. It was a very exciting time for me. There was electricity in the air. I could feel the energy, and in my heart, I knew something *good* was about to happen.

~ **June 2000** ~

The end of the school year culminated with my two eighth grade girls trying out for the basketball team and making it. They were voted team captains by their peers, and got to see me compete live at the Hilton Hawaiian Village for the title of Miss Hawai'i 2000.

I may have taught Rachael and Emerisa a significant life lesson, but more importantly, they taught *me* one, which I now refer to as **The 3 Ds to Success: Dare, Dream, and Do.** I needed to dare myself to dream again, and then I had to go out and just do it.

But later on, I realized **3 more Ds** were necessary to *really* make it happen—things that I learned through my involvement in sports: **Desire, Dedication, and Discipline.** The formula for winning: the **6 Ds** was so simple—and yet so powerful.

Once, at a speech, I shared the 6 Ds with college students and a young man came up to me afterward and said, "6 Ds: Dare, Dream, Do, Desire, Dedication, Discipline…sounds easy, but it's not, right?" I smiled and said, "No, it's not. But if you follow it, it works."

If Rachael and Emerisa didn't dare me to step out of my comfort zone, I never would have had the courage to compete in my final year. As the first teacher to win, I will always attribute my last attempt in the pageant system to the two students who challenged me to be more than I ever imagined. The saying is true: to the world you may be one person, but to one person you might mean the world. They have told me how much I meant to them, but they may never realize just how much *they* affected *my* life in a positive way.

I entered Miss Hawai'i for the third time, setting into motion a course of events that would put me on a new and irreversible course. Because I had been on that stage twice before, I was considered a "returning veteran" to the pageant. I psyched myself up. This year, I'd be ready. I had to be—it was my *last chance*.

~ Third Time's a Charm ~

As humans, we think we can always be in control of our lives. Sometimes we impose our will on God, but that never works. For those truly living a spirit-filled life, when we empty ourselves and ask God to fill our void, we find ourselves experiencing something bigger than ourselves— something unimaginably joyful. That's when God reveals His working wonders in our lives. I had no clue that my destiny was leading me to a more expansive territory.

~ June 9, 2000 ~

Backstage, before the Miss Hawai'i 2000 pageant, all ten of us contestants said a prayer together for each other, and ultimately, the winner—whoever she was. We agreed that God, in His Infinite Wisdom, already knew who was going to be crowned. And since she was already predestined to serve as Miss Hawai'i, all *we* could do was be our best, and support each other throughout the night. We cheered each other on backstage and there was such camaraderie, which is not typical of most pageants.

Personally, my goal was to walk away that night knowing that I did my best in every single phase of competition. It wasn't about how I matched up to the other girls. I had to compete against myself. I felt good about my twelve-minute interview with the seven judges the day before the telecast, so being onstage during the final night was the fun part.

Swimsuit was our first competition. I wore a red two-piece with a red chrysanthemum in my hair. My suit was tailor made by Ann Tongg, who also used to design the Miss America one-piece "supersuits" back in the eighties. I had no idea there was a science to making a girl look her best during this phase!

Trying not to look at Mama in the audience, I found out later she could not believe her eyes when I came out…that was expected. However, I didn't want to think about her reaction so I could focus on the rest of the competition. I prayed that she would be all right.

That night was was the first time I ever wore false eyelashes. During pageant week I had to practice walking in my four-inch heels onstage because I kept tripping on them! It was all so foreign to me, but it was clear that I had to play the part if I wanted to win. In Swimsuit, contestants walked out to Madonna's song "Rain." We created our own choreography to the song as we paused for a pose, before walking downstage with pareaus draping over our shoulders. I had never felt better about the way I looked, because I worked hard to get fit for that pageant. I was so proud of myself, and it showed.

At this third attempt at Miss Hawai'i, my vocal rendition of the Spanish Gloria Estefan love song, "Con Los Años Que Me Quedan," seemed to appropriately fit the theme of the opening song of the night, "Mambo No. 5." As I sang the first lines of my song, I felt every word. In my mind, I was singing to Tini and, although I wasn't ready to become a recording artist overnight, my performance was better than any of my past two deliveries of the same song. It was the best I could have done at the time, and I walked off the stage contented. Talent was my most challenging competition that night—even *more* than Swimsuit—but I overcame my nerves.

As the night progressed, I felt confident that I had done my personal best in each phase of competition. It was like checking things off my list. If I was happy with my performance in every category, I was already a winner.

Then it was time for Evening Gown. I wore the same black dress with the criss-crossed front bodice and rhinestones on the sheer sleeves, that I wore onstage at Miss Leeward 2000, and I loved the way it felt on me. Tini's group Reign was serenading the contestants during this segment. They had been performing around town and were releasing their first album that year. I was so excited that the pageant producers asked them to be the chosen group that night!

The five guys of Reign and their band members all came looking sharp, dressed in tuxedoes. They took turns lending a hand to escort each contestant as we appeared onstage for Evening Gown. I couldn't have been happier that Tini and I were together during my special moment. It was so romantic! Tini took my hand and led me onstage as I did my competition walk and headed down the long runway in my black dress. *I felt like a princess*. It was a night I'd never forget, if only for that reason.

Next, we were asked our onstage questions by fifth-graders. As a teacher, I felt right at home. The questions weren't rocket science, but it showed the audience and the judges how well each woman related to young children, since Miss Hawai'i's job includes visiting schools and working with youth on a regular basis. A little girl asked me what I would do if she were my sister and she came home after a bad day. I told her that I already had six sisters, but I'd love one more. The audience laughed. Then I said that I would first talk to her and try to make her feel better, then I'd put the crown on her and make her feel like a queen.

Throughout the live show, I felt like I was on top of my game. With a positive attitude the whole time I was there, I began to live in the moment because I realized this would be the very last time I'd compete at Miss Hawai'i.

The television spectacle unfolded over the course of two hours on KFVE. Then finally, it was time for the announcement of winners. Emcee Howard Dashefsky declared that ALL ten contestants received the Congeniality award, a first in the pageant's history! In fact, we all got along so well that we agreed to vote for the contestant before and after us in the lineup, because it was too hard to choose just one person.

Then he called a tie for Talent between *two* contestants: Billie Takaki, Miss Diamond Head 2000, and Liane Mark, Miss O'ahu 2000, which accounted for forty percent of a contestant's overall score. Liane was also named Swimsuit Winner. By all accounts, it seemed she was the obvious winner, but still, anything was possible, because not all the scores were revealed. In any case, my demeanor changed. I sensed the end of a journey and another disappointing finish, to which I had grown accustomed.

Meanwhile, the emcee announced the finalists. Confident in my interview, the most crucial phase of competition (but a category in which the winner is not announced publicly, for the sake of building suspense before announcing the overall winner), I was pretty sure I had a good chance of making it into the Top Five. But now self-doubt got a hold of me. I had not been announced for *any* award onstage, aside from the Congeniality Award that everyone got.

Howard called Fourth Runner-up . . . Miss West O'ahu, Juliet Lighter! Then Third Runner-up . . . Miss Honolulu, Alicia Lopes! Both *not* me, but my fellow preliminary pageant sisters. I was happy for them, but I started to get nervous. It was time for the Second Runner-up . . . I braced myself and got ready to possibly be called. Instead he announced, "Miss Diamond Head, Billie Takaki!" *What!? How can that be? She won Talent with Liane! Shouldn't she be at least First Runner-up?* At that point, I thought First Runner-up might possibly be me. OR . . . it could be *anyone* else on that stage. Who knew what the judges were looking for? This was unnerving.

I was puzzled because Billie just won Talent, a huge chunk of the score. It's common knowledge that the strategy to win overall is to score high in *every* phase, across the board, and I thought both Billie and Liane had done just that, *so where did I fall in?*

That night, my students, co-teachers, family and friends were all in the ballroom watching the pageant live. I worked out the facts in my head: I might still be able to win *if* I scored first in Interview (even if the winner wasn't announced), and *if* I won Evening Gown and Onstage Question, I *might* still have a chance, but *only* if I placed high in Talent and Swimsuit as well. Even if I didn't win those categories, I might have come in a close second to Liane and Billie. *Oh boy!* I was tired of speculating. At that point, I thought, *It's fine, I just might be called First Runner-up.* Then my mind switched gears.

Desperately trying to keep my composure, I thought of the possibility of a repeat at the Miss O'ahu preliminary pageant, where Liane surged ahead to make me her First Runner-up just months before, in front of my students.

I was near tears. I thought, *So close, and yet so far.*

Then the emcee said, "The First-Runner up is . . . Miss O'ahu, Liane Mark!" Completely baffled, Liane accepted her award and walked to the corner of the stage. I was still standing with six other contestants onstage and was just as perplexed as she was, if not more. *Then who won?* I thought.

In my head, according to any kind of speculation or calculation, my biggest competitors were already called, but the remaining contestants were incredibly intelligent, beautiful, and talented as well. Between the rest of the girls standing, they had all won onstage awards including: the People's Choice Internet Award, the Quality of Life Award, the Spirit Award, and Academic Achievement Awards. Except me.

At that point, it could have been *anyone* on that stage. We all knew that you can never guess exactly what the judges are looking for in a winner. On any given night, with a different set of judges, the outcome could be different. I knew this, but the suspense was unbearable. Because I had not been announced as a winner in Talent or Swimsuit, I thought, *What if I scored LOW across the board and didn't even place?!*

My nerves were getting the best of me. All the possibilities rushed through my head of who might be named the new state representative. I stood onstage trying to figure it out. I was hoping for this moment for so long. At first I shuddered at the thought of coming in second. Now, the reality was that I might not even be mentioned—in front of everybody! Twice before, I stood on the same Miss Hawai'i stage and never made it into the Top Five. I was not so sure tonight would be any different.

That's when I stopped to find my center, and put it all in His hands. I prayed in my mind: *Dear God, give me the strength to get through this if I don't win. I don't want to cry in front of everyone . . . let Your Will be done, and help me to accept it, whatever it is.*

It took a lot of guts to get to this point at Miss Hawai'i, and now it was the moment of truth (I was glad I had used the "Vaseline trick" before the show, smearing the balm on my teeth to keep the smiles effortlessly coming, amidst the anxiety I was experiencing inside). The announcer was running down the laundry list of prizes that Miss Hawai'i would receive, all totaling up to more than fifty-thousand dollars and all I could do was just breathe and keep my composure. *Could this take any longer? Geez!* The suspense was grueling.

My self-coaching kicked in with full force, *Ok, Angie. If you don't win, you will be the best teacher ever. You'll be fine. Just think, you were able to be onstage with Tini tonight, as he and Reign serenaded you during Evening Gown, you made some lifelong friends, and you showed courage getting this far. You're already a winner.*

Hoping and praying that the winner might be me, but knowing that the alternative was that I would walk away without placing once again, I decided not to be attached to the outcome. I had to let it go. I would accept God's Will for me, no matter what.

My pageant sisters and I were looking at each other wondering whose name would be called. One of the girls looked at me and pointed to me signaling that she thought the winner would be me. I tried to disregard her prediction because I didn't want to psych myself out for no reason. There was no more speculation now—only acceptance for whatever outcome. *God, help me, it's in Your Hands.*

My stream of thoughts were interrupted when the emcee said, "The new Miss Hawai'i is . . . Miss Leeward, Angela Perez Baraquio!" I almost collapsed with shock, squeezed my pageant sisters' hands, and threw my head back in sheer excitement and giddiness. I hugged my fellow contestants and thanked the judges. The moment was surreal!

As the Miss Hawai'i theme song began to play over the loud speakers in the Coral Ballroom, the crowd broke out in applause. My students, family, and friends, the entire ballroom was cheering for ME. I was so deeply humbled!

Candes Gentry, Miss Hawai'i 1999, placed the crown on my head, and I was presented with the official Miss Hawai'i koa bowl by Hilton Hawaiian Village President Peter Schall.

Making my way down the runway, the pageant's theme song played, "Miss Hawai'i, oh so lovely . . . " I couldn't believe this moment that I had dreamed of was *actually* happening in real time! I had worked so hard to get here and wished that one day I could represent my state at the national level. I remember walking the runway, smiling, waving, with tears welling up in my eyes because I was overcome with such emotion and gratitude. *This was incredible!* I thought, *Now everywhere I go, I am Hawai'i. I can't believe I will be representing our beautiful state at Miss America in Atlantic City this year!* My students, co-workers and all my supporters were clapping and waving at me as I took my victory walk to the end of the stage.

With the power of prayer, belief in myself, and positive thinking, I had finally attained the long awaited STATE TITLE! Seven years after the heartbreaking loss at the Kamehameha basketball game, I found some kind of redemption, and I discovered a way to make my peace with the outcome.

That winning moment was a culmination of all I had been through in my life up to that point. And it was so sweet!

I was greeted at the end of the runway by hundreds of supporters for the new Miss Hawai'i and was covered up to my eyes in fragrant flower lei by close friends and family. I still couldn't believe it—*I* was the Millennium Miss Hawai'i!

My Traveling Companion (TC) for the week at the Hilton, "Aunty" Leatrice, met me afterward. She was beaming with pride. And why not? She was a former Miss Leeward as well. Later, I discovered that my good friend, Natalie Brown-Aiwohi, who helped in my pageant preparation, was also a former Miss Leeward, so the legacy of our shared title continued with me. I was overcome with gratitude, and I had a flashback of all my former TCs during my past two tries at Miss Hawai'i: Davey Ann Basque and Bonnie Parsons were the ladies who took care of me as I readied myself for competition in 1995 and 1996. All their hard work and belief in me paid off. I stood there proud to represent all of them—and now, all of Hawai'i.

A string of lei cascaded down my arms, and it was like graduation night all over again. I felt incredibly thankful for the title, but the best part came when the former Miss Hawai'i winners gathered around me and said, "Welcome to the sisterhood!" There was so much love everywhere. At that moment, I realized I had begun a new chapter of my life.

After the pageant, the CEO of Miss America, Bob Renneisen came to congratulate me. He then asked, "Angela, what's your platform?" "Character Education—with a focus on America's youth," I replied. He cautioned, "Well, I hope you're passionate about it because if you win Miss America, you'll be talking about it all year long, and that passion will have to sustain you on the days when you feel like you can't go on." His advice took root in me and would be a gentle reminder when difficult times arose in the coming year.

Tini met me in the lobby. We hugged and took photos together. As happy as he was for me, we both knew that now, any plans of marriage would have to be put on hold. We said good night and Aunty Leatrice and I returned to our hotel room.

I was over the moon! Aunty Leatrice and I tried the coveted Miss

Hawai'i crown on in our pajamas and took silly pictures together. Then I had to get some rest and to wake up bright and early to prepare for all the interviews on the news stations at the crack of dawn.

As I closed my eyes in bed that night, I thought about all that transpired, and the roller coaster of emotions I experienced. That night was the beginning of my new destiny. Thankfully, my third and last try at Miss Hawai'i proved to be the lucky one. It was clear that in anything, you literally need to be *in it*, in order to *win it*. And now, I was on my way to Atlantic City to compete in the 80th Anniversary Miss America Pageant!

CHAPTER 7

PREPPING FOR THE BIG LEAGUE

After coming down from the high of being crowned Miss Hawai'i, reality set in immediately. In contrast to popular thinking, the time between winning a state title and preparing for Miss America is not glamorous nor is it an easy path.

The spiritual, mental, and physical preparation for my journey to the national crown continued. With so many expectations upon me, it was the most stressful time in my entire life. Stepping into the unknown was the difficult part, and it was hard to plan ahead.

There was no guarantee that I'd win in October 2000, so I had a backup plan to return to Holy Family Catholic Academy the following fall as a second-year PE teacher, sports coach and Athletic Director. My pastor, Father Mac, assured me that regardless of the outcome I would always have a job at my alma mater, so that was reassuring.

I was scheduled to leave late September 2000 to meet the contestants at Walt Disney World in Orlando, Florida. Father Mac hired a replacement teacher for me, just in case. He had every faith in me that I would bring home the crown. In the meantime, he said I was garnering great publicity for the school, especially with my character education platform. As a former graduate of Holy Family and a current teacher, I was attracting positive media attention, which eventually led to increased enrollment on our campus. It was a win-win situation, and I was happy that I had one less thing to worry about if I didn't win, but if I did, all my bases were covered.

As one of my Miss Hawai'i prizes, I was given a Franklin Covey seminar. For two eight-hour days, I attended the "What Matters Most" workshop. There I set my short-term and long-term goals, and learned how to "Sharpen the Saw" in all areas of my life. That experience changed forever the way I organized my life. Personally, I liked having multiple projects going on simultaneously, because they kept my mind and body active. But I needed to learn time management. The course taught me that in setting goals, I needed to start with the end in mind and work backwards. It all made so much sense to me and increased my efficiency. I talked to Tini afterward about the workshop and we discussed our short and long term goals individually and as a couple, and then we set timelines to meet our goals.

An exercise at the workshop asked us to imagine ourselves at eighty years old. The trainer asked, "What are you doing? Who are you with? Where do you live? Are you healthy?" Once we had a clear vision of where we wanted to be at that age, we started working backwards, figuring out what we needed to do today in order to take baby steps and get where we wanted to be. It was that simple. Later I read, *Seven Habits of Highly Effective People* by Stephen R. Covey. The book and the workshop were transformational for me.

I listed the things I wanted to accomplish in the short term: (1) Be Miss America 2001, (2) Earn my master's degree, (3) Marry Tini. I remember writing my goals down and closing my notebook quickly, hoping no one would see them. Time management and goal-setting were two skills I walked away with after the intensive retreat. I was armed and ready to tackle the world.

That night, I went home and meditated on my purpose for competing in the pageant. I wanted to make a difference on a larger scale and positively impact youth worldwide. Miss America gave me a platform to do just that. I felt I was becoming well-rounded and more worldly through my pageant involvement. I was watching the news and keeping up with current events, forming my worldview, and learning how to validate my opinions.

My intent was to serve others, especially our youth, in the greatest capacity possible. I had my reservations about competing in Swimsuit, but I knew that it was part of the scoring and I had to do it if I wanted to win.

A book publisher once told me, "We sell 'em what they want, and give 'em what they need." I had a game plan to accomplish my goals. I'd wear a swimsuit on stage to give the television viewers and pageant fans what they *wanted*, but my platform on character education was giving the world what it *needed*.

That summer of 2000, I woke up one morning from a dream that I had about winning the Swimsuit competition at Miss America. I called Tini to tell him about it, and he told me to try not to psych myself out and just stay focused. I knew he was right. Just like Coach Dana always said, "Play your game, and focus on the task at hand."

He didn't want to get my hopes up prematurely, so I put that delusion out of my head. Anyway, it seemed like a long shot. I had never won a preliminary Swimsuit competition at any local pageant, or even at Miss Hawai'i the year I won, so why would I have a chance at winning Swimsuit at the national level? It seemed silly, so I focused on the bigger picture.

Just as I had done for years in our basketball locker rooms, I began to visualize me winning, to see myself as the new Miss America. I imagined what it would be like to sign my first autograph as the winner. So I got a piece of paper and wrote, "Love and Aloha, Angela Perez Baraquio, Miss America 2001." Just seeing it gave me chills up my spine. To see it in black and white was surreal. I immediately tore up the paper to avoid having anyone see it.

Well, maybe it wasn't so crazy. The next time I signed my autograph in that way, I was the newly crowned winner, about to walk onstage for my interview at the David Letterman show in New York City. My advice: If you have a dream, visualize it and write it down! The written word has tremendous power.

Months later, as Miss America, I would meet bestselling author Harvey MacKay on the road. I never forgot his words, "Angela, remember that a dream is just a dream. A goal is a dream with a plan and a deadline." I had all those things. Now I just needed to execute.

Being physically, spiritually, and mentally prepared was imperative. I was working out every day on my body, but Swimsuit was only fifteen percent of the overall score. Evening Gown was fifteen percent, Interview was thirty percent and Talent was forty percent, so I had to gauge my time and prepare accordingly.

Many contestants think that pageants are all glamour. For me, this was furthest from the truth. The reality was that at the time I was competing I was a first-year teacher living downstairs from my parents. I trained every single day on each phase of competition, and I had little time for anything else outside of church, gym workouts, talent practice, and interview preparations.

On the other hand, I was pleasantly surprised and even impressed at the results I saw when I really put my mind to being my best self in all areas. I realized that I was capable of doing much more than I thought possible. I took my body where my mind wanted to go. Working out that much was an exhilarating experience. To be honest, I have never trained as hard or as frequently as I did when I was preparing for Miss America. This was not a team sport like basketball, but an individual one, which required lots of help from trainers and supporters.

Todd, my pageant director once told me that ultimately, I was the one on that stage who had to deal with the outcome, as well as the consequences of every single choice I made leading up to that point. When he put it that way, I continued to listen to the advice of others, but even more importantly, I had to listen to my heart and do what was right for me.

So for my last year of competition, I was no longer a puppet. I did things *my way*, with no apologies.

When preparing for Miss Hawai'i and Miss America, I was amazed at what resulted from self-discipline and focus. An hour a day of Billy Blanks' Tae Bo (kickboxing), adhering to a strict diet (no fries, sweets or sodas), reading the newspaper, keeping up with world news each night and meeting several times a week with my mentors proved to be a formula for success. I became my own coach when no one else was around, and pushed myself farther than I ever believed I could.

What surprised me was my overall endurance in all aspects, and that made me proud of my accomplishments. I was extremely grateful for the team of people that helped me get to the highest level in the system. I could never have done it alone.

Spiritually, I prepared by attending Mass and reading my daily devotions, meditating on what God wanted me to do. I prayed every day for the wisdom to know what was right, to care about it, and to do it. And I always asked God to help me accept His Will. Mama asked for prayers from all the churches she was involved with on O'ahu. Everyone's prayers gave me peace of mind and lifted me up as I was competing. I often felt angels all around me.

Before I left for Atlantic City, New Jersey to compete, I had my official photo shoot at Nate's Photography, the same studio I took my senior portraits just six years earlier. My, how things had changed since I was last there. I remember posing for Nate with my gown and crown, and then in my red interview business suit, thinking, *These are the pictures that will be in the program book and the same photos the judges will be seeing with my bio as they are judging all fifty-one contestants. The images will go down in history as a snapshot of who I am right now. I don't want to smile like Miss Hawai'i vying for the title. I want to smile as if I am already Miss America.* That's exactly what I was thinking when he began snapping those photos. When the prints came back, people commented on my picture and told me I looked like a Miss America. Little did they know I was "acting as if" I already was.

My mentor teacher and close friend, Valerie Elefante, told me that she and her friends visualized then-current Miss America, Heather French, crowning me. They became my prayer warriors. I also remember praying often, asking God to use me as an instrument. I knew I had a lot of work ahead of me, but the good news was that I didn't have to do it alone. I had a solid team of supporters beside me.

Of course I wanted to do well, but ultimately, it wasn't about what I wanted, but what *He* wanted for me. So I put the outcome in His Hands. Sometimes that's all we can do; trust, and know that God has a plan for us.

~ With A Little Help From My Friends ~

From the moment I began competing in pageants I knew this was "my thing"—something that would define me as unique from my siblings. No one else tried it, so why not me? I went from being the child in the family who was typically forgotten, unnoticed, or overlooked to the one who was being fussed over and cared for. I felt beautiful on the inside, but to feel like royalty on the outside was strange and new to me.

During my pageant years, I was fortunate to be constantly surrounded by an army of friends and family who rallied to my support, eager to help in any way. Countless volunteers and sponsors helped sustain the program I had grown to love. It was impossible to express the fullness of my gratitude.

I believe that no one can win anything completely on their own. The African adage is true, "It takes a village to raise a child." I credit my family and friends for shaping me, but so many others helped me along the way. In my first press conference as Miss America 2001 in Atlantic City, I thanked "everyone I ever came in contact with." When I said it, I meant it.

During my third time competing at state, it was announced to the contestants that the girl who was crowned Miss Hawai'i 2000 would have an official dress designer to prepare and sponsor her wardrobe for the national pageant. After I won, I was excited to work with Lisa Hutchinson of Monalisa Designs. She was like my fairy godmother that year. We worked closely together in design meetings and fittings to create and finalize a dazzling wardrobe for the national show.

My favorite dress was my competition evening gown, which Lisa allowed me to design myself (with her help and expertise, of course). To see it onstage and be able to get crowned in it was fantastic!

At our first meeting, I told her that I envisioned wearing a long red gown for the evening wear competition. Knowing what style was most flattering to my body type at the time, I asked for a halter-style, backless gown with a slit and train. Slowly, but surely, the gown took shape and Lisa was able to bring my vision to life!

My personal style was classic, simple, and elegant. Lisa orchestrated and executed the design beautifully. She assured me that the crimson color of the satin fabric she used looked great onstage because she had used it before with other Miss Hawai'is. From prior experience, she learned that when the lights hit the dress on the Boardwalk Hall stage, it would create a mesmerizing effect.

Her expertise proved to be spot-on, because when I walked out in my gown for the first time, jaws dropped. Although I didn't have it bedecked with jewels like my fellow contestants, it was still stunning and I was proud to wear it. It was a magnificent feeling to wear an elegant gown and float onstage like a princess on the most memorable day of my life!

During my year as Miss America, the Sheraton Atlantic City kept my dress on display in a glass showcase, beside my competition earrings. Behind the items was a full-sized color photo of me wearing the gown. They returned the items to me after my year, so I have all of them in my possession and will keep them for my daughter (if Keilah ever wants to play "dress up" someday).

At the time, all the former Miss Americas had their winning moment shown in a video loop on the TV in the lobby. My winning moment had not yet been added, but it was so amazing to know that I was a part of that grand legacy.

My Talent outfit was a strapless wedding gown with silver beading intricately sewn into the bodice. Lisa had designed it with a bride in mind, but the moment I tried it on at her boutique, I knew I wanted to dance my hula 'auana (modern hula) in it for the Talent portion.

I had sponsors who had handmade beautiful realistic flower headpieces and lei for my competition. I surely wouldn't find fresh Hawaiian flowers in Atlantic City, so they created a custom-made puakenikeni (golden-colored fragrant flowers from Hawai'i) ensemble for me. Because the flowers change color from white to yellow to orange, my flower necklace and headpieces represented the multi-colors of each phase. During Talent the flowers I had onstage looked so natural and stunning. I wore them with pride to my appearances throughout the year because that was my way of representing the Aloha State everywhere I went.

For Swimsuit, I wore a yellow two-piece designed once again by Ann Tongg, the specialist who designed my red Miss Hawai'i competition suit. This one was also tailored specifically to my body which gave me more confidence while competing.

Thankfully, my trainers collectively whipped me into the best shape I'd ever been, mostly with squats, pushups, bench presses, and Tae Bo (which I loved to do on my own time, even though it went against my trainers' advice because they thought it would make my legs look too muscular). I was extremely proud of the progress I made physically—it took a lot of discipline to stay fit. To finish my competition look, in my hair I wore a yellow hibiscus, Hawai'i's state flower.

I was so lucky to have former Miss Hawai'is open up their wardrobe closets to me. Jennifer Hera, Miss Hawai'i 1998, lent me gowns for events during Miss Hawai'i pageant week. On my request, she even took a day to show me pictures and videos of her time in Atlantic City, which allowed me to envision what it was like to be at nationals. It was crucial for my visualizations.

After I won I was humbled when Miss Hawai'i 1996, Melissa Short, invited me to her home and generously offered to loan me gowns for my appearances as Miss Hawai'i before I went to Atlantic City (I officially served as Miss Hawai'i 2000 for four months before crowning Billie Takaki as the new titleholder). Melissa even gave me brand new shoes from her own closet!

Candes Gentry, Miss Hawai'i 1999, sent me off with aloha attire for my contestant arrival ceremony in New Jersey, which I also wore after I won during my appearances on the road. Through it all, my pageant sisters and were extremely supportive. I remembered their kindness and good example, and did the same for other girls who were to come after me.

Part of the prize package for Miss Hawai'i included an official hair and make-up artist. Pattie Kuamo'o and Dennis Guillermo of Salon 808 made up my "Glam Team." Before I met them, I didn't even know how to do my own makeup!

In fact, backstage at Miss Hawai'i, they saw me made up and ready for competition. Because I didn't have a budget to pay for professional hair and makeup services, a friend of mine who sold makeup said she'd do it for me at no charge. She admitted she never did stage makeup before, but I was grateful to her because I didn't know how to do my own pageant makeup.

Suddenly, without saying a word, Pattie and Dennis motioned me to sit down and told me they just wanted to "touch me up." I was confused when they began nonchalantly removing all my makeup. Then they started over!

Clearly, *they* were the professionals, so I let them do their thing. They told me later that when they saw me during rehearsals onstage before the telecast, my heavy makeup made me look like a drag queen under the lights. I had no idea! But that night, I ended up looking flawless on TV, especially during my crowning moment, all thanks to them.

After I won Miss Hawai'i, Pattie met me in the salon for a makeup consultation. She said every Miss Hawai'i needed to know how to do her own face for appearances, so she told me to bring in all my makeup, and we would play with it. To her shock, all the makeup I owned was stuffed into a tiny pink zippered pouch, the size of a hot dog bun. In it, was a half-sharpened Wet N Wild black eyeliner pencil, an almost dried-up mascara wand, and some clear ChapStick lip balm, not even tinted lip gloss!

As a PE teacher, I didn't need a ton of makeup, and there was nothing pretentious about my presentation. Pattie casually took my pouch and asked me, "Is this ALL your makeup?" I said, "Yes," and she gently plopped it in the wastebasket beside her station.

I was appalled and was about to dig it out. She stopped me. "No worries, honey," she reassured me, "I'll take care of you." I gave in trustingly. At twenty-four, after nine pageants, playing in a band, and hosting a TV show, I still didn't know how to do my own camera-ready or full-face stage makeup. I needed to learn—fast.

At our next session at the salon, Pattie surprised me with a full palette of M.A.C. eye shadows, and a small collection of lipstick, glosses, lip liner pencils, and professional brushes. She then made a list of things for me to request from Shiseido, one of our pageant sponsors (I had unlimited Shiseido makeup and facial care that year.) Pattie, once again, saved the day. That makeup lasted me the entire year of Miss America, and thanks to her lessons, I was able to appear in full-face makeup, appropriate for my speeches and appearances on the road, all year long. To this day, we still laugh about my first consultation, and we remain good friends.

In the weeks following Miss Hawai'i, I began to pick up the prizes and gifts from my sponsors. Hawaiian Airlines gave me a year travel pass, so I took advantage of it by attending several character education workshops in California to prepare me for my Miss America platform.

One of my most cherished winnings included something that every Miss Hawai'i treasures: her breathtaking gift from Steven Lee Designs. When I received my very own official 14-carat gold Official Miss Hawai'i coin pendant surrounded with diamonds, I squealed in excitement! I had seen and admired it from afar, the diamond-and-gold coin pendants that lay on former Miss Hawai'is' necks when they would come to appearances. Now I had one of my very own!

Then, after I won Miss America, Steven Lee surprised me with *another* diamond-and-gold pendant and chain! This time, it was a gold coin with me wearing the Miss America crown on the front, and the words "Miss America 2001" on the back of it. The fact that it was personalized just for me meant so much. I was extremely touched by the thoughtful gesture.

Other jewelry I received from Miss Hawai'i sponsors was an exquisite set of earrings, a necklace, and bracelet made of black pearls from LuCoral Museum. Brenda Reichel from Carats and Karats gifted me with a 14-carat gold Hawaiian bracelet with "Miss Hawai'i 2000" engraved on it, and later after my win, she gave me another one that said "Miss America 2001" with a rare pink diamond set in it.

As I traveled the country, I wore those two bracelets together with such pride. There were so many other prizes that I won, which totaled up to about fifty-thousand dollars, in addition to the roughly thirty-two thousand dollars I had collectively earned in scholarship grants from the Miss Hawai'i Organization alone. In the three years I competed in the Miss America Organization, I earned more than one-hundred-thousand dollars in scholarship assistance. It was pretty remarkable.

A few weeks after winning in my state, I was surprised to learn that I had an anonymous shoe and jewelry donor, so shopping for those items was *ridiculously* fun! The committee members and I stopped at Nieman Marcus where I bought some very posh heels for my Interview and Evening Gown competitions. And I found the perfect jewelry for my wardrobe at Miss America. I got to keep my entire sponsored wardrobe, shoes, jewelry, and accessories!

My Top Five outfit was an elegant, Asian-inspired two-piece pants suit, sponsored by Villa Roma. Mamo Howell, a well-renowned Hawaiian designer, also donated at least ten stunning outfits that were my go-to dresses when events called for aloha attire. For my "Show me Your Shoes" parade outfit that ended pageant week in Atlantic City, I wore a gorgeous, high-neck traditional white lace holoku with a train, courtesy of Princess Ka'iulani Designs. The dress was reminiscent of those worn by Hawaiian ali'i (royalty) used at the turn of the century in old Hawai'i.

I felt so grateful for everyone that I had the chance to meet and work with, and for all I had been given. Never in my life had I been spoiled like that. Certainly, not in my household! It was a welcome change to what I was used to, and I was happily receiving the blessings that came my way.

~ To Sing or Dance Hula? That is the Question ~

One of the biggest decisions a state contestant must make is to choose a talent to perform at Miss America. Each young woman has only ninety seconds to showcase her gifts. I will never forget being torn about singing or dancing hula. Random people would come up and tell me that I should sing because Miss America *always* sings. While many winners were singers, the talents have been varied. When I found out that Kaye Lani Rae Rafko became Miss America 1988 with a Tahitian dance, I was inspired. In 2000, I was the first to Miss America to win with a Hawaiian hula dance as my talent.

The summer of 2000, before the big pageant, another state's executive director came into town and she gave me some valuable advice during her visit. I told her I wasn't sure about what to do for Talent and she put it bluntly, saying I should do for Talent what I could *still* do even if I was injured. She explained that some girls choose talents that are too challenging for them and when they get to Miss America, the added stress and rigorous schedule causes them to crack under pressure.

I decided to do what came most naturally to me: hula. Growing up, I danced for fun at family parties, after learning how to dance in junior high during our May Day celebrations.

Then in college, I fell in love with the cultural significance of hula. One of my state directors, Raymond Abregano, Jr., convinced me to perform the dance, choreographed by his hula brother, Kala Gongob. Some people didn't consider it a real talent when, in fact, it is a cultural dance that takes years to master. I felt hula was the best way to represent my state as the current Miss Hawai'i.

During Pageant Week at Miss America, we each were given just one ten-minute rehearsal on the large stage in Boardwalk Hall, in front of all the other contestants, professional dancers, emcees, Heather French, and anyone else who would be a part of the production. Years later, Heather told me that on that day, one of the male dancers said to her, "What is Miss Hawai'i's talent—tai chi?" Heather replied, "No, it's hula, a Hawaiian dance." Then Cris Judd, one of the dancers who had roots in Hawai'i and later married J.Lo, said, "She's beautiful, she doesn't need a talent." Heather was tickled to share that story with me. I thought, *That's so sweet, but how interesting that the other dancer thought my talent was tai chi* . . . I was glad to have been able to make the finals and present a cultural dance, that was once banned in the islands, to a worldwide audience.

A few months before the nationals, a woman approached me saying, "I read in the paper that you are going to dance hula at Miss America. Honey, no one has ever won with a hula!" I replied, "Well, that may be true, but I have already decided to dance, thank you." Her unsolicited comments rang in my head. Deep in my heart, I knew hula was the best choice for me, no matter what anyone else thought.

When I returned for my Homecoming celebration at the Hilton Hawaiian Village, just two months after being crowned Miss America, the same woman came up to me at the luau, which the hotel hosted for me and said, "Hi Angela, I'm not sure if you remember me. I was the one who told you that no one has ever won the pageant with a hula." Smiling at her, I thought to myself, *Oh yes . . . how could I forget?* She continued, "Well, I saw you dance and win that night. It was so beautiful. I couldn't have been more wrong. I just wanted to say congratulations!" I gave her a heartfelt hug. It felt good that I trusted myself even when other people doubted me.

The song I danced to was chosen specifically because it was reminiscent of how I felt walking down the runway when I won the state title. It was appropriately named, "I Am Hawai'i" a medley of film themes from the movies *Mutiny on the Bounty* and *Hawai'i*.

I chose a version sung by Cathy Foy, Miss Hawai'i 1975. Cathy had performed at Miss America on the same stage in Atlantic City as Miss Hawai'i exactly twenty-five years earlier. Everything I chose for that pageant had profound significance, and all the pieces seemed to fit.

~ Tough Love is Still Love ~

During my year of service in 2000, the Miss Hawai'i Executive Committee rallied around me when I was crowned, but immediately cracked the whip, and got me prepared for all phases of competition.

The committee members never sugar-coated anything, but they each had big hearts, and their collective coaching style helped me in the long run. I may not have realized it then, but now I see that I would have never been as prepared for the year ahead if it weren't for the training I received from my state committee. I will always be thankful for their guidance, advice, and feedback.

Even though there were many moments I felt gratitude for their extreme generosity and selflessness, there were also moments I felt misunderstood. Like any family, we weren't perfect, but we were there for each other when it mattered. They would open up their homes to me, spend time away from their families to help me prepare, hold weekly meetings to be sure I was on the right track, and make sure I had everything I needed to be fully prepared when I went to Atlantic City representing our beautiful state.

My interview coach and I had weekly meetings discussing current events. She helped me formulate my opinions on issues and articulate my thoughts regarding global news. To score high in Interview I first needed to be on top of current events, then form an opinion and be able to validate it.

The judges, I was reminded, scored contestants not necessarily on their stance, but their presentation, and how well she backed up her position.

The committee frequently told state contestants that they were waiting to see who the next woman would be to put Hawai'i "back on the map" because we were due for another winner. I accepted that challenge.

However, I truly didn't know what to expect afterward if I became Miss America. Since they were all there when Carolyn Sapp won in 1991, I asked the committee what happens after the winner is crowned. They basically told me I didn't need to worry about that because they wanted me to be prepared for the competition and focus on the task at hand. Although I understood and accepted their position, I still wanted to plan ahead—just in case.

A fifth-grader, who overcame her own stage fright, enlightened me before I went on stage at Miss Hawai'i. She said, "When you're prepared, you won't be scared." I just wanted to be prepared.

At the time, I was under a lot of stress and it started to show on my face. I'm sure other state winners went through something similar because it is undoubtedly a stressful time for any woman preparing to compete at the national level. I felt like I was in a pressure cooker. My skin was breaking out like never before. It was worse than anything I experienced in high school, so I visited a dermatologist in the months leading up to Miss America. I think my body was trying to let go of everything I was holding inside for years. Thankfully, my doctor prescribed me medicine and it all cleared up just weeks before I left for Atlantic City.

One of the toughest moments I endured before leaving for the pageant happened two weeks prior to my sendoff. The committee arranged a mock interview for me with a panel of judges to prepare me for nationals.

86

After the debriefing, I went home. The executive director called me on the phone telling me that overall, my performance was basically unimpressive. I was crushed! His unexpected words made my heart sink and rattled my confidence. Tears began to flow, and I couldn't breathe. Now I was really feeling the pressure.

I suppose it was frustrating for him to know my capabilities, and see me *not* living up to my potential. Maybe he saw that I could win if I just pushed a little harder to be at my best. Still, I was just days away from leaving for the biggest competition of my life and I felt deflated. I know he was speaking his truth, but I had a hard time accepting it.

This was nothing new to me, though. I had been here before with other "coaches" who prepared me for life. Like Mama and Coach Dana, who expected excellence from me, my committee would not accept anything less either, because they wanted to see me succeed. I see clearly now that they pushed me to my limits, but for a good purpose and with good intent.

After listening to the full critique about my shortcomings in Interview, which I was growing increasingly sensitive to, we finally hung up. Blinded by my own tears, I buried my face in my arms after that harsh reality check. As much as I didn't want to admit it, my state director was right. I needed to step it up before the nationals.

I was told in the past by my mock judges that I had a strong interview, and interviews win these pageants. Apparently, at this one, I was rusty on current events, and my answers were not articulate. Plus, I spoke really fast. They constantly reminded me to slow down, but I really felt as if I *was* speaking slowly. I realized I could have done better. The criticism stung, but I resolved to be more conscious of my committee's comments, and not take everything so personally.

Deeply discouraged, I had to find a way to move past that moment of weakness. I had to decompress and stop putting undue pressure on myself. I knew that if I went in and gave my personal best, I would be just fine. There was no time to waste. I told myself, *Come on, Angie! Step it up, you're Miss Hawai'i.*

It was time to prove what I was made of; I was ready for redemption. My mind went back to the 1993 Kamehameha basketball game all over again. The situation: last quarter of the game, 5.5 seconds left, time to go "all-in." I needed to crank it up a notch. Coach Dana used to say, "When you're not in shape, you get tired, when you're tired, you make mistakes. When you make too many mistakes, you lose games." I *was* tired, but I had to be prepared and it was my last chance to surge ahead.

I wiped my tears and flashed back to my friend Candes's comforting words of encouragement after she had crowned me the new Miss Hawai'i. When she was the current winner, she said she was also critiqued for speaking quickly in Interview. She reassured me on the side, "Angie, don't let anyone change you. If you talk fast, you talk fast. That's you. Everyone's always telling me to slow down. I try, but that's just the way I am." I loved her for telling me to just be myself and embrace that. It gave me the sense to be aware of people's comments and advice, but the courage to accept me for the way I am. Such simple advice, but so true. *Be Yourself.*

Meanwhile, Tini was patiently waiting in the wings. He was working at an architecture firm in downtown Honolulu. Once, while I was visiting a sponsor in downtown, I parked in a garage near Tini's office building. During lunch he asked where I was, and I told him. But I was busy and couldn't meet him, so he said he'd meet up with me later. When I got to my car after my meeting, I found two dozen red roses on my backseat and a note that simply read, "I miss you." Through it all, Tini was loving me in his own special way. More than ever, I needed that kind of tender love from someone who knew me best.

Before I left for the pageant, the committee and I hashed things out. I admitted I was a headstrong contestant, but I was also extremely focused and eager to learn *how* to be Number One. I couldn't do it alone. I needed their help. They conceded that although their words may have been harsh in my eyes, they wanted me to be at my best. They added that I had a strong interview overall, but I needed to be prepared for nationals.

Although I had an "off" day, I still had time. I had to listen to all the things my committee was telling me to do, and if I did, I would do well. We reconciled our differences before I left for the pageant, and by the time I saw them again in Atlantic City, we were all totally different people.

I felt very much supported at Miss America. The whole committee and the Hawai'i delegation came together to celebrate at the State Visitation, where all the state winners gathered at the end of each night with their supporters. Ours was the only state that had a group carrying ukuleles, lei, and waving ti leaves. Every evening after preliminaries, we'd all get in a circle while I danced hula. We sang songs and laughed together, and we gave lei to each preliminary winner. The spirit of aloha was strong among us.

And when I came back to Honolulu for Homecoming, the committee planned everything down to the last detail. I'm sure there were so many things they did for me behind the scenes that I never knew about. But somehow I always knew they gave all they had to provide the best of everything for me and all their Miss Hawai'is.

As a mother now, I see the importance of tough love and there are times I use it with my own children, *sprinkled in with some tender love here and there!*

The entire committee showed me tough love, but it was still LOVE. I realize that they all had good intentions—it just wasn't evident to me at the time. They may not have supported me *the way* I wanted to be supported, but in the end, they always had my back.

Today, I can say I'm a better person, specifically because of the preparation I was given by my Miss Hawai'i state committee, and I am grateful for the countless hours they volunteered to push me to my limits, allowing me to become the best state representative I could be at Miss America. Those experiences prepared me for what was to come.

~ The Sendoff ~
September 2000

The day I left for the competition festivities, my school marching band and cheerleaders surprised me at the airport gate. (This was a year before 9/11 and the new security regulations, so this was completely allowed). The kids were decked out in full uniform, performing for me once again, like they had at school a week earlier. They were sending me off in style, and I felt so honored. Just like the day I won, I was covered up to my neck in lei and filled with overwhelming gratitude.

My TC Leilani Keough carefully bagged each lei to keep it fresh for our arrival on the East Coast. She reminded me to preserve them so I could give them away to people when we landed, a tradition that each Miss Hawai'i continues each year.

I'll never forget how the cheerleaders made signs for me and morphed into a three-tiered human pyramid. On the bottom, the sign read, "Miss Angie," the middle tier read, "Miss Hawai'i" and the top tier said, "Miss America." That *visual* was imprinted on my mind. The K-8 student body presented me with letters of encouragement and love wishing me well at the pageant. They assured me they would all be watching and cheering me on, and no matter what, I was a winner in their eyes. Their support spoke volumes. Feeling so much love and support from so many people, how could I not give my all to represent the people I was leaving behind?

After I was crowned Miss America I found out that Holy Family coordinated a viewing party at the school, cheering me on while the pageant aired live from New Jersey. Eight hundred parents, students, and teachers watched me compete and win on three huge screens with a mock runway, even though the Hawai'i telecast had a slight delay because of the difference in time zones. There were news cameras there, however, interviewing my students in real time, and the school went wild with pride as the competition progressed. Some of my family members who couldn't make it to Atlantic City attended that event. It felt great to know that so many people supported me.

My TC Leilani and I boarded the plane, and we were headed for Orlando, Florida (my first time on the east coast) on the way to meet the rest of the contestants at Walt Disney World. When we were checking in to the resort, Leilani said, "Angie, this is the best time of your life. Enjoy every moment. You will never pass this way again." I remember saying, "I'll definitely be back to Disney World." To which she replied, "But not as the current Miss Hawai'i." The words sunk in. I knew she was right. I soaked up every moment and took twelve rolls of film over the next two weeks.

I read one of my student's letters later that day and she wrote, "Dear Coach Angie, No matter what happens, you'll always be Miss America to us." I held my students close to me on that entire trip knowing that they were a big reason I was doing any of this. I took their notes and flowers with me to Atlantic City, along with their hopes, dreams, and their aloha.

The extreme pressure seemed to fade once I landed on the east coast. It was my first time away from my family, and it felt liberating to be independent. This was my time to grow, my time to shine. I was in charge of my own destiny, and it was electrifying.

~ September 26, 2000 ~

Once I arrived to the east coast, my main goals were to have fun and make friends, and that's what I did. Walt Disney World was truly magical. It was my first time there, and I enjoyed the park with all my fellow contestants. During that first week, I called Todd (my pageant director at the time) telling him, "The girls are all terrific, and I feel like we are all on a leveled playing field. I can *do* this." Todd later told me that when he heard me say those words, he knew that I was different and he had a feeling that I was going to win. My confidence was building, and so was the excitement.

~ Atlantic City Festivities ~
October 2000

We were chartered by plane from Orlando to Atlantic City, and then we rode on a private bus to meet the press at the Sheraton. As our bus entered the city, there was a huge sign, which read, "Welcome to Atlantic City! Home of the Miss America Pageant." I had to pinch myself. I loved being on the Boardwalk and couldn't believe I was there! I wondered if at any given moment I would wake up from this wonderful dream.

The first week in New Jersey was filled with dance rehearsals, fittings, and TV shoots preparing for the final night's show. The second week, the mood changed when Preliminary Competitions commenced.

By lottery, I was chosen to be contestant No. 50. I was excited for several reasons. Hawai'i is known as the fiftieth state, so that had significance for me. Also, Heather French, Miss America 2000, visited Hawai'i a few months earlier and told me that *she* was contestant No. 50 in the lottery the year before, and to her surprise, she won a Swimsuit Preliminary at Miss America before winning the title.

I remember visiting her in her suite in Honolulu as the newly crowned Miss Hawai'i. Heather told me *her* theory of why she won. It all started during preliminary week: being placed in the Sigma Group, she did her Judges' Interview on Tuesday. Being seen second-to-the-last in the entire group of contestants by the judges, she felt her interview was memorable, not only because she was confident and knew her platform inside and out, but also since she was still top of mind for the judges, when she competed the following day in Swimsuit, they must have remembered her and scored her high in that category *because* of her strong interview.

She admitted that the downside of being the fiftieth contestant was that the panel of judges might be tired by then, but she took the opportunity to really "wow" them in Interview, so they could get excited about her and her platform message of Homeless Veterans. Heather was well aware that she needed to stand out. She believed that if her interview was weak after the judges had already seen forty-nine other contestants with strong interviews, that placement might have worked against her. But she made a really good impression on them in that first competition in Interview, from the first moment the judges saw her. As Heather spoke, I hung on her every word.

I temporarily forgot about that conversation until we arrived in Atlantic City, and Heather asked all the contestants what numbers we were in the lineup. When I told her I was No. 50, she got so excited and jokingly said, "It's a sign! Now, if you win your Swimsuit preliminary like me, you just might win the whole thing!" Remembering Tini's advice when I told him about my dream of winning Swimsuit at Miss America, I tried not to psych myself out. However, I knew that starting from the all-important interview, if the judges like you, you have a better chance of advancing to the Top Ten.

For pageant week, just like Heather did the year before, I competed in Interview on Tuesday, Swimsuit on Wednesday, Evening Gown on Wednesday, and Talent on Thursday. The night before my interview, I spoke with my state committee downstairs in the lobby of Caesar's Palace, my host hotel. They tried to motivate me before the big day. "This is it! Are you ready for your interview tomorrow? This is where you can win it. If they like you in Interview, they'll score you high across the board. You have a strong interview, and you'll do well in Evening Gown and Talent, but you HAVE to score high in Swimsuit on Wednesday. That's your weakest competition." *Wow, thanks.*

But it was the bitter truth. I had never won a Swimsuit competition before—not in a preliminary, or even at State. But I had a goal and strategy to get into the Top Ten.

To prepare for Interview, I had to keep asking myself what I wanted out of my time at Miss America. What was my purpose? I wrote in my journal a list of all the things I wanted to get across to the judges. My bullet points were my "must-airs," which included my family background, teaching career, platform, and anything else that made me unique from the other contestants. I practiced my thirty-second introduction and my ninety-second closing in front of the mirror and tried to get as comfortable as I could on my platform and current events.

I needed to "act as if" I was already Miss America from the second I walked into that room. This was a job interview, and this would have to be the best one of my life. But how do you let seven judges "see" you in twelve minutes? That was the challenge. I had to be deliberate, purposeful, and above all, prepared. When I was finished making final preparations, I turned off my lights and visualized myself walking into the room.

My main source of motivation came from my students. During the summer before the national pageant, just after I was crowned Miss Hawai'i, a TV crew was sent to each state to do the up-close-and-personal video shoot for each contestant. I asked my church youth choir kids, my students from school, and my whole family to film the segment with me. Those who attended the video shoot sacrificed their Saturday afternoon. The entire day of shooting would be edited down to a minute and a half and only the women who made the finals would get their segment shown on TV. That fact alone compelled me to aim for the semi-finals so my students could see themselves on national television.

After my Private Interview with the first judges' panel (the second panel of seven celebrity judges took over during the telecast), I walked out feeling like I had done my personal best. I said everything I wanted to say to the judges and felt I represented my family, school, and state well.

During the interview, I got emotional when I talked about my students because I wanted the judges to know that if I could make it to the finals, it would be proof to my students that anything is possible. The underlying message to my students was that they would never know what they are capable of accomplishing unless they try. Walking out of the interview with no regrets was a great feeling. I breathed a sigh of relief. That was one competition down, three more to go! If I kept performing at this rate, I would be a winner in my own eyes, which is what mattered the most to me.

Physically, I didn't look like a typical pageant girl. Compared to the other girls, I wasn't tall and thin. I was short and had muscular thighs, but I looked physically fit. I was also brown-skinned and proud of it. My attitude was, "This is me, take it or leave it." I told myself I was going to score as high as I could by walking with confidence. It may have been my weakest phase, but I was determined to have fun and give it my all. I was doing my Tae Bo workout video every day once pageant week arrived, and was determined to at least look "presentable" on Wednesday during Swimsuit. No matter what, I was starting to feel comfortable in my own skin.

Despite our strict diets, the hostesses kept us well fed. We had healthy food and snacks set out on tables, and we ate between rehearsals. Unfortunately, there was *no white rice*...the island girl in me missed it! Actually, it was a good thing. Since I didn't eat bread, it was easy to stay away from carbs.

During the preliminary week Evening Gown competition in Atlantic City, all the contestants stood on stage on a spinning platform, facing a huge screen, which showed our edited-down video. Preliminary week was the first time we and the whole live audience saw it, but only the Top Ten would have theirs shown on final night in front of the world on the live telecast.

When I saw my up-close-and-personal video, I got so emotional because I was homesick and hadn't seen my family and friends for almost two weeks! It propelled me to do even better on the final night. I held back tears of joy and beamed as I competed that night. I was giving my all for my students.

As for Talent, well, that was my least stressful phase because I enjoyed it the most. I couldn't wait to dance hula on that huge stage in Boardwalk Hall.

After all the pageant preliminaries were over for all fifty-one contestants, we prepared our state costumes for the "Show Me Your Shoes Parade" and were excited to ride in our own convertibles down the Boardwalk before a throng of pageant fans. It was a great diversion from the intensity of competition.

Following two weeks of making friends with contestants who had become my close friends and confidantes, it was bittersweet to think we were only a day away from crowning the new Miss America—the speculation began among contestants who they thought would be in the Top Ten, the Top Five, and who they would pick as the winner. It became obvious that there were three types of contestants: the ones who wanted to win, the ones who didn't want to win, and the ones who were fine either way. I knew that I wanted to be Number One.

~ Mirror, Mirror ~

The day before I competed in Swimsuit, I looked in the mirror and all my flaws seemed magnified. In a vulnerable moment, I wished I were taller, lighter, thinner, and prettier. Although I had grown into a young woman, in a flash, I saw a glimpse of the little girl I used to see in the looking glass.

Even the scale, which displayed my diminishing weight, couldn't prove to me that I was fit and in the healthiest shape of my life. I think back now how sad it was that I could not fully accept and love the person I had become. As women, I suppose we all sometimes fall prey to the same trap.

I knew who I was on the inside, but it took some time to accept my uniqueness and embrace my looks. When I genuinely started to feel beautiful both on the inside and out, my confidence grew and others began to view me differently as well. The "act as if" principle was once again in full effect. Winning Miss Hawai'i made me realize that I could do anything. I was more self-assured because it gave me validation that I was indeed on the right path. I continued to pray to the Holy Spirit to lead me where God wanted and if it *wasn't* His Will, to make it as clear as possible.

The day after I was crowned Miss America 2001, I looked in the mirror, and for the first time I allowed myself to see me as others saw me. I had found the niche I was searching for within my family and it felt good to stand out. The entire process I had gone through to become Miss America over a span of six years was transformative. Yet the crown didn't change me. I changed the way I perceived myself and that realization was key.

Our mirrors remind us of who we currently are, where we've been and are an indication of where we are going. Success to me is defined as being able to see myself clearly in my mirror and honestly saying that I like what I see. If I truly have self-love and know my worth, I can mirror back that love of self to love for others and the world around me.

Preparing for my Swimsuit competition the next evening, I reminded myself to be conscious of who and what I was representing as I walked on stage during pageant week. I envisioned myself to be a woman full of confidence. My hope was to authentically reflect back to the world on the *outside,* who I truly was on the *inside.* Knowing that winning would mean overcoming insurmountable odds, I felt like nothing could stop me from doing my best. And slowly, the feelings of insecurity started to melt away.

~ Three Little Birds ~

On Wednesday morning, October 11, 2000, I woke up around five a.m. to read my daily inspiration from the angel book Tini had given me the day he kissed me at the airport when he left for college in 1994. The message of the day had an angel reminder about BIRDS. It said, "Birds have often been thought of as divine messengers, and they may have a message for you." The book continued, "Imagine that the birds are the eyes and ears of the angels. They will entertain you with their spirits and they may relay a message from the angels. Next time a bird touches your heart remember how loved you are in Heaven. You may want to get a bird feeder to attract your favorites to your window." I thought to myself, *I'll keep a close eye out for birds today.*

Feeling strong after my interview the day before, I honestly felt that I wouldn't have changed a thing. Now I had to gear up for the Swimsuit competition that evening.

Pattie and Dennis were there bright and early in my suite, ready to do my hair and makeup before rehearsals. As I sat in front of my hotel window, high above the Atlantic Ocean, on the thirty-second floor, I thought about the exciting and important day ahead. Pattie had her back to the window as she rubbed the liquid foundation onto my face. Dennis was busy with a bottle of spray and a hairnet, shaping my perfect chignon.

All of a sudden, I saw three white birds outside my window. I told Pattie and Dennis, "Guys, look outside the window. Hurry!" They stopped their work on me. It was still dark because the sun wasn't up yet, but it was clear that there were three white birds hovering outside our window flapping their wings and staring at the three of us inside. They didn't go anywhere. They just looked at us for a solid minute. We were watching them as intensely as they were watching us. Finally, the stare down finished, and they flew away.

The three of us were in awe at what we just witnessed together. Without missing a beat, Pattie smiled and said excitedly, "That's a good omen! Maybe it means you're gonna win tonight." I laughed and said, "Yeah right!" I thought, *Swimsuit is my weakest phase.* Still, of all the neighboring hotels and the countless hotel rooms in the building, it was remarkable that those three white birds stopped by to see us at that particular time, on the thirty-second floor.

Later that night, I was floored when they called "Miss Hawai'i" as the winner of the Preliminary Swimsuit Award! As I stood onstage receiving the unexpected honor and the one thousand dollar scholarship that came with along with it, I thought back to the dream I had earlier that summer about winning Swimsuit at Miss America. Tini told me not to psych myself out so I could stay focused, and I did. So to work extremely hard at overcoming my "weakest" category, and then not just overcoming it, but *winning* it, was incredible!

I made it on the front page of the Atlantic City Weekly "WHOOT!" Newspaper the following morning, and the buzz had begun. Mama seemed proud of me, but I could tell she was torn. She didn't like that a picture of her daughter in a two-piece swimsuit was plastered on the cover of the local papers for all to see. I understood her feelings but continued to stay focused.

Papa told me later that Mama took as many free magazines off the stands as she could and stuck them in her tote bag. All my relatives were laughing, but Mama didn't think it was funny! She was just being protective of me, and I *so* appreciate that now, especially as a mother.

States held up signs cheering for their state representative and added, "OR MISS HAWAI'I!" Among a sea of winners, I was noticed. After

95

winning Swimsuit, I felt I could go home happy. Anything else would be icing on the cake.

Perhaps the angel wisdom book Tini gave me was right and the white birds came to give me a message to get ready for the whirlwind ahead and to remain focused on God and the larger goal. I wondered, "Why *three* birds?" The first thing that came to mind was the Holy Trinity: three persons in one God.

Sometimes we can't see the big picture when involved in our daily routines. But the stakes are high when you are competing at a national level. For me, the gospel and my daily devotional readings gave me perspective. When I kept my priorities straight and put God's Will for me first in my mind, everything fell into place. Those who had doubts did not affect me; I knew that I had the Lord's support in my decision.

CHAPTER 8

AN ASIAN-AMERICAN EXPERIENCE

I believe there are two types of people: those who think *everything* is a miracle and those who think *nothing* is a miracle. I'm the former . . . I'm also proud to say I'm a former Miss Hawai'i *and* Miss America, albeit an *unlikely* one.

Thankfully the American perception of beauty is constantly changing and becoming more diverse. My win at the turn of the century was an obvious departure from the standards of traditional beauty. I wasn't a typical winner, so when the judges named *me* Miss America, it was a time in history that allowed Asians—especially Filipinos like myself—to celebrate the diversity in our country.

I didn't realize the extent of it then, but my win proved to be groundbreaking, especially in the Filipino community. In many ways, my own people saw it as a miracle because there were so many odds against me. Even *I* saw it as a miracle and was grateful for the opportunity to represent them on the international stage. As I traveled the country and visited my homeland, Filipinos, Asians of all backgrounds, teachers, students, and locals from Hawai'i expressed their pride and admiration for this breakthrough. It *meant* something to them, and that meant *everything* to me, to be seen as a symbol of hope and encouragement.

Just as when Bess Myserson became the first Jewish Miss America in 1945 and When Vanessa Williams won the title in 1983, my victory was also a significant milestone for the pageant and for my culture.

Collectively, all my Miss America sisters represent and are reflections of the changing face of America. I admire and respect each one of them and I honor the contributions they make to enhance our program each year. But what I realize now is: no other Miss America has walked in my shoes before—because I tried *this particular* pair on first. I had to learn to walk in them, and break them in, hoping that others would follow.

In 2014, another woman walked in my same shoes *and* got a new pair herself. Nina Davuluri, broke barriers of her own when she was crowned the country's first Indian-American Miss America, and the second woman of Asian descent to capture the title. I was thrilled when I watched her win!

But that thrill quickly turned into sadness when some of the hateful and racist comments started to appear on American social media. While many celebrated her victory, along with me, there were some ignorant, intolerant, and hurtful comments, some that questioned her nationality. Nina spoke her truth on the national media circuit so eloquently and with such grace to her detractors and I was impressed by her strength of character. She has continued to represent America well throughout her year of service and I couldn't be more proud of my sister.

As the Miss America pageant anticipates its 100th anniversary in 2021, there is much to celebrate. However, only fifty-two years before my win in 2000 and sixty-six years before Nina's win, the climate in America was *very* different. We can't see our progress unless we take a look back at how far we've come. And as we saw from those social media comments, we still have a long way to go.

Before shedding some light on the pageant's history, let's revisit the rules in the 1948 Miss America contract.

~ Breaking Ground ~

A few years ago I watched a film on PBS called *American Experience: Miss America*. After the show, I went online to read more about the film and found the 1948 contract for Miss America hopefuls back then. In it, eight rules were laid out for the contestants. Here's the gist of it:

One, you must live in the state you represent for at least six months prior to the contest.

Two, you must be single and never married.

Three, you must have completed or be in your final year of high school.

Four, you must be 18 to 28 years old.

Five, you must be of "good character," possessing "poise, personality, intelligence, charm and beauty of face and figure."

Six, you must possess talent, as displayed in a three-minute routine. (Your options were limited to "singing, dancing, playing a musical instrument, dramatic reading or . . . a three minute talk.")

I'll jump to number eight next, which was simple, permitting both amateurs and professionals.

And then there was the seventh rule: **"Contestant must be in good**

health and of the white race."

The words on the page jumped out at me, and I was appalled!

But this was life in post-World War II America.

Reading the words of Rule No. Seven, makes me feel disqualified, unequal, second class. It's jarring to see an unspoken prejudice spelled out so pointedly.

When we establish a rigid definition of beauty, we shun the alternatives. In 1948, a girl like me was the alternative. History shows us that it wasn't until 1970 that the Miss America Organization repealed its ban on non-white contestants. *Think of all the bright, beautiful women who had been turned away prior to that repeal!* Up until that moment, people of color seemed to be looking for acceptance.

I didn't immediately grasp the significance of my win, but it sunk in pretty quickly. The very first request for my autograph came at the beginning of my New York media tour, outside the set of *The Late Show with David Letterman*.

I arrived greeted by a cheering, wailing crowd. "Angela! You're our first Asian Miss America! We're so proud of you!" "I'm Thai!" "I'm Korean!" "We're Vietnamese!" they proclaimed. Up close, I was stunned to see tears streaming down their cheeks. They had been there, waiting to see me, since five-thirty in the morning! And they were there because they identified with me. In their eyes, my victory was *their* victory.

That incredible thought thrilled and sobered me. Suddenly, I was representing Asians across the country, from Chinese in Alaska to Koreans in Pennsylvania. I would later hear stories of bullied Filipino kids in Hawai'i refuting back at their tormentors, "Yeah, well, Miss America's Filipino!"

In Angela Saulino Osborne's book, *Miss America: The Dream Lives On*, it states that after so many years of being shut out by the pageant, two black women represented Miss America in 1983. Vanessa Williams was the winner, but when she resigned, her First Runner-up, Suzette Charles, reigned the last eight weeks of that year.

Osborne (1995) goes on to say that Yun Tau Zane (the first woman to represent Hawai'i at Miss America) was also the first Asian woman to vie for the crown in Atlantic City in 1948. Years later Virginia Cha, Miss Maryland 1989, would be the first Asian-American to be First Runner-up at the national competition.

Of her accomplishment, Cha commented, "Twenty or thirty years ago it wasn't possible to have women of all races and ethnic backgrounds in the Pageant, but now that we do, we shouldn't be surprised that the Pageant is in step with the rest of the world." Indeed, the pageant wasn't the only entity that had practiced segregation. Thankfully, by 1970, America was changing with the times. Ironically, that same year, my parents landed on U.S. soil.

The Asian-American comedian Margaret Cho told PBS in the Miss America documentary that she grew up watching the pageant as a little girl and told her dad she wanted to enter the pageant one day. He said, "No, oh no, you cannot do that, no." And she took it to mean that the beauty pageant was not open to all women. Cho says, "I mean, my father thought that this whole pageant was fascinating and we would pick out the winners, but I was not allowed to even entertain the fantasy of becoming one of these women. And I thought well maybe I'm just not pretty enough. Maybe I'm just not white."

I understood that feeling all too well. When I was a girl, popular American culture never presented a model of beauty that looked like me. I wanted to resemble the girls on TV, but most of them were white, blonde, or brunette, tall, and thin. My friends' Barbie dolls never looked anything like me, so unlike many young girls I never really had a connection with those toys when I was growing up.

In those days I didn't see so much as a brunette Barbie doll—that's how wide the chasm stood between the American ideal and the reflection in my mirror. *Now if Barbie were Filipina, then maybe I'd have a bunch of dolls!* With my slanted eyes, broad nose, brown skin, short frame and muscular thighs, it was hard to find any feature in common with Barbie, a Miss America or even a fictional character like Cinderella—except for the fact that she and I both dreamed of a better life and hoped to one day live out our fantasies of happiness with our very own Prince Charming.

The best I could do was to produce a twinkle in my eye, which seemed to emerge whenever I smiled. On a good day, I was cute, never gorgeous or even pretty . . . and there is a difference. Cute is the comical sidekick, the bubbly back-up singer. Pretty is center stage, in the spotlight.

We Asian-Americans, like every other non-white American, had to wait a long time to see ourselves elevated in the mainstream imagination. Mattel didn't introduce an Asian-American Barbie doll until 1990 when Kira, Barbie's friend, hit the scene. She was a safe, subtle step toward Asian culture, with hazel eyes and smoky eye shadow that made it hard to trace the exact shape of her lids.

Disney introduced us to Princess Jasmine in 1992, Pocahontas in 1995, and Esmeralda in 1996. Then its first Asian heroine in 1998, in the fierce and fearless Chinese Disney Princess, Mulan. Now those were girls I could get behind!

And then Miss America crowned its first Asian-American winner in 2000: me. What an amazing experience!

The pageant has been a mirror for what is going on in the world around us. Every year the winner becomes a representative for the country and has the unique position of encapsulating what was happening in that particular time and being a part of the snapshot of that era. I won at the turn of the century in October 2000, which very well indicated that we as a nation were getting less hung up on race and color.

It took a while for me to view my Filipino ethnicity as an asset, something to be embraced and celebrated. My parents were determined to see all ten of their children succeed and assimilate to American culture.

As an immigrant to Hawai'i, Mama, an English teacher from the Philippines, made it a point to correct our "Pidgin English," the vernacular language spoken by locals in Hawai'i. The six p.m. news and *Sesame Street* helped us learn proper English.

Mama ingrained in us that if we wanted to succeed in business and in life, we had to work twice as hard as our counterparts. It was part of the work ethic instilled in us at a young age. My parents wanted us to learn to speak our Filipino language, but after Ceci's teacher advised Ma and Pa to stop speaking to us in Tagalog, we only heard them converse with each other and not to us directly. That's why we understand a little, but are unfortunately, not fluent in Tagalog.

Slowly, I began to love my Filipino self. When I was eighteen, I went to Seattle. People commented on my Hawaiian accent. *What accent?* I thought, and raved about magical visits to my hometown. "The most beautiful girls are from Hawai'i," Washington locals told me.

Huh? This was something to chew on.

My friend, who was half Filipino and half Caucasian repeatedly complimented my dark skin. To her, it was a built-in, year-round tan, an exotic touch. "I'm jealous," she said. *Jealous of my tan?* That was an eye opener. I had developed an insecurity about my skin color.

Winning Miss Hawai'i in June 2000 was a major confidence booster. Looking back, I see it as a turning point that solidified my Filipino pride. I didn't look like the other Miss America contestants I would soon face, and I was glad. It was empowering to stand out.

Soon after I was crowned Miss Hawai'i, I received a call from Melissa Short, Miss Hawai'i 1996. "Don't wait until you get to Atlantic City to realize you could win it all," she told me.

There was a sense of urgency in her voice. She didn't want me to make the same mistake she had made. She hadn't recognized all the Miss America contestants were on the same playing field until the pageant had begun, and by then, it was too late. I needed to arrive with confidence, she said, with the knowledge that I had as good a chance as any, and maybe even more of a chance because of my exotic look. I took her advice to heart, visualizing myself as Miss America.

The judges aren't going to crown someone who doesn't believe she could or should be Miss America. They pick up on that quickly.

By the time I was interviewed for a Filipino newspaper as the brand new Miss Hawai'i, I was feeling confident. I had my head on straight and my heart open wide. That's a powerful combination.

"There's never been an Asian Miss America," the reporter said. "What makes you think you're going to win?"

"There's always room for a first," I answered. I wasn't trying to be cocky, I just really believed in myself. I recognized the possibility and spoke about it confidently.

Imagine, fifty-two years after the 1948 contract was written, someone like me would actually have the opportunity to make history as the first Asian woman, first teacher, and first Filipina to win Miss America with Hula as my talent!

Over the years the pageant has morphed into what it is today: the largest scholarship provider for young women in the world. I am humbled to be considered a role model for the young and old, and to be able to speak to audiences about causes that are dear to my heart that affects positive change.

According to former Atlantic City Chamber of Commerce President Frederick Hickman, "Miss America represents the highest ideals. She is a real combination of beauty, grace, and intelligence, artistic, and refined. She is a type which the American Girl might well emulate." *Wow, what an honor!*

A few years after I won the national title, one of the state contestants who competed with me told me she saw my name on a card, as she and her family were playing the twentieth anniversary edition of the board game *Trivial Pursuit.* The question: "What title was Angela Perez Baraquio the first Asian-American to hold?" The answer: "Miss America." We found it amusing because her team got the question and of course she knew the answer because we competed at Miss America together!

Today, social media is a great way to keep in touch with friends. My friend from high school messaged me on Facebook from New York telling me that my name was in a Double Jeopardy clue for the "They Came from Hawai'i" category. The clue: "In 2000, Miss Hawai'i Angela Perez Baraquio was crowned this, becoming the first Asian-American to win the title."

As folks in California and Hawai'i saw the same show, people started taking pictures of the screen with the clue texting me, posting it online, and sharing it with others. It was very cool to be recognized on national TV on a game show *fourteen years* after my win! It never occurred to me that my winning Miss America would actually make history.

I remember attending the ninetieth anniversary of the Miss America Pageant in Las Vegas, where about forty former winners returned. We posed for a photo together holding the crowns we each received during our year.

After our group photo, all the African-American Miss Americas got together for their own group picture. It was astonishing to see all the beautiful women of color, my sisters, who were in that snapshot. I marveled at the diverse and changing faces of Miss America. It was something to celebrate.

Being the only Asian-American in the room, it was obvious that my presence among these women was truly a privilege. I watched on the side and thought, *What a beautiful sisterhood we have. I hope that one day I can take a picture with "all the Asian-American winners."* I'm excited to now have a sister to add to that picture: Nina Davuluri, Miss America 2014! Now she and I can take photos together as representatives of the Asian-American population, and hopefully we will welcome even more diverse winners in the years to come.

In my eyes, all of it has been a miracle and a grace from God.

Miss America 2001

State Competion
Magazine
Official Photo, 2000

National Competion
Magazine
Official Photo, 2000

Crowned by Heather French,
Miss America 2000,
October 14, 2000

Talent Competition
October 14, 2000

Miss America 2001 Preliminary
Swimsuit Winner, October 2000

Ma and Pa on their Wedding Day, June 6, 1965

Courtesy of Dino Deschaine

Uncle Normand Deschaine, 1967

Courtesy of Remy Freer

Uncle Normand, Tita Emy, and Grandma Teresita at Disneyland, 1967

Ma and Pa with firstborn, Maria Cecilia (Ceci), Manila, 1966

Ma (pregnant with John) and Pa leaving Manila for America with Ceci, Jerome, and Lucy, 1970

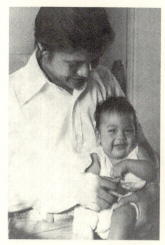
Papa and "Angie Bebe",
December 1976

Family photo in Papa's "ABLE" work truck, 1978
(Albert's the baby)

Me, Rose, Tess, and Berna, 1976

My Second Birthday Baraquio style, 1978

Performing in our outfits sewn by Grandma Teresita, 1979

Grandma Teresita and Baraquio
Family, 1979

Visiting Uncle Normand's grave at
Punchbowl Cemetery, 1979

Gloria, me and Albert at my
First Communion, 1984

1980

1985

1986

2002

2002

E4 Wednesday, May 5, 1993 The Honolulu Advertiser

STATE GIRLS BASKETBALL TOUR

Menehunes
hope to take
the next step
Top-seeded

● Saturday, May 8, 1993 □ C-5

| PREP BEAT

Kamehameha, Iolani
reach state title game

By Pat Bigold
Star-Bulletin

The pendulum has swung both ways in the dramatic Kamehameha vs. Iolani girls prep basketball series this year.

Tonight, one of these teams will get the final away. The Interscholastic League of Honolulu's Warriors and Raiders (16-4) will

na Takahara, her face also wet with tears.

Suddenly sensing its own doom, Kamehameha raced the ball downcourt and apparently lost it out of bounds with 5.5 seconds left.

But because officials could not determine which team the ball last touched, they ruled a jump ball and Kamehameha was awarded it on the alternating possession ar...

...llon, who led points, then ...der the bas-...gina Kaahili

Moanalua coach Dana Takahara and her Menehunes won't be satisfied with a second-place finish this time around.

Advertiser photo

OIA Back-to-Back Champions, 1993

Moanalua Girls' Basketball Team, 1993

Playing Beach Volleyball,
2003

Moanalua High School Varsity
Basketball Drills, 1994

High School Cross
Country Meet, 1994

Father Mac and me, my 8th Grade Graduation from
Holy Family, Class of 1990

High Tide by Diamond Head, 1997

My friend Preston, the altar boy-turned-priest, 1997

Playing Keyboard and Percussion for High Tide, 1998

Hosting Hit-TV from California, 1997

Attending Rachael and Emerisa's Holy Family
8th Grade Graduation, June 2000

St. Augustine Tongan Youth Choir, 2000

Holy Family Cheerleaders at
Sendoff, 2000

My VERY first pageant:
Second Runner-Up,
Miss Asian Universal 1994

Performing Hula as Miss Island
Paradise, 1995

First Miss Hawai'i
Preliminary Pageant, 1995

My BFF Maxinne Anselmo Pacheco,
Tino Montero, and me, 1996

Miss Hawai'i 1996
Contestants at Governor's
Mansion Appearance with
Brook Lee

Photo courtesy of Nate's Photography
Miss Hawai'i 2000

Moment of Truth,
Miss Hawai'i 2000 Announcement

Tini and Reign Serenade Miss
Hawai'i 2000 Contestants in
Evening Gown Competition

Miss America Top Five Finalists in Hawai'i
Homecoming Luau, 2000

My Miss America TCs Bonnie Sirgany and
Joann Silver, September 2001

Performing at Homecoming Luau, 2000

Miss America Organization Staff, October 2000

Homecoming Parade in Waikiki, 2000

Homecoming Parade in Waikiki, 2000

Former Miss Americas at Pageant Luncheon, Las Vegas 2011

Miss Hawai'i Committee in Caesar's Penthouse
Suite, October 14, 2000

Pattie and Dennis, my "Glam Team",
October 14, 2000

Lisa Hutchinson in front of my Miss America
Showcase in Atlantic City, September 2001

Miss Hawai'i Contingent before Preliminary
Interview, October 2000

Jennifer Hera and Billie Takaki
at APBEF "Sparkle" Event, October 2001

Miss Hawai'i Sisters at Airport Sendoff to
Atlantic City, September 2000

Todd Oshiro at Miss Hawai'i Airport Sendoff to
Atlantic City, September 2000

Meeting General Colin Powell at America's Promise
Headquarters, Washington, D.C. October 2000

Private meeting with First Lady Laura Bush
at the White House, April 4, 2000

First time meeting President Bush
at The Rose Garden for Children's
Miracle Network Event, April 4,
2000

Meeting Philippine President
Gloria Macapagal-Arroyo at
Malacanang Palace, Manila, April
2001

All Photos Courtesy of the Miss America Organization

State Dinner Honoring Philippine President and Attorney Arroyo
May 19, 2003

Tini, Mr. Arroyo, Mrs. Bush, President Macapagal-Arroyo, President Bush, and me, 2003

Meeting Vice President Dick Cheney, State Dinner, 2003

Tom Brokaw, me, Tini, State Dinner, 2003

Donald Rumsfeld, Brian Viloria, me, and Tini, State Dinner, 2003

My new husband and me dancing at the White House State Dinner to a Marine Band, 2003

Joan Lunden after the Pageant,
October 14, 2000

Romp in the Atlantic Ocean
Photo Shoot, 2000

On set at Good Morning
America after Diane Sawyer
Interview, 2000

Macy's Thanksgiving Day Parade, 2000

With Kevin Johnson from
Phoenix Suns in D.C., 2001

With Mary Lou Retton at
Children's Miracle Network
Celebration in Orlando, 2001

With Whoopi Goldberg, 2001

Mark McGwire of the St. Louis
Cardinals before I threw out
first pitch, 2001

Wheel of Fortune in Hawai'i, January 2001

Throwing out the First Pitch at St. Louis
Cardinals Game, 2001

Speaking to Holy Family Students in Honolulu
During Homecoming, 2000

Official Platform Launch at National Press
Club, Washington D.C., 2000

Lolo Alejo and me in Manila, Philippines,
April 2001

Singing National Anthem at Denver Nuggets NBA
Season Opener, 2001

University of Hawaiʻi Commencement
Speaker, 2001

Gilbert Gottfried, Mimi Kennedy, me and Vivica A. Fox,
2001 Hollywood Squares

In my own Hollywood Square, 2001

Tini's Altar Boy Days,
1993

"White Christmas"
Moanalua Winter Ball
December 20, 1993

Mine and Tini's FIRST DATE
at the Moanalua High Winter
Fantasy, December 20, 1993

At Tini's St. Louis High
School Sr. Prom, 1994

Albert, Tini and me before the
"Airport Kiss",
September 1994

Meeting Tini after winning Miss
Hawai'i 2000, June 9, 2000

Celebrating Swimsuit win
at Miss America with Tini,
Preliminary Week, October
2000

The Onstage Proposal at
Miss Hawai'i 2001,
June 15, 2001

Wedding Day,
June 15, 2002

Me and Tini entering limo as the
new Mr. and Mrs. Grey outside St.
Augustine Church in Waikiki, 2002

My Grey Family,
June 15, 2002

Baraquio Sisters before my wedding,
June 15, 2002

Rachael, Hana and Emerisa from Holy Family
at my wedding, June 15, 2002

Celebrating my Master's Degree paid in full by the
Miss America Organization, December, 2004

Tini and my beautiful children – my heart
December, 2013

The Baraquio Siblings
Just the Ten of Us

Tess, Berna, me, Gloria and Rose on Living Local Set,
2006

Albert and me in California,
June 2006

Baraquio Sisters,
1991

Baraquio Sisters (I'm 8 months pregnant with
Micah), October 2006

Baraquio Brothers Jerome, Albert and John,
1989

Baraquio Brothers John, Albert and Jerome,
November 2006

CHAPTER 9

BEAUTY AND BRAINS

The pageant business is undeniably huge. In the U.S. alone the commercial beauty pageant industry organizes local and regional events for all ages. Each year, more than twelve thousand young women enter the 1,200 regional Miss America franchise pageants, and thousands of other pageants from small towns to global, Internet-based contests.

As a child, I was never a big fan of pageants, in general. I never considered myself a pageant girl not only because I felt far removed from the winners who didn't look anything like me, but also because in my household each day was filled with church, school, and sports. There wasn't room for much else.

However, when I finally got involved in the Miss America Organization at eighteen, I learned that there were distinct differences between Miss USA and Miss America. *I* always thought they were one and the same! Traveling the country, I found that many people had the same misperception. The fact is the two entities are *completely separate*.

I believe the Miss America Organization is unique from other pageants, specifically because it provides women with scholarships to further their education so they can become professionals in their chosen field.

While I can only speak from my own experience about the Miss America Organization (MAO), in comparison to what I know about the Miss USA/Universe Organization, I will hopefully shed some light on the differences, in case you are thinking of becoming involved in one or both of these systems.

No doubt, both organizations empower women, but the Miss America system was my preference mostly because it fell into my lap at age eighteen!

To be honest, I never had the opportunity to compete in the Miss USA/Universe system, but my friends that *have* can attest to the fact that it has enhanced their lives and I am fully supportive of them.

Today Miss America remains a non-profit organization run by a national paid staff and more than 300,000 volunteers nationwide. There is no entrance fee. The Miss USA/Universe Organization is a for-profit organization and there is a fee to enter. The Miss Universe Organization is also currently owned by Donald Trump.

When Miss USA wins she shares an apartment in New York City with Miss Teen USA and Miss Universe throughout their year. Miss America titleholders live out of a suitcase and travel from one hotel to the next, always on a one-way ticket to another city.

Both Miss America and Miss USA winners end up paying a lot in taxes on monies earned during their year, so it's necessary to retain a professional tax preparer when the year is over.

An important thing for prospective contestants to consider is that Miss America's age range is seventeen to twenty-four and Miss USA's age limit is eighteen to twenty-six.

Local pageants in the MAO lead up to state competitions and culminate at Miss America. Meanwhile, local preliminaries in the Miss USA system lead up to the Miss USA Pageant. Then the winner from each participating nation goes on to represent her country at the international Miss Universe competition. Only Miss USA, *not* Miss America winners, compete at Miss Universe.

Miss USA gets valuable prizes from her sponsors and some winners get acting and modeling contracts, but the focus is not on scholarship winnings. A Miss USA titleholder's year includes travel, VIP and red carpet events, photo shoots, and media exposure. Many Miss USAs typically go on to have successful modeling or entertainment careers.

What's great about the MAO is that it's a scholarship-based program. The grants I earned through Miss America helped me pay for school without depending on my parents' financial assistance—and, I liked the scoring system.

I believe the Miss America system attracts a certain type of woman because of its scoring, which is reflective of the values of today's pageant. This was the breakdown when I was competing: in addition to the Formal Interview (30 percent), Evening Gown (15 percent), and Swimsuit (15 percent) competitions, there was also a Talent portion that was the most heavily weighted (40 percent).

With Swimsuit being a *part* of the score, but worth a minimal 15 percent, women competing for Miss America must focus *more* on the phases of competition that are worth more: Talent and Interview, if they want to win a preliminary, before advancing to their state title and then going on to Miss America. That was what attracted *me* to the program. The way the scores were weighted at the time I started competing back in 1995, I felt I had a chance to do well.

Miss USA/Universe contestants compete only in the phases of Interview, Swimsuit, and Evening Gown. Unlike Miss America, there is no platform requirement for Miss USA or Miss Universe, since there isn't any subsequent platform-based speaking tour to follow. It's true that many Miss America contestants go on to become doctors, lawyers, teachers, legislators, and professional speakers.

Immediately after she is crowned, Miss America embarks on a yearlong 20,000 mile a month nationwide speaking tour, and most winners have the opportunity to showcase the talent they performed in the competition throughout their travels, on a regular basis. For example, I danced hula at many of my appearances and sang at several events along the way. Talent, however, is not a requirement in the Miss USA pageant, although many women in the system possess great talent.

~ Pageant History ~

Miss America and Miss USA may *seem* similar in title, but they are two totally different and unrelated systems. However, one relation they *may* have is their shared history.

Miss America began in 1921 on the shores of Atlantic City as a Bathing Beauty Contest, which served as a way for businesses to attract and keep tourists in the city well beyond the Labor Day weekend.

However, both the Miss America pageant and our nation have made great strides since 1948. The four points on the Miss America crown symbolize the cornerstones of today's pageant: Style, Service, Scholarship, and Success. Over the years the pageant has evolved, placing more emphasis on the Formal Interview, a woman's talent, and its mission to provide significant scholarship awards to women, all of which are now hallmarks of the organization.

When Miss America historian Ric Ferentz was alive, he told me how Miss USA was born. I had no idea until then! He explained that Miss America 1951, Yolande Betbeze, was an opera singer who was reluctant to pose in a swimsuit but did so for the pageant competition. Yolande was brought up Catholic and educated in a convent school (just like my mother).

After she won, however, Yolande refused to pose in a swimsuit again as the new Miss America. That led the swimsuit pageant sponsor to withdraw their sponsorship that year and begin their own beauty pageant in 1952: Miss USA and Miss Universe, as a product promotion. The new pageants did not include the facets of talent or scholarship as did Miss

America. It was my first time learning of this, and I thought the history was fascinating.

As a Catholic school teacher, I didn't want to have to be seen wearing a swimsuit in public again either after I won, so I understood exactly how Yolande must have felt when she refused to appear in one again after winning Miss America. Although she had her reservations before the pageant, after her win she stood her ground. Following her decision, she was embraced by feminists. Personally, I was impressed by her courage to stand up for what she believed.

In my opinion, Yolande's actions were a positive turning point in the Miss America pageant's progress and they quite possibly resulted in the distinction between the two programs today. In the Miss America scoring breakdown, contestants are clearly recognized for their intellect, values, and leadership abilities in Interview. In Talent, women get to showcase their God-given gifts and prepare a performance. *That* excited me.

~ Why I Love Miss America ~

Some people wonder why girls compete over and over in the Miss America system. Well yes, it's first and foremost a beauty pageant, let's call it for what it is. From my perspective, Miss America is an "overall beauty" pageant, and that's why I was happy to be a part of it. It allows young women to strive to be their best self.

But it's not for everyone. In order to do well you need focus, determination to be your best, and thick-skin to be able to take a lot of criticism. You also have to be willing to change and grow because that's inevitable.

The reality is the more you compete in the MAO, the more scholarship money you can earn toward higher education. I don't see anything wrong with striving to be beautiful inside and out and paying for college in the process. I would definitely recommend participation in this scholarship program to young women of all backgrounds, who can benefit from an organization that gives away more than forty million dollars in scholarships each year.

I ended up winning more than fourteen thousand dollars during the first two years I competed. In the three years of my pageant involvement, I had earned more than one hundred thousand dollars in scholarship assistance. The money I earned helped me pay off my entire debt accrued from my bachelor's and master's degrees, paid off my California teaching credential in full, and helped me purchase a needed laptop computer and my required school books.

Thankfully, my parents and husband never had to worry about how they'd pay off my student loans or wonder how they would put me through my master's program. Because of the Miss America Organization, I graduated debt free! Critics of the pageant can say what they want, but let's be honest, if that's not empowering for a young woman who wants to advance her opportunities for the future, I don't know what is.

And while the results are not the same for every contestant, the possibilities are endless. You reap what you sow. What that means is your biggest prizes consist of scholarship tuition grants and cash prizes that can *only* go toward furthering your education at an accredited institution.

An important thing to note is that Miss America contestants typically do not win cash to do whatever they want with it. Winners can only use this money toward school and school-related expenses or they can't use it at all. If money goes unused within a certain time frame, it goes back "into the pot" to be used for future contestants. To me, these cash grants were a godsend.

Once, a fourth grade boy raised his hand at one of my school appearances during my year, after I had shared about the scholarship aspect of the program. He asked in all sincerity, "Miss America that's so cool you got to pay off all your college expenses. Do you know if there's a *Mr. America* Pageant?" Even the young boy recognized the power of this program.

If you're thinking of competing, all these differences are important things to keep in mind depending on your reasons for running and what direction your life path is leading you.

Some women compete in *both* Miss America and Miss USA, many times because the cutoff age is two years later for Miss USA. When this happens, I've noticed that contestants are already prepared for the rigor of competition at Miss USA/Universe and do very well in that system.

I have witnessed how each of the programs has been beneficial to young women. Neither one is better, they are just different. Because many of my friends have competed in both Miss America and Miss USA systems I don't agree when people peg one against the other. We are all sisters and we should support one another because each system has value. It's simply a matter of preference. Miss America was just a better fit for me.

Whether you're Miss America or Miss USA, one thing remains constant. Both programs offer phenomenal opportunities for the career advancement of women. Both pageant systems require that you have beauty and brains and both can also teach valuable life lessons to women who *don't* win. I know that firsthand. If you are thinking about competing in one of the systems, choose the program that is right for you and make sure you read the fine print in the contracts. Do your research and ask a lot of questions.

From my experience, I can say that nothing and no one can ever fully prepare you for the reality of the job of Miss America. This is why I am honored to be a part of this sisterhood. Only another former national titleholder can understand and empathize with what you have been through, and what challenges and opportunities lie ahead.

When you look at any of the past winners of Miss America and Miss USA, you'll find that none of them could have gotten that far without beauty *and* brains—and a winning mindset.

~ Thoughts on Swimsuit ~

When I first competed in pageants at eighteen, I was a bit conflicted with the Swimsuit portion embedded in the pageant scoring, because I didn't understand the purpose behind it. The biggest conflict I grappled with was that Mama taught us to be modest and I didn't want to walk around, in what's meant to be beachwear, on stage in high heels and makeup!

After getting involved in the Miss America system, my whole paradigm shifted when I, quite surprisingly, came to believe the Swimsuit competition truly improved my own personal ideas of overall health and wellness and led to a boost of confidence in any challenging situation.

The Swimsuit competition at Miss America is now known as the "Lifestyle and Fitness" category. Judges are asked to score a contestant based on overall first impression, beauty of face, and figure, confidence, and poise. When I was competing for Miss Hawai'i 2000 and Miss America 2001, I felt that it *was* beautiful to be healthy. And if Beauty equaled Health, then I wanted to be both.

For my first few pageants, I wore a one-piece. Based on my scores, Swimsuit *was* my weakest category. I knew I wasn't at my best fitness level, which is why I wore one-pieces. My mentors told me I had to really get fit and suggested wearing a two-piece to showcase my commitment to fitness. I had a lot of fear and anxiety come up around it: (1) Mama, (2) my students.

But I needed confirmation that it was ok to move ahead, even though I knew in my heart what I wanted and needed to do. After consulting with my parish priest, he told me basically what I felt all along: It's a game, so wear the uniform and when you win do something good with it. It was just the push I needed to make up my mind. I realized . . . I was up for the challenge, and why not feel beautiful? I never really felt beautiful growing up so I went for it.

After considering many issues, I ultimately decided to wear a two-piece bathing suit during the Swimsuit competition of the pageant. Let me tell you, it wasn't easy. But the results were astounding and I felt it was worth it because I reached many personal goals while looking and feeling really healthy in the process.

In the end, I was proud of how far I had come. From the moment I decided to run for Miss Hawai'i in 1999 to the moment I was crowned in October 2000, I had lost thirty pounds, which naturally increased my self-esteem! My arms, legs, and abs were the most toned they had ever been. And my face looked chiseled, not round. For the first time in my life, I *really did* feel pretty. *That was something to celebrate!*

Despite my inner conflict, I was proud of my accomplishment of winning the Preliminary Swimsuit Award at the national level because I worked hard for it. I wasn't parading anything but health, wellness, and fitness. At twenty-four, I was young and I had a fit body.

As I write this, I ask myself if I'd be comfortable walking around in a two-piece swimsuit in public at this moment. Right now, I wouldn't be, but when I was at my *best*, before four kids, and in the competition mindset, I wasn't afraid. That's what the program allowed me to do: sharpen my skills and abilities in every aspect of competition. I love a well-sculpted body because it's God's artwork, and being at my physical peak, I felt I showcased it in a pure way. If I were strictly competing in a bikini contest, that would be one thing—and *that's* hard enough in itself. But this was *not just* a bikini contest. It was a chance for the judges to see how a woman handles herself in an intrinsically difficult situation. If you want to become Miss America, you have to be well rounded, and physical fitness is an important aspect.

Swimsuit is only worth fifteen percent of your score, but it's still part of it. I believe it's there to show that you can handle yourself with grace under pressure and scrutiny—even when you are in a vulnerable situation, something Miss America has to do in real life every day after she wins. In many ways, the Swimsuit competition prepared me for the job of Miss America and for life after it.

At Miss America, because I was being judged on the categories of Interview, Evening Gown (with an onstage question), and Talent, the preparation to excel in ALL those categories forced me to be well-rounded. There was an importance placed on having a healthy balance in *all* things. And on top of all that, I wanted to be public servant with a message.

After my private judges' Interview on that Tuesday during Miss America preliminary week, I'm sure the judges liked me, but making an impression in Interview is one thing. To do that with minimal clothing in the Swimsuit competition, is quite another.

I didn't lose that same confidence onstage on the next day when they saw me compete on Wednesday night in Swimsuit. I had the same demeanor and confidence that I had in Interview. They could tell I was the same person, just in a different competition.

Even though I had a strict mom, was a practicing Catholic, an elementary educator at a private, Catholic school, I still thought pageantry was fun. It allowed me to integrate the different parts of me and express myself in different ways.

To me, Miss America was celebrating beauty and brains, health and fitness, and American ideals: let's face it, there are certain freedoms women have in America that women in other countries don't have. Public dress for one. There are still places in the world in which women are not allowed to wear anything less than long sleeves, long skirts, and head coverings. If you think about it, the Swimsuit competition is a representation of America: a free country.

From a teacher's perspective, there's a fine line between teacher and student, and I felt the kids respected me. They knew the real reasons behind me competing the third time: they were the ones who challenged and compelled me to run again, so it was exciting for them to follow my journey. I believed that my students and co-workers saw me as a role model as I left for Atlantic City.

I knew if I respected myself, and behaved in a professional manner at school as I readied myself for competition, they would respect my decision to run. My principal, pastor, and several teachers actually flew to Atlantic City to watch me win and came back the following year, after 9/11, to see me crown a new winner. That support spoke volumes and I was deeply grateful to know that I had the blessing of my school to compete.

When Joan Lunden and I were backstage together at *Late Night with David Letterman*, she asked if I was nervous before they introduced me on camera. I told her, "I'm good! If I can walk on stage in a swimsuit in front of millions of people, I can do *anything!*" Knowing I worked hard to earn the right to be there, I was proud and confident.

What I learned from the whole experience is that I was very critical and judgmental of pageants at first, but specifically, I couldn't understand why there was a Swimsuit competition in the pageant. I thought it could be eliminated. While this is true, there are reasons that it's kept in: for the telecast because it boosts ratings, and ratings equate to sponsorship dollars, which allow the show to stay on the air and pay the bills. And then, it's kept in for all the reasons I just mentioned. I understand all that and I believe that women can actually learn a lot about themselves and take away something positive from being a part of this experience.

When it comes to something I initially don't know much about, have no experience with, or just don't get, I try to be more understanding. Today, I am much more compassionate of people who have different thoughts, views, and opinions from me.

~ Thoughts on Beauty ~

I've made great leaps and bounds, since my first consultation with Pattie, my makeup artist. By now, I'm no stranger to cosmetic treatments and I've mastered applying false eyelashes and maneuvering curling irons. However, I do feel there is a time and place to sport a completely natural look with little or no makeup, which is always liberating and definitely low maintenance, especially when you're a mom on the go!

Like most women, I also enjoy jewelry and shoes, but I like to say that my favorite accessory is my smile. Mama used to tell us girls, "Your eyes are the windows to your soul," and "Your face is your fortune." I tend to smile with my eyes, and I find that it's a lot more fun than frowning. It also makes you more approachable to others. True beauty starts from within and when you are comfortable with yourself, that shines through, making you more beautiful on the outside.

Once, I was hired to do an appearance at the Horseshoe Casino in Indiana. Former football player for the Chicago Bears, Dick Butkus, was seated at our table and he sat beside a woman who never introduced herself. The host of the casino presented me to them as Miss America. I noticed the woman kept glaring at me and I felt a bit uncomfortable.

When she left the table, socialite Ivana Trump, who was also sitting at our table said to me, "That woman doesn't like you because of your plastic surgery."

"What plastic surgery?" I asked.

"Oh you didn't have anything done on yourself?"

"No," I replied.

Then Ivana said, "Ohhh, she saw you on a TV show the other day and you said you had a lot of plastic surgery done."

I laughed, "I think I know who she's talking about. Miss Brazil was on *PrimeTime* recently and admitted to having nineteen procedures done in one year. She thinks I'm Miss Brazil!"

I was thinking, *Ha! I guess I should be flattered—I was born this way!* At least we got to the bottom of that . . . Needless to say, that lady made my night, even though she wasn't very nice to me.

So my thoughts regarding plastic surgery, Botox, and such: while that isn't for me, I say, to each her own. I don't judge anyone who has work done on them. Personally, I think *I* would be too chicken to get plastic surgery done on myself. Also, I'm pretty simple. I'm an athlete and a local girl from Hawai'i. As much as possible, I try to be natural and make the best of what God gave me.

I *will* admit to several surgeries, though: I've had four cesarean sections, and thankfully I got healthy babies out of those events. So although recovery was difficult for a few weeks, it was worth getting cut open! However, to this day, I have never had any cosmetic surgery done.

Overall, I am a big proponent of doing what you feel is right for you when it comes to appearance and self-esteem. As long as you respect and value yourself, others will respond accordingly.

Many girls get their fashion and style tips from magazines. Pageant contestants look to former winners for ideas of how to win and how best to present themselves in an upcoming competition. There's nothing wrong with that, I did the same thing. But it's important to make sure you don't look like everyone else. It's easy to get caught up in what society's idea of beauty is.

Keep in mind that judges look for the "whole package." Beauty comes from within, so aim to be your Best Self vs. your Worst Self. We all know what those two individuals look like for us, so it starts with awareness of our internal shortcomings. I love actress Judy Garland's advice, "Always be a first rate version of yourself and not a second rate version of someone else."

In competition, amid pressure to conform, I'm proud to say I remained an original, celebrating my uniqueness and individuality, especially the third time around. While almost every other contestant sported big pageant hair, I chose to wear mine through each phase of competition in a classic chignon (a low bun). Simplicity was my trademark.

After winning Miss Hawai'i, many contestants started requesting and modeling what my hairdresser, Dennis, jokingly coined, "The Angie Baraquio Hairstyle." I can't stress enough how important it is in these contests to stay true to yourself and not try to emulate a past winner. You are an individual so don't be afraid to express yourself!

I remember how Father Mac reminded parishioners during daily Mass in his homilies that there has never been anyone exactly like us in the history of the world and there will never be anyone like us in the future. His words resonated and struck a chord in me, "You are beautiful and special. God loves you more than you love yourself." It's a lesson I teach my own children today.

Through the years, our bodies require more maintenance to stay healthy and in good shape. In terms of nutrition, I realize that I have to be more conscious of healthy habits for my kids and me, especially if I want to prevent any sicknesses that already run in my family. As far as fitness goes, realistically, I will never again work out the way I did when I was preparing for Miss America, but I try to get in at least thirty minutes of exercise or cardio a day and eat sensibly with a diet high in fruits and veggies.

As I approach forty, I sport a very different version of my body. Although I liked the way I looked when I was twenty-four, I also like who I am today—and so does my husband. It's all about being comfortable in your own skin and rocking what you've got, at *any* age!

If you become a titleholder at some point in life, remember that you define the crown, not the other way around. I know women who have competed in the past and become so attached to the outcome. If they don't win a pageant, they lose their self-worth. Then other women win and feel as if they are suddenly superior to others, once they earn a title. Don't take yourself or any pageant too seriously.

Every girl brings something special to a local, state, or national title, so your year is what you make of it. If you strive to continuously improve yourself you can't lose. No matter what, stay humble and remember to be kind to the people you see on the way up, because you will probably see the same people on the way down.

To stay on the healthy track, it's important to always find balance in life spiritually, physically, and mentally. Author and former editor of *Vogue*, Mignon McLaughlin once said, "It's wonderful to watch a pretty woman with character grow beautiful." When you work on the internal before the external your outside can't help but shine and attract others.

~ A Teacher with a Microphone ~

The first Miss Hawai'i, Yun Tau Zane, was the first Asian woman to vie for the crown in Atlantic City in 1948. Fifty-two years later, I became the first Asian-American woman and the second Miss Hawai'i to win the title in the pageant's history.

From an Asian perspective, I was completely honored to be the first one to accomplish this feat, but I didn't want my race or ethnicity to define my year of service. Instead, I wanted people to focus on my message of building character in our nation's youth and I aimed to focus on the important role educators have in schools and communities.

My friend and Miss America 1995, Heather Whitestone, once said that in the moments after you are crowned Miss America, it is the only time in your life that you will have that kind of national spotlight unless you run for office or win an Oscar. She cautioned future Miss Americas to use it wisely, and I felt I did.

Some critics said it seemed like I didn't care about being a pioneer for Filipinos. Quite possibly because in an interview right after I won, my words were taken out of context. I made a comment to a reporter when asked about my win. I said that the beauty of living in Hawai'i is that it is so multicultural and diverse. It's a melting pot of people from all over the world. I also said that in Hawai'i, we are colorblind.

Referring to my character education platform, I told the Associated Press reporter that it doesn't matter *what* you look like on the outside, what matters is *who* you are on the inside. That comment was edited down to a sound byte that made me seem like I was ashamed of my ethnicity, which was clearly not the case.

The upside, however, was that using the spotlight to say that people in Hawai'i saw *people* instead of *races*, allowed me to steer clear of any public backlash that might have taken place because of my ethnicity as the first

Asian to win.

Then another headline caused a stir in the islands. The headline, "Hawaiian Wins Miss America" upset some people in the Hawaiian community because they thought I was claiming to be Native Hawaiian, when I never gave that impression at all. Without my permission or knowledge, the media constantly referred to me as Hawaiian just as they would refer to anyone from California as a Californian. People just needed to be educated that Native Hawaiians are actually a *race*, and unless you have Hawaiian blood, you are not considered Hawaiian, even if you were born in Hawai'i. You are considered "local." To set the record straight, I am a Filipina-American, born and raised in Hawai'i. And I am very proud to be of Philippine ancestry.

I believe the Miss America program is a celebration of our country's diversity and all that it represents. It empowers women and allows them to reach for ideals. If it didn't, I wouldn't be a part of it.

During my year as Miss America I learned so much about the human experience and I was grateful to travel the country as its representative. While on my 2000-2001 speaking tour, I met professional teachers all over the nation, and it was an honor to champion the cause, "Character in the Classroom: Teaching Values, Valuing Teachers."

Educators deserved to be appreciated and recognized for their work. I acknowledged their passion for teaching, reminded them of why they became educators in the first place. A lot of teachers and administrators I addressed thanked me for my platform of promoting character education and valuing teachers—they felt undervalued, underpaid, and under-appreciated. I was their national voice and advocate for a year, and I was honored to speak on their behalf. My mission was to champion the children, the educators, and character education issues on Capitol Hill and beyond.

My specific focus that year was on implementing character education initiatives into existing school cultures and curriculum. I felt schools needed a *proactive* versus a *reactive* approach to discipline that would help improve student behavior. That personal passion stemmed from my knowledge and awareness of tragic incidents like the Columbine High School massacre in Littleton, Colorado, and other acts of violence in schools.

As I visited hundreds of schools across the country in more than forty states, I reminded teachers that building a positive school culture and climate, starting from its administrative leadership team, is key to academic success achievement. It was not one more thing to *add* to their plate. As teachers, this *is* our plate. Nobody becomes a teacher to become rich. Teaching is about making a difference every day, one student at time.

It's my strong belief that character education, encouragement of civic duty and community service should be a part of all schools' requirements, starting at the primary grade levels and continuing through post-secondary education. Students need to learn how to give back at a young age because if they serve others and volunteer as children, they'll continue to serve their society as adults, and that benefits everyone in the long run. My parents taught us the importance of service at a young age, when we started singing and playing music in our church choir and cleaning the church every weekend. Helping the nuns in their bookstore and feeding the homeless all taught us how good it felt to be of service to others.

Winning Miss America catapulted me into the spotlight overnight. While it may seem like all glitz and glamour, the truth is, Miss America is a public servant. She is a classy woman who truly cares about giving back to the community around her. It's what I *still* do as a teacher even today.

Being constantly in the public eye forced me to overcome stage fright and lingering insecurities. Praying calmed me and gave me clarity when I needed it most. Before every speech and every competition, I recited the Holy Spirit prayer: "Come Holy Spirit, fill the hearts of your faithful, and enkindle in them the fire of your love, send forth your spirit and you shall be created, and you shall renew the face of the earth." Prayer has always been my strength, a remedy for worry, a way to remain calm, which has never failed to produce a fountain of blessings in my life.

As the first teacher to win the title, a memorable moment for me was the day I launched my platform in Washington, D.C. at the National Press Club. My speech was recorded live on C-SPAN and heard across the country on National Public Radio (NPR). That was definitely a pivotal moment that signified in my career that I had arrived. I knew that the crown would be my microphone, given the platform of Miss America, which enabled me to speak loudly and clearly about what I strongly believe is right.

On the National Day of Prayer on May 3, 2001, I was the special guest speaker addressing the families of the Department of Defense at the Pentagon. Hours later, I testified before the Education Caucus on Capitol Hill in support of the H.R.1 Education Bill for national character education funding. The bill, sponsored by Representatives Wamp (TN) and Etheridge (NC), was in the process of getting passed, and eventually did. The federal government earmarked fifty million dollars for national character education initiatives, and I couldn't have been more thrilled!

Afterward, on that same day, I made my way to the White House to share the stage with President George W. Bush. I remember sitting in my hotel room later that night at the Capitol Hilton watching the movie, *The American President*. I had watched the movie many times in college, but to be in the federal district, as Miss America, speaking at the White House, on Capitol Hill and at the Pentagon, and meeting the commander-in-chief was a transcendent experience.

In Providence, Rhode Island, I was told that I was the first Miss America to testify at the National Governors' Association Conference. It was a humbling experience to take my character education platform to all the governors in each state. Later, I attended a gala at the Vanderbilt Mansion in Providence, where I met all the governors and even got to teach their families hula under the stars.

When I visited Iowa a few weeks later, Governor Vilsack told me he remembered how I taught him and the other attendees hula at the conference. What an ice breaker! The power of the Miss America crown is that it opens doors to opportunities for women. For a woman like me, with my upbringing and background, to have had the access I've had since winning is astounding.

I often speak of the crown as my microphone because I always had a voice—but with the crown, that voice was amplified for a much greater audience. From Washington, D.C., to hundreds of schools and legislatures across the country, I took my message of character everywhere I went.

~ All My Sisters ~

Coming from a family of seven girls and three boys, I have firsthand experience of the importance and benefits of women supporting and lifting one another up instead of tearing each other down. It's hard enough to compete against ourselves every day without having to size up to someone else. There is a serious danger in comparing ourselves to others. When we do that, we always fall short, and the results are unhealthy.

Good or bad, we reflect ourselves in each other. If we love ourselves, our capacity to love others is great. If we don't like ourselves and know deep down we are flawed, we pinpoint those flaws in others. We should be aware that what we fail to see clearly in ourselves, we easily see in others.

By guarding against quick judgment and finding the faults of our neighbor, we prevent our remaining fingers from consequently pointing back at us and recognizing the proverbial "planks" we have in our own eyes that prevent us from seeing clearly. When we cast out the darkness in our lives, we become the light.

Marianne Williamson, spiritual teacher and author, put it best in this statement that I love: "It is our light not our darkness that most frightens us. Our deepest fear is not that we are inadequate. Our deepest fear is that we are powerful beyond measure."

I used to think that I shouldn't share my accomplishments with the world. As girls we were taught by society to be quiet, subdued, and submissive. After I won, I felt shy about sharing my accomplishments so others wouldn't feel as if I were showing off or that they didn't measure up to what I had done. But Williamson thinks otherwise: "Your playing small does not serve the world. There's nothing enlightened about shrinking so that other people won't feel insecure around you. We were born to make manifest the glory of God that is within us. It's not just in some of us; it's in everyone. And as we let our own light shine, we unconsciously give other people permission to do the same. As we are liberated from our own fear, our presence automatically liberates others."

That said, I still use my discretion and try to know my audience. But I don't let anyone dim my light, because I know how dangerous it is to risk having that light in our lives diminish.

We have power as a sisterhood and we get stronger when we share it with others and lift each other up. As a sister, a mother, a friend and former Miss America, I feel it's my job to inspire and give hope to other women, and pave the way for others to come.

Whatever you see in me, is what's already inside you. At the end of the day, we all serve as mirrors for one another. Think about it: If you didn't already have it in you, you'd be unable to see it in me. So let's look for the beauty in others, by starting first with the beauty we see in ourselves.

While competing in pageants, I've met women that believe that other women are out to sabotage them, so they go out and do the same before they can get hurt. Yet they only end up hurting themselves in the long run. They believe that they can only have success at the expense of a fellow woman. That could not be further from the truth.

Once I ran with a contestant who asked my opinion on which picture she should use for an ad of hers in the pageant program book. I genuinely gave her an opinion that would make her portray her best self. She ended up using the other picture which wasn't very flattering. When I confronted her about it, she said, "I thought you were sabotaging me, so I did the opposite." My intentions were only good, but for some reason she assumed they were not.

I have respect for all women, whom I truly feel are innately beautiful creatures and the backbone of society. Women have a tremendous capacity to love, to multitask, to endure—in good times and in bad. I know because I come from a lineage of strong women in my family. Those like Grandma Teresita, Grandma "Lola" Severina (Binay), Mama, and my sisters are the sources of my strength.

Likewise, we have inherited our power from our feminine ancestors who came before us, tracing all the way back through generations of our family tree. The fortitude that I have within me is only a tribute to the countless sacrifices they made for me, some known, and some unknown.

Ladies, let's remember we share in the same sisterhood and there's great influence in solidarity, so we must stand together and continue to raise each other up. We are all beautiful and we are all worthy of love and respect.

CHAPTER 10

GLASS SLIPPER FITS

Becoming Miss America was one my greatest achievements, and the best gift I could have received as a young, single woman. I tried not to second-guess the judges' choice in choosing me, especially as the first Asian-American to wear the crown. But many times I asked, *Really, why me? So many other girls were more deserving.* Then I'd catch my negative train of thought and counter it with, *You deserved to win as much as anyone else. Embrace it and be grateful for the opportunity.*

Just weeks after being crowned, I sat in a hotel room flipping through channels when I came across the telecast of *Behind Closed Doors with Joan Lunden,* the A&E special that was filmed following my coronation, chronicling the first forty-eight hours of my reign. It was the first time a documentary like this had ever been done for any winner, so I was anxious to see what was captured and how they would portray those first two days. The moments after my win were a blur and I had forgotten all the details. Watching the two-hour special reminded me of everything I did. I watched in wonderment as if I were observing someone else. And then I heard something that stopped me in my tracks.

The Miss America Pageant CEO Robert Renneisen said in a clip, "It's very much like a real-life Cinderella story. Think about it for a minute. Her mom and dad emigrated to Hawai'i from the Philippines thirty years ago—and thirty years later, one of their ten children IS Miss America. If that's not the American dream, I don't know what is."

I never saw my life as a fairy tale. Through all the ups and downs, it seemed highly unlikely that my life could ever remotely resemble something so magical—after all, fairy tales are not reality. And I certainly never viewed my life in that manner, even if I loved all those Disney movies. After the bitter disappointment of the big state championship basketball game in 1993 and my multiple pageant losses in the past, I knew this truth. I had come so close to victories, only to see them slip through my hands.

Hearing an outsider's perspective verbalize my win like that reminded me of my mother's words spoken that day next to my entertainment center filled with Disney figurines, **"Angie, if you obey God and do His will, your life will be better than a fairy tale."** In that moment, I realized that Mama had been right—my faith in God and myself had helped me achieve my dream; my life *was better* than a fairy tale, because it *wasn't* a fantasy. It was my new reality.

Every day felt surreal. It was an adventurous time filled with excitement, and yet it didn't take long before I felt isolated on the road. I had two Traveling Companions (TCs), Bonnie Sirgany, and Joann Silver, who alternated each month, chaperoning me everywhere I went, but I was homesick and missed my family and Tini. The crown had its perks, but there were many responsibilities. The travel schedule was grueling, and I learned quickly how demanding the job of Miss America could be.

I had visualized myself winning, not knowing how it would actually play out in real life after the crowning moment. Before the confetti on stage could settle, I found myself being rushed off in a limo on its way to New York City. Everywhere we went we traveled first class, and I got paid well for speeches and appearances. It was a long way from the starting salary I received as a first year teacher, which was why I appreciated the opportunity so much.

It also reaffirmed my desire to proudly champion the work that educators do each day to serve parents, students, and communities. In comparison, this new job seemed much easier than teaching—at first. I would find out soon enough that being Miss America was *not easier* than teaching in a classroom. Both were challenging. They were just different types of work and now I had more influence. As Miss America 2001, I was still teaching, but my classroom just got bigger and *a bit* more glamorous!

It wasn't until I got on the road that I realized how challenging the day-to-day work really was. I had to be mindful that I was expected to be "on" at a moment's notice. I might be the only Miss America a person might ever meet, so I always tried to make a good impression. It didn't matter if I was sick, tired, or grumpy. I had to exude the Miss America ideal at ALL TIMES. There were days when I was just simply exhausted because I gave my all to make everyone feel special, but it was worth it. No one saw me plop on my bed at the end of long day. On those days I knew I had given my all, and it was a good feeling.

Sometimes I had five to twelve appearances scheduled in a single day! My activities included speechwriting, speaking at events, holding press conferences, meeting people for lunch or dinner, doing wardrobe fittings, giving interviews, signing autographs, participating in satellite media tours, taking pictures with children, answering fan mail, posing for magazine photo shoots, visiting with friends and family in the local area I was visiting, greeting sponsors, running through airports to catch connecting flights, and writing thank you notes. My days and nights were spent on airplanes, limousines, and in hotels.

As glamorous as it appeared, it was also a lot of work. And of course, I wished I could share this once-in-a lifetime experience with my loved ones in Hawai'i. Instead, I poured my emotions into my journal, spent quiet time alone, and savored personal conversations alone with God.

In between appearances, I would call Tini, Todd, Mama, and my friends back home just to hear their voices and touch base—regardless of the six hour time difference when I was on the east coast.

The Miss America staff would send my schedule to my TC a month in advance so that I wouldn't become overwhelmed with my duties. No longer was I just Coach Angie or Miss Baraquio, I had become an American ambassador.

~ Experiencing Celebrity from a Catholic Perspective ~

My Catholic faith has always been a gift, and as I mature, I become more aware of how my beliefs have shaped every aspect of my life. When I meet someone who has no faith—in any religion—I realize how lucky I am because mine has given me strength in the face of adversity and discernment in times of uncertainty.

Sure, I basked in moments when I enjoyed celebrity status, and while that was enjoyable, there were times I felt confined to a fishbowl, with all eyes on me. I realized that when people say they want to be rich and famous, what I think they *probably* mean is that they would like to be rich and influential. The famous part can sometimes be overrated!

It didn't take long for me to discover that external beauty may help win the crown, but something deeper would be necessary to sustain me during the twelve-month whirlwind I was about to face. I knew I needed to lean on God like never before. I was away from everything familiar, and it was up to me to sink or swim. Not being a traveler before this point, there was no time for self-doubt or fear anymore. I was Miss America. And with the title came responsibility and the opportunity to have a bigger classroom with greater influence.

Joan Lunden asked me in my interview how I planned to keep my head on straight. I told her my friends and family would make sure of it. Knowing my family, they would keep me in check, for better or for worse. When I was leaving Caesar's Palace as I headed for New York, someone yelled out as I climbed in my limo, "Don't let 'em change you, Angela!" To which I playfully responded, "Yeah, right. I'm gonna change them!"

My whirlwind tour of states was intended to start bright and early that Sunday morning. The A&E *Behind Closed Doors with Joan Lunden* special showed most of what I did in that time frame, but what the audience at home never saw was the part when my entourage and I quietly left the cameras for a few hours to attend Mass at a church down the street from our hotel.

Miss America officials had arranged for a limousine to pick me up from my hotel and whisk me away to New York, but there was one problem: I told pageant officials that I would meet all my scheduled obligations on time, but I couldn't leave right away for New York because I wanted to go to Mass. I assured them I'd still make it in time to meet Regis, Letterman, and Diane Sawyer at *Good Morning America.*

They were initially surprised, but my request was approved. My walk with God was important to me and just because I had won I didn't want to stop living out my Catholic faith. I just needed to have my new identity work around my core, the "big rock" in my life that was non-negotiable. I had to continue to stand up for what I believed, and I did it respectfully, and confidently.

When I got to the church, I wore my red business skirt suit, which I wore for my Interview competition. I greeted the priest celebrating Mass and took my seat in one of the center pews. Several security guards, my traveling companion, and top Miss America officials escorted me to the service, and we all reverently piled into the row one by one. Surprisingly, almost every one of us recited the prayers together. Later, I found out that the majority of them were Catholic, and they were happy to attend Mass with me. The readings that day were taken from the book of Wisdom. It started out, *I pleaded, and the spirit of wisdom came to me. I preferred her to scepter and throne, and deemed riches nothing in comparison with her.* When the Lord appeared to Solomon in a dream and offered to grant him anything he desired, he preferred wisdom to these things. In fact, he chose that God grant him wisdom and an understanding heart. Because of this humble request, many other blessings flowed.

The Scriptures were timely and appropriate for me that day, and the message was exactly what I needed to hear. The night before, I was given a rhinestone crown and a crystal Waterford scepter, crowned as America's sweetheart. And today, I sat before the Blessed Sacrament, asking God for his protection and grace to grant me courage, wisdom, and guidance for the year ahead.

I looked to my right and saw a statue of Our Blessed Mother Mary. She was wearing a crown on her head, and I lovingly sought her intercession to keep me safe and grounded during my year. After all, she is considered the Queen of Heaven and Earth. I was merely Miss America. It was a humbling moment to be in that church, and I felt blessed to spend some quiet time at Mass, before embarking on my inaugural journey to the Big Apple.

It was hard to be incognito. People recognized me as I walked in, but everyone was courteous and respectful throughout the service. After the recessional hymn, my entourage and I snuck out the side door on the left. On the way out, though, we were caught off guard when we heard the organ play the tune, "There She Is, Miss America" as we were leaving church. I thought to myself playfully, *What? Oh no, they didn't!* Thankfully, most of the congregation had exited by then. I'm sure it was intended to be a nice gesture but it took me by surprise.

That year, I would attend Mass every Sunday with Joann and Bonnie, my two Traveling Companions (TCs) regardless of the city we were in. I was grateful to have such a supportive staff at Miss America, who could have technically denied my request, based on the fact that my decision resulted in less paid appearances, which affected the organization's bottom line.

In any case, it prepared me spiritually for my intensive travels and most importantly, for what I was about to encounter at the tail end of my year. To be at my best, I knew I couldn't do it alone. I needed the help of God, Mother Mary, and all the angels and saints throughout my year, if I wanted to best utilize this opportunity to serve and inspire others.

Recently, a friend put on his Facebook wall an image that sums up my feelings the day after I won. It was a picture of a Spiderman action figure kneeling in front of a crucifix. The heading said, "Real Heroes know the Real Hero."

As humans, we are made in the image of God. I actually felt like a superhero after I was given such an enormous responsibility and gift. Heroes are courageous and powerful. While it felt good to win, it also felt good to stand up for what I believed. Sometimes being powerful means recognizing who our Source of power really is, humbling ourselves before Him, and allowing Him to use us as instruments.

~ Life on the Road ~

While competing at the local level, my wardrobe consisted of friends' borrowed prom dresses or "loaners" from former titleholders. I was on a shoestring budget as a college student, but once I won my local title, Miss Leeward, I was given a budget from the executive director to purchase a tailor-made swimsuit for my third time at the state pageant, was loaned two dresses for the Evening Gown and Talent competitions, and borrowed a business suit for my Personal Interview phase at the Miss Hawai'i competition.

After becoming Miss America, however, things changed drastically. I went on a wardrobe shopping spree in New York City, an experience that would make any girl go nuts, in the *best* way possible! Aside from my face makeup, my whole wardrobe got a makeover as well, and that was insanely fun!

One of the best perks of being Miss America was going on two separate shopping trips to designer studios like Kasper/Anne Klein, ABS, Donnybrook, XOXO, Laundry, Chetta B., Mary McFadden, Alberto Makali, Carmen Marc Valvo and other pageant sponsors. I know you're wondering if I got to keep the majority of the clothes and the answer is YES, I did. It was very *Devil Wears Prada*-ish visiting the studios in New York and picking out whatever I wanted with their stylists.

Every so often I'd get loaners for some photo shoots and appearances, but I had no problem, because pictures last forever and I didn't mind wearing outfits only once. Designers considered me a walking billboard for them anytime I wore their line, and that was fine with me!

I was stoked to get a cellular phone, laptop, and printer from the Miss America Organization for business and personal use during my year. On my new computer, I wrote and printed out all my speeches and kept in touch with loved ones via email.

My luggage was also part of the prize package, so I traveled with TUMI brand suitcases, which took a beating on all those airport carousels and car trunks. Traveling was enjoyable, (except the time I freaked out when I learned I was riding in a six-passenger private Cessna airplane), but I did miss home-cooked meals.

My home away from home was Atlantic City, NJ, so when I was there, I would repack for each travel leg. I packed mostly business suits for my speeches and appearances and for the occasional black tie event, a gown or two. Typically, I wore business skirt suits or pantsuits and my Miss America lapel crown pin—rarely ever the crown on my head, unless there was a special request for me to wear it in a parade or photo shoot.

My jam-packed itinerary for the following month would arrive via fax to our hotel thirty-days in advance, so I wouldn't become overwhelmed. My TCs and I were usually on the road together for at least four weeks at a time; we were literally crisscrossing the U.S. constantly.

For instance, I might have breakfast in New York, lunch in Chicago, dinner in Las Vegas, do an appearance in Vegas the next day, then fly to Washington, D.C.—all in a matter of three days.

And traveling was not always glamorous. My TCs and I would run frantically from one terminal to another to catch a connecting flight if the previous one was delayed (talk about the necessity of being in shape). If a flight was canceled we sometimes lost our luggage for a day and had to live off what was in our carry-ons until it was delivered to our rooms. Living out of suitcases proved challenging at times but we made the best out of it.

So let's talk logistics. I did my laundry by hand at hotels, at friends' homes, or when I went home to Hawai'i (which was six times that year). It was great to eat out at and order room service, but I missed the flavors of home. On the road, I had my cravings of li hing mui, mochi crunch, and spam musubi, all things readily available in Hawai'i. Every time I went home, I had to stock up for my travels.

I was always looking for Asian restaurants in the area so I could eat some white sticky rice, a staple in Hawai'i. In Boston, I was excited to see a Japanese breakfast on my hotel menu so I could have salmon, rice, miso soup, and pickled vegetables every morning while I was there. Once I was in Utica, New York, and a client left me a thoughtful welcome gift that had spam musubi and local snacks in a gift basket outside my door! And when I went home, I always visited Rainbow Drive Inn or Zippy's to get my local-style "plate lunch" fix!

As for hair and makeup, those consultations with Pattie and Dennis paid off, because I had to do my own hair and makeup on the road. Luckily, I kept my look simple and it was easy to maintain. I was expending a lot of energy, and at the end of a long day, I felt like I was running on vapor.

When I would come back from an appearance, I'd immediately plop on my bed and feel like my spirit completely left my body. The constant overlapping cases of jet lag caught up with me, and I learned to "sleep" standing up in elevators. The pace was frenetic! There were times I daydreamed of "vegging out," being back home, surrounded by family, and sleeping endlessly. But it was on to the next city, and I was constantly preparing for my next speech.

In the thick of Miss America activity, I was in Washington, D.C. for an appearance and at a youth event I met NBA all-star Kevin Johnson, formerly with the Phoenix Suns. He and I talked for a bit and when he sensed my lackluster attitude when we had some downtime out of the public eye, he told me, "I know it's not easy, but on days when you're tired, you have to remember it's only a year, then it's over. Enjoy the ride. So many girls would give anything to have your crown, so don't take it for granted. Remember that every day, and be grateful for this experience." He was right and I appreciated his candor and advice. He rejuvenated my spirit, and I was resolute about making the rest of my year the best.

~ Go the Distance ~

Halfway through my year, I was infused with a jolt of energy when I found out my request to visit the Philippines was granted. I had never been to the Philippine Islands before and this would be an exotic change from all the domestic travel I was doing. My parents had always wanted to take us to see the motherland, but with ten kids, that wasn't an easy, affordable thing to do, so this was a special treat. I mentioned several times to Bob, my CEO, that I would love to go as the current Miss America to visit my parents' homeland and possibly meet the Philippine President. I wasn't sure it was even a possibility, but I just thought I'd ask.

Even though Miss America usually travels within the U.S. during her year, the organization wanted to celebrate that I was the first Asian-American winner. I was ecstatic when I was told that plans were underway for my travel itinerary! They gave me some suggested reading materials to prepare for my trip before TC and I were scheduled to visit the Philippine Consulate in New York.

I would see my parents again and together we would fly to the Philippines to visit our homeland for the first time. When we arrived in Manila, the Filipino press greeted us. Among them were my uncle and cousin on my mom's side, (the Perez clan) who worked for *Manila Bulletin*. Walking through the airport, I thought, *Cool. Everyone looks like me!* I felt right at home among my people.

My father's family from Bocboc, Aguilar in Pangasinan drove six hours to meet us in Manila. It was quite an experience meeting my cousins for the first time. The similarities were striking. They all looked like my siblings and me, some spoke English, but they mostly spoke in their native tongue, Pangasinense. The cousins from Manila spoke Tagalog and English to me, while my cousins from the province spoke little English, but we all hugged and no words were needed.

My family from Pangasinan brought with them my only living grandparent at the time, Papa's father, Grandpa "Lolo" Alejo, who had just turned eighty. It was priceless to meet him for the first time and for him to be reunited with my dad after so many years. Papa is the oldest boy of his eight siblings, and he was the only child who left for America in 1970.

Now, here he was, thirty years later, returning with his daughter who had been crowned the first Asian and first Filipina-American in Miss America history. Both sides of my family were so proud and gave me such a warm welcome.

My aunties Tita Remy and Tita Curie called my dad "kuya," a term for the eldest boy, who is traditionally the most respected and most responsible in the family. The aunties told me, "Your Papa is a hero here." *Well, he was always one in my eyes.*

Papa and Grandpa held both my hands the whole day as we toured Intramuros together, playing tourist. It was a rare sight to have three generations of Baraquios in the same place. Basking in the moment, I felt spoiled to have my Dad and Lolo all to myself for a few short hours, and I loved every minute. When it was time to say goodbye, Lolo and I cried tears of joy and hugged. My grandpa later told my Tita Curie, "I may not have mansions, but I feel like I'm the richest man alive."

We had lunch on a pier, drank water out of coconuts with straws, and laughed a lot. We danced, we smiled, and my grandpa even took a picture wearing the crown. That day will go down as one of my favorite memories of all time.

Lolo Alejo's satisfaction was evident, and he couldn't stop smiling from ear to ear. Grandpa had turned eighty that year, which means he was born the year of the pageant's inception, 1921. It was the first and last time I would spend quality time with him because the next time I would see my beloved grandfather would be two years later, when I returned to the Philippines for his funeral.

The weather was humid, and the heat almost unbearable in April, but I stayed at the Manila Hotel and received unparalleled hospitality by everyone in the city, including the Manila Mayor Lito Atienza. The State Department helped us set up our itinerary for the week, and one of the highlights of that trip was being escorted by motorcade down the busy streets of Manila to Malacañang Palace in heavy traffic, to meet with the president in office, Gloria Macapagal-Arroyo.

Madame President welcomed our small Miss America entourage (my TC, pageant officials and me) and told us that she and the whole country, all eighty million Filipinos, were so excited when they saw a Filipina woman crowned Miss America. She explained how proud she was of me for this major accomplishment, and that everyone was on the edge of their seats watching and rooting for me.

I could hardly believe that in a matter of months, I had the opportunity to greet former Philippine President Estrada during his visit to Honolulu just weeks after I was crowned Miss Hawai'i 2000, and now I was in the palace with another president. This visit would mark the first of three occasions that I would meet President Macapagal-Arroyo. The second time we met, I welcomed her to Hawai'i and greeted her with a lei when she arrived at the Hilton Hawaiian Village. The third time would be together with our spouses at the White House, two years after I had crowned a new winner.

~ Miss America Highlights ~

Often I am asked to share the highlights of my year. What I mention below are just the main things that stand out to me, but the full memories are all in my head and in my journals. Understand that what I'm about to share is not to impress you but to impress upon you how beautiful your life can be if you put it in God's Hands and let Him lead. I am an *ordinary* person who has lived an *extraordinary* life, by the grace of God.

I must say that meeting two sitting presidents from two different

144

countries was more than I ever dared to put on my bucket list. I wanted to meet at least *one* U.S. President once in my life or at least take a tour of the White House. What a privilege to be able to do that and more! I remember seeing photos of former Miss Americas meeting presidents and thought, *if I ever won I would want to meet the current president at the White House.*

The influence I had as Miss America was far-reaching, and I used it to put our youth at the forefront of our nation's priorities. I realized that I had been able to do more in one year than some people might ever do in a lifetime. I felt incredibly fortunate to be able to live life to the fullest, and I offered all I did back to God.

I mentioned before that I had an audience with President Macapagal-Arroyo three times, but I also met President George W. Bush on three occasions: while he was our nation's current president with Marie Osmond and the kids of Children's Miracle Network at the White House Rose Garden; while sharing the dais at the White House for the National Day of Prayer; and at a White House State Dinner in May 2003.

In person, President George W. Bush seemed like he had a passion to do the right thing. He told me he really appreciated all the prayers said for him. He said that's what keeps him going, since he had one of the toughest jobs in the world. I admire President Bush for his faith, courage, focus on the family, and inner strength especially during the 9/11 tragedy.

Going to New York City for the first time and being interviewed on the most popular talk shows right after I was crowned was exhilarating.

Then being in the Macy's Thanksgiving Parade was a huge honor, since I watched the parade every year as a child. I rode on the Old Lahaina Luau float with the hula dancers from Mau'i. I didn't expect to be outdoors for so long in the forty-degree weather. Equipped with hand and feet warmers in my gloves and boots, I was still freezing!

Seeing local folks again, dancing hula and representing the Hawaiian culture was heartwarming. I had no reason to complain, because the dancers on the float had to throw off all their sweaters and scarves at the two-minute warning before they went live on the air. The dancers were pros, smiling and performing for a few minutes, acting as if they were under the hot Mau'i sun.

In the weeks after my crowning, I visited the headquarters of AOL, Southwest Airlines, *Redbook*, *Seventeen* magazine, and Clairol. I got to ring the opening bell at the Chicago Board of Trade and at the New York Stock Exchange.

Once, I was on the cover of USA Today, and while I was flying in first class, the man sitting next to me held up his newspaper and I had to do a double-take because I saw my face on the front page and had to nudge my Traveling Companion to tell her about it. It was so surreal, and to be quite honest, a little bit awkward because my neighbor was looking at me funny but neither of us said anything!

Visiting Gettysburg in Pennsylvania, walking the Freedom Trail in Boston and visiting the witch museum in Salem, Massachusetts really put me in touch with American history. Living in Hawai'i, and being so far removed geographically from the mainland U.S., I didn't have the opportunity to learn about our nation so intimately. These were unforgettable experiences for me.

Experiencing the different seasons in various states was thoroughly enjoyable. From the sun in Florida to the snow in Minnesota and North Dakota, I remember when temperatures would sometimes reach below forty-five degrees with the wind chill factor. *Brrrr!* That was way too cold for this island girl. I had to ask my driver to take me right up to the front door of my appearances or I'd turn into a popsicle.

Every chance I got, I took advantage of seeing the local landmarks. Whenever we'd drive through or fly over bordering states, I'd instinctively sing "America the Beautiful" in my head and get emotional because I was filled with such patriotism and love for my country. I sent home packages I had received from the road, filled with goodies and gift baskets from sponsors and fans. There was such abundance in my life and I wanted to share it with my family.

The outpouring of love I experienced was overwhelming. I would receive flower arrangements, bouquets of roses, and gifts at every stop. Sometimes I'd leave little gifts and treats I couldn't take along with me for the hotel workers and housekeepers to share in my abundance, and they were always very appreciative. I loved seeing their grateful faces. It felt so good to give back in small ways, whenever I could.

Attending star-studded events was always exciting! Although I'm not a huge football fan, it was mind-blowing to be able to fly to Tampa to attend Superbowl XXXV as a special guest. I shared a skybox with General Schwarzkopf and football greats, Don Shula and Joe Namath while watching the Ravens beat the Giants.

With a weeklong itinerary of festivities leading up to the Superbowl, one of the most notable events was "The Taste of the NFL." Wayne Kostroski was our gracious host. Top chefs from all over the country came together with the NFL teams and donated money raised from this fundraiser to local food banks. That week, I also volunteered with the Buccaneers to help out Habitat for Humanity, and co-emceed a Youth Town Center event with 49ers legend, Steve Young.

It was an honor to be invited as a celebrity model at the Gridiron Glamour Fashion Show hosted by Holly Robinson Peete and her husband Rodney. When I got there, I met other celebrity models including Daisy Fuentes, Ananda Lewis, Star Jones, Marion Jones, and Pattie LaBelle (yes, the "New Attitude" singer!)

In the spring, when cherry blossoms are blooming in Washington D.C., it's also time for the White House Correspondents' Dinner. As the April 28, 2001 dinner guest list began to circulate, I found myself on it, and was jazzed to be part of one of the most anticipated events on the Hill. In the International Ballroom at the Hilton, I enjoyed sharing a table with Pat Robertson from the 700 Club and Jaime Daremblum, the U.S. Ambassador to Costa Rica.

Saturday Night Live comedian, Darrell Hammond did impersonations of Bill Clinton and Al Gore, and it was hilarious—at least President George W. Bush thought so! Both he and Mr. Hammond delivered humorous remarks about political culture and current events. The media outlet and celebrity pairings at each table were amusing, and it made for a memorable night.

Growing up, I had been a huge fan of game shows, so I have to admit, having a celebrity square for a whole week on *Hollywood Squares* was pretty cool. Meeting host Tom Bergeron, and fellow guests Whoopi Goldberg, Brad Garrett, Gilbert Gottfried, Mimi Kennedy, Martin Mull, Seth Peterson, Alan Rachins, and Vivica A. Fox was simply *a-mazing!* I was floored when I arrived to my own star dressing room complete with my name and title on the door. A huge gift basket filled with cool "celebrity swag" welcomed me into my private space.

During one of my visits to Hawai'i in January 2001, I was asked to make an appearance on *Wheel of Fortune*, which was filming at the Hilton Hawaiian Village. I met Pat Sajak and Vanna White and got to dance hula with some audience members at the end of the show. The tiles even read "Welcome Miss America!"

Then in 2003, the *Pyramid* show called. I used to watch it when it was called the *$25,000 Pyramid*. Donny Osmond was hosting the show at the time, so it was great to see him again. The show was putting on a friendly competition between former Miss Americas and current Miss America contestants. I lived in Hawai'i so the producers flew me to L.A. for filming and I loved competing on one of my favorite game shows!

Sporting events are also filled with excitement. I was invited to throw the first pitch at a St. Louis Cardinal baseball game and I actually got it to the plate! An instant reply was shown on the Jumbotron, and afterward, I got to meet Mark McGwire. The team manager gave me a Cardinals baseball cap and Mark signed it before taking a picture with me.

Singing the national anthem at the NBA season opener game for the Denver Nuggets in front of 20,000 people was something I'll never forget. Another fun memory was competing with John Salley on *ESPN's 2-Minute Drill*.

When I was in Washington, D.C., as the Goodwill Ambassador for the

Children's Miracle Network, I was able to have a private fifteen-minute meeting with First Lady Laura Bush in the White House. Since she was a former schoolteacher and librarian, we had a lot in common because of our work with children. We talked about my platform on character education and she was both interested and supportive. Her demeanor was very classy. I even told her that she looked and acted like a Miss America. We took a picture of us holding the crown together.

That same trip, Marie Osmond took me out to dinner with her husband at their favorite Thai restaurant in D.C., and we had a lovely time. It was hard to believe I was having dinner with Marie Osmond! We used to watch her and her family perform on TV as kids and my brothers had crushes on her! A few weeks later, Marie and I met up again in Orlando at Walt Disney World for another Children's Miracle Network event where I did satellite media tours with Jeff Foxworthy. I also got to meet Mary Hart, Mary Lou Retton, Brian McKnight, John Schneider, and Larry King—all incredible moments!

At the Kennedy Center in D.C., Alma Powell, wife of General Colin Powell, presented me with the Best Friends Foundation Award onstage. We sat next to each other in the audience and before we went on I whispered to her that I had met her husband at the America's Promise Headquarters. She said, "I know! When he met you he came home and told me, 'I met Miss America!'" It was too cute.

General Powell sent me a personalized photo that said, "To Angela, with mutual admiration," and he sent me a little red wagon, the symbol for America's Promise, that had my name and title printed on it. The irony is that before I won Miss America, I told myself that I wanted to meet him if I won, and there I was in his office five days after being crowned. *My visualization worked!* However, he had to leave America's Promise soon after he had been appointed as the new Secretary of State by President Bush.

The Prudential Spirit of Community Awards was held at the National Museum of Natural History. I was one of the keynote speakers, and had to follow Secretary Madeleine Albright. *No pressure, right!?* She was a phenomenal speaker and was so inspiring that even *I* considered serving in high office after I heard her address. After I spoke, the crowd gave me a standing ovation. I was so humbled.

On July 4, 2001 I was in Washington, D.C. for the Independence Day Parade. The event organizers requested me to be the Grand Marshall, which I willingly accepted. I just remember getting on my float, and before the parade began, I passed by about a hundred Caucasian high school cheerleaders from California, who screamed in unison when I passed by, "Aloha, Miss America!" I marveled at how far I had come to get here, and how wonderful it was that the pageant had chosen a winner that reflected the diversity of our nation. It was a dichotomy that a Filipina woman wore the title of Miss America and the Caucasian cheerleaders were waving back at her. I could only think of my parents and grandparents, and all the sacrifices they made to bring our family to America. Then I thought about our military men and women who serve our country so we can be free. It was a moment when I felt so proud to be an American.

Savannah, Georgia was where I toured Gulfstream, a plant where about seventy private jets are assembled each year. Folks like John Travolta and Oprah Winfrey get their private jets from here and we even saw the President's private plane, Air Force One on property. Afterward, I went to Flight Safety Systems, where the pilots allowed me to fly a simulated jet. I practiced taking off and landing, something I never thought I'd be able to do. After all that flying, I toured downtown Savannah's historic district in a horse-drawn carriage, an educational and enlightening experience. I told myself, *I definitely want to come with Tini someday!*

Once, I had the opportunity to meet with twelve executives from the Wall Street Journal. A Texas reporter heard about this and told me during our interview, "Some people would do anything to land a meeting with *one* executive from there, and you sat with twelve of them?" Yes, I did. And when I left I hugged them all. *That's just "living local" no matter where you are!*

I took my aloha all over the country and was beaming with pride for my beautiful state. Many schools would ask me to dance hula after my speeches or teach the crowd a few moves. People were mesmerized by the cultural dance. Many students I met had never been to Hawai'i before, so having a luau theme at my speeches was big, and for some, it was the closest they'd ever get to the Aloha State. I loved sharing our Hawaiian culture with the world.

A memory I will always cherish is when I returned to Hawai'i for my Homecoming after winning. The other four finalists from Miss America were flown in to celebrate with me and we had the best time together! We rode around town in stretch limousine together watched a movie, ate at a sushi restaurant, and attended the UH football game together at Aloha Stadium. The half-time show was in honor of my win. The time, effort, and attention put into all my Homecoming festivities was unbelievable! I knew the Miss Hawai'i Committee, the governor, and the mayor played huge roles in executing all the activities and I was extremely grateful.

There was a parade held in my honor that started by Fort DeRussy and went down Kalakaua Avenue ending at Kapi'olani Park. My car was a gold jaguar convertible. I felt like a queen in my green and gold Mamo Howell-designed dress and dozen roses. I carried an umbrella with the design of the Philippine flag. Thousands of people came out to welcome me home and even tourists watched from their hotel windows throughout Waikiki. When I saw the Tongan church choir members, my students from Holy Family, and students of all the Hawai'i high schools displaying banners with positive character traits like Respect, Perseverance, Honesty, Integrity, and Citizenship, I was deeply moved. I looked at all the natural beauty and people that surrounded me and the famous phrase popped into my head, *Lucky We Live Hawai'i*. I felt truly blessed.

The Hilton Hawaiian Village hosted a ceremony when I officially crowned Billie Takaki as the new Miss Hawai'i 2000 on her birthday. She served beautifully as our ambassadress of Hawai'i for eight months, and I could not have been more proud of her.

Billie and I became instant friends from the moment we met. A few years earlier, in 1998, she introduced herself to me in college when we were both dancing during a class hula performance. She said she recognized me from TV as a contestant for Miss Hawai'i 1996. She was a huge fan of the pageant and dreamed of being Miss Hawai'i someday. What an incredible irony—who knew that two years later we would find ourselves vying for the same state title in June 2000 and then five months later we'd share the same stage again, while I crowned her the new Miss Hawai'i as the current Miss America?

There were so many other highlights in my year, but if I were to list them all, this book would never end. All my dreams were coming true and some were even exceeding my expectations. So the glass slipper fit, and that made me ecstatic! Each new day brought new and exciting adventures, and I grew accustomed to the continual high.

CHAPTER 11

THE CLOCK STRIKES TWELVE

Two months after winning, I returned home. Knowing the year would fly by quickly, I didn't waste any time. Plans were underway for my transition back to "normalcy." I met with a public relations company and commissioned their help in mapping out my future, specifically my five-year plan after passing on the title to a new winner.

We did a SWOT (Strengths, Weaknesses, Opportunities, and Threats) Analysis together. In it, I listed things I wanted to do which included getting married to Tini; earning my master's degree; having children; becoming a professional motivational speaker; starting a non-profit organization; traveling to new places; hosting my own TV show; becoming a presidential appointee or goodwill ambassador; and staying involved in education. My list was ambitious, but I had to dream big because I'd already proven that *anything* is possible!

However, sharing my timeline with others was not the best idea. I was told that my goals were too lofty and not focused enough—that it couldn't be done. But in five years, with committed focus, I checked all those items off my list and began setting new goals.

I was told "you *can't* do it all" but I believe you CAN do it all, just not all at once. I've learned that as long as I had a timeline with deadlines for each of my goals, I could start checking things off my list, one by one. By the time my year of service starting winding down, my five-year plan was about to go into effect. I had lots to do if I wanted to put all those goals in motion.

It was early September 2001, and I was in the process of leasing my very own condo in Downtown Honolulu and readying myself for my post-year transition. My sister Tess, who had helped me all along behind-the-scenes became my scheduling manager post-reign.

After being managed by the Miss America Organization's twenty-three paid staff members for an entire year, whittling my "staff" down to two: my sister Tess and me, was a huge adjustment. It was like college graduation all over again, having to endure the dizzying pace in the last days before commencement and anticipating the excitement of the pomp and circumstance. Then experiencing the reality that sets in the day after, was a wake-up call reminding me that I was in the real world and that I had better figure things out fast. I wasn't quite sure what would happen to me after I crowned my successor on September 22, 2001, but I was hopeful.

Being on my own was a rather frightening thought after all I'd experienced. Although I was twenty-five years old, I felt an *exhausted* forty! Still, I had matured and learned so much in one year, and I owed it all to the Miss America system.

All at once, the reality of my job as Miss America hit me: In a split second your life changes when you win, and in that second you crown your successor a year later, it changes again. I felt I had finally found my niche, but at the same time, the girl I had worked hard to become was in the past.

To the public I became "Miss America," and suddenly, I lost my name. People wanted to know all about the title, the job, but rarely ever called me by my name anymore. After years of being child number eight, and reminding Mama, "I'm Angie," I was named Miss America and had to remind people, "I'm *still* Angie!" I felt like I was on top of my game at twenty-four, and had worked so hard to define who I was, just to have people only refer to me as a title. I had heard people refer to formers as "ex-Miss Americas." I definitely wasn't ready for *that*.

Preparing to crown a new Miss America was like entering into unchartered territory. It seemed as though I had to figure out "life after the crown" on my own, even though I knew my sisterhood of Miss Americas would be there for me if necessary. The uncertainty was nerve-wracking, but I tried not to dwell on it.

My year was unforgettable, and I knew that with God, all things were possible. And yet this unsettling feeling in the pit of my stomach kept nagging at me, warning that, like all dreams, this one must come to an end.

Navigating through post-year issues would be tricky but it was part of my growing pains. With only two weeks away from the final night when the nation would crown a new Miss America, my friend Justin Yoshino decided to host a Mahalo (thank you) party for my friends, family, sponsors, and me on September 7, 2001, at the Hanohano Room, atop the Sheraton Waikiki. I agreed that it would be a perfect way to say goodbye to one chapter and usher me into the next. It gave me the chance to thank everyone who had been there for me and to celebrate what was to come. We sang, ate, hugged, laughed, and danced. I was surrounded by everyone I loved.

A few days before I left Hawai'i, I was commissioned by the CEO to call and congratulate each Miss America contestant and answer any of their questions. Several contestants felt compelled to thank me for being an inspiration to them specifically because, like me, they had athletic body types (natural looking muscular bodies, thick legs, not wafer-thin), and after seeing me win the Swimsuit Preliminary Award and overall title, they knew they had a fighting chance as well. It felt good to know that I was helping to change the perception of beauty in the pageant, and build self-esteem in other contestants.

My bags were packed and I knew that the next time I'd be back home would be as a former Miss America. The thought was humbling. I could hardly believe everything I had experienced in the past several months. I knew I would treasure this year forever, but I had mixed feelings about my future. *What would life be like after this major high in my personal timeline? What's next?*

Traveling with my sister Tess from Hawai'i, we planned to stay a few days with our eldest sister Ceci before heading to the east coast for pageant week. We settled into her house in Orange County, California on September 10, 2001, and spent a quiet evening together catching up on life. I was excited to see what would come of my meeting with TV executives in Los Angeles in just two days.

In the famous fairy tale, prior to the ball, Cinderella's fairy godmother warned her, "You'll only have until midnight and the spell will be broken. Everything will be as it was before." My "pixie dust" was running out and I didn't know what to expect after September 22, when I settled back into normal life.

Well, I'd find out soon enough that life would not resemble anything close to normal for *all* Americans—not for quite some time. That night would be the calm before the storm. We had no idea what tomorrow would bring.

~ The Fallout ~

In the early hours of September 11, 2001, a tragedy of global significance occurred. It was an infamous day that will be etched into our collective minds till the end of time. Nineteen terrorists hijacked four planes and carried out suicide attacks against U.S. targets. Two of the planes were flown into the World Trade Center in New York City. A third plane hit the Pentagon, just outside Washington, D.C, and a fourth crashed in a field in Pennsylvania. That unforgettable day, now referred to as 9/11, resulted in widespread death and destruction.

This single act defined George W. Bush's presidency and triggered major U.S. initiatives to combat terrorism. According to news reports, more than three thousand people were killed during the attacks in New York City and Washington, D.C, including more than four hundred police officers and firefighters. Life as we knew it changed in an instant.

I still remember vividly how my sister Tess shook me from my sleep around 6:45 a.m., California time. She told me to hurry up and come downstairs to watch the news. "Angie, get up! America's under attack!" I had no idea what she was talking about. I thought I was having a bad dream, when in fact, it turned out to be a real-life nightmare.

My sisters and I watched Katie Couric on the *Today Show* deliver the horrific news, blow by blow, from my sister Ceci's living room in shock, disbelief, and utter sadness. Half awake, I adjusted my eyes and tuned in intently. The now-famous images of President Bush, when he first heard the news of the hijacking, flashed worldwide across all the news stations.

Forgetting my jetlag, my tiredness switched to empathy for the innocent passengers on the planes who made frantic calls to their loved ones in their last moments and the hardworking people in the Twin Towers and surrounding buildings, who woke up that morning thinking they were going to work as they would on any other day.

But this would go down in American history as a day like no other. It was as if we were watching a movie about the end of the world, but the terrifying scenes weren't contrived. Tears streamed down our faces as we watched the heart-wrenching drama unfold. The North Tower had a gaping hole near the eightieth floor of its 110-story structure, created by the burning plane, which protruded out of the side of the skyscraper. Hundreds were killed by its impact, while others were stuck on higher floors. Hundreds of people rushed in panic and terror to escape the burning building.

Like the rest of the country, I thought the initial plane crash was a freak accident and that we had seen the worst of it, but I was wrong. According to the news, eighteen minutes after the first plane crashed into the North Tower, a second airliner came out of nowhere and sliced into South Tower near the sixtieth floor. The explosion caused a shower of burning debris over surrounding buildings and the streets below. People were screaming and running for their lives on the ground. Then breaking news informed us that the Pentagon had been hit by another plane that caused structural damage to the building. By then, it was clear that America was under attack. I thought, *I was just at the Pentagon.*

Less than fifteen minutes after the Pentagon was struck by another airliner, the South Tower of the World Trade Center collapsed like a deck of cards in a massive cloud of smoke and dust. The tower's steel structure could not withstand the tremendous heat generated by the burning jet fuel. Another fifteen minutes later, the second Trade Center tower collapsed with sinister precision. Everything was happening so fast.

Meanwhile, a fourth plane bound for California, leaving Newark, New Jersey was hijacked forty minutes after takeoff. Because the flight was delayed, passengers onboard knew about the other hijackings taking place in New York and in D.C. Passengers and flight attendants heroically planned an insurrection in the cabin and fought the hijackers. They were suspected to have attacked the cockpit with a fire extinguisher. The plane crashed in a rural field in Pennsylvania and everyone onboard was killed.

The intended target was unknown, but theories include the White House, the U.S. Capitol, the Camp David presidential retreat in Maryland, or one of several nuclear power plants along the eastern seaboard. My mind flashed to the amount of miles I had traveled throughout the year, and how often I had flown in and out of those same airports on those airlines. *It could have been me on any one of those planes.* I felt survivor's guilt for those who lost their lives on the hijacked planes, and remembered how I had prayed for protection during my year that day at Mass, the morning after I was crowned.

Back on the TV set, the devastating effects were incomprehensible. Live shots of people jumping out of buildings, shrieking, and running frantically through the streets covered in dust and debris, with thousands of pieces of paper flying to the ground had everyone glued to their TVs. What I witnessed on television that morning were horrific scenes that I had never before witnessed, and they had made an indelible mark on my memory.

It's hard to explain how I felt at the time, being in my position as Miss America. As an ambassador for our country, who was about to pass on the crown only two weeks later, I felt helpless and my heart ached for the victims who would never see their families again—for all the survivors that were left behind. I was offended, confused, and angry. I felt personally attacked. I didn't know how to make sense of what was happening. The tragic events perplexed me to imagine what must have been going through people's minds in their last moments. Even if I wasn't personally in the Trade Center or near any of those planes, I felt directly impacted emotionally, spiritually, and mentally.

I sat dumbfounded in my pajamas, eyes swollen, following the headlines up to the minute trying to keep up with the breaking news. Wallowing in misery, the local newsfeed broke through my wistfulness.

The anchor teased, "Coming up, Miss America visits local high schools." My sisters and I looked at each other in bewilderment. When the local news returned, it was an obvious mix-up because they showed clips of a young Caucasian woman with a huge crown speaking to high school kids. The graphic below her echoed what the anchor said before.

They kept referring to the woman as Miss America and here I was, the current Miss America in my pajamas at my sister's home. I literally spun around to see if there were cameras outside telling me I was getting "punked." Was I on some kind of *Candid Camera* show? I secretly hoped this was the case, that all of it was all really a horrible joke, which would include all I had seen on the news. *So was I in an alternate universe?* No, the news station just didn't do a good job of fact checking. I still don't know who the girl was. In any case, the day continued on, muddled with confusion and conflicting realities.

Just days before, I was in paradise, enjoying life with my family and friends in Waikiki, celebrating my year as Miss America, and now my country, the nation I represented as the "face" of America, was under attack. It was a frightening and disheartening time.

Many people believe there is good in the world, but for every yin, there's a yang, and pure evil exists as well. That's why I believe it's important to shield myself spiritually and continually ask God for His protection and grace in all circumstances, especially at the hour of death, whenever that time may come.

~ Divided We Fall, United We Stand ~

On September 11, 2001 at 9 p.m. Eastern Standard Time, America watched and waited for word from the White House. President George W. Bush delivered a televised address from the Oval Office. He declared, "Terrorist attacks can shake the foundations of our biggest buildings, but they cannot touch the foundation of America. These acts shatter steel, but they cannot dent the steel of American resolve."

The CEO of Miss America called me earlier in the day, as we were glued to the television. He asked me how I was doing and said I needed to get to Atlantic City as soon as possible. The contestants were given the option to cast votes to decide if the show would go on, be postponed, or put off indefinitely, given the circumstances. The contestants voted for the show to go on and the pageant stood behind it. Initially, I was against it, with all that was happening, but later had a change of heart when I realized that the contestants were determined to prove they would not be intimidated by this heinous act. Their courage was admirable.

Certainly, it was a challenge to be Miss America at such a precarious time in our nation's history. I felt a heavy burden on my shoulders, with the next group of pageant contenders looking to me for leadership, but my load was nothing compared to thousands of families who lost loved ones that day and would have to find a way to move on with a new void in their lives.

Heroism was rampant in every news story. Acts of humanity and selflessness by firefighters, medical workers, police officers, and civilians risking their lives to help their fellow man was beyond inspiring. God gives each of us the crosses he knows we can bear and what determines our destiny is how we embrace those crosses. Each person in the line of fire rose to the occasion, and it was my responsibility to do the same.

My flight bound for Philadelphia was supposed to leave on September 13, but planes were grounded for three days. I didn't leave Los Angeles until September 14. The entire flight was deafeningly silent. Passengers didn't say a word. To no one's surprise, everyone was on edge, including the flight attendants. I just closed my eyes and said my prayers. The moment we landed, a collective gasp of relief was felt as the entire cabin instinctively broke into an applause at our safe landing.

I couldn't help but think about the new Miss America I would crown in nine days. I was no longer sad about passing on the title. Now I was concerned for her safety and well-being, once she stepped into this position—a job that was already tough, even before 9/11. I was on a plane several times a day during my year. I wondered how things would change for her as she traveled the country.

A few months prior, I met a man named Jay Magazine at a trade show in New Jersey. He gave me his card and introduced himself as the manager of the restaurant located on the top floor of the World Trade Center. He sent me a note and some memorabilia from his restaurant to keep as a souvenir. Then he offered an open invitation for me to visit him anytime I was in town or if I wanted to have dinner there with friends.

When I visited New York City a few weeks prior to September 11, I almost went to visit Jay at the World Trade Center, but another event came up. I never got to see him again. When the first newspaper reports were released of the initial casualties confirmed at Ground Zero, I was crushed when my finger scanned across his name. I said a prayer for his soul and thought about the loved ones he and the other victims left behind.

I arrived in Philadelphia a week before the pageant, but by then, all the contestants had been shuttled to Atlantic City. My driver took me to the Sheraton and as we drove there, huge American flags were displayed on every street corner, on countless front lawns, and draped across hotels in bright lights, beaming with American pride. Brought to tears by the outpouring of love and display of patriotism for a nation by its people, I whispered to myself, "God bless America."

The Miss America pageant was the only national telecast to air as scheduled that year, on September 22. Even the Oscars postponed their telecast, because of the tragic state of our country . . . but our show went on. I remember seeing the announcement on *Entertainment Tonight*. Watching a clip of me winning from my hotel room was surreal. It seemed almost inappropriate for me to remember a celebratory moment like that at such a contrastingly mournful time. In comparison, my win seemed almost insignificant.

Upon arrival to New Jersey, I had a slew of scheduled appearances and events leading up to the final night, including interviews, satellite media tours, the parent breakfast, emcee duties, and hula performances during each night of preliminaries.

The fathers of the contestants escorted their daughters onstage during Evening Gown that year, so Papa was able to join me onstage as well during the three preliminary nights during pageant week. I was so happy to see my parents and Hawai'i supporters there, since many people canceled their travel plans after 9/11.

It was a fast-paced week and I had to prepare once again physically, spiritually, and mentally to have the stamina to get through the week. The initial plan for the final night's telecast was to have the contestants and me frolic near the Atlantic Ocean, playing on the beach in homage to my Hawai'i roots. Then we were all supposed to bring back the classic glamour of the pageant and enter Boardwalk Hall in white ball gowns, reminiscent of the 1950s.

At the eleventh hour, though, plans had changed. Producers decided to scrap the entire script, and instead, decided to pay special tribute to the heroes and victims of September 11 and hold a telethon during the telecast to help with the cause.

The rehearsals in the Hall were in complete contrast to the year before when I had pyro and confetti during my runway walk as the new Miss America. This year, the stage was strewn with security guards and bomb sniffing dogs.

I had heard that one of the women in the Miss America Organization had a relative who was a pilot onboard one of the hijacked aircrafts. Many other hostesses shared stories of how they had friends or relatives who were called to help in New York and many lost their lives.

The catastrophe was too close to home for me. If I were in Hawai'i, I might have felt far removed from it all, but here the casualties had actual names and faces attached to them. There were too many stories, including a former Miss America and close friend who lost her son in the World Trade Center. For her and countless others, it's something they may never get over. My heart aches every time I think of that kind of loss.

I was a co-host with Tony Danza that year. In the middle of the show, I was assigned backstage with the contestants in the Jury Room, and it was a classic moment when Tony said, "Yo, Angela!" and I replied, "Yo, Tony!" in *Who's the Boss* fashion. The pageant was actually praised for being a welcome diversion for the American public at such a traumatic time. Our nation came together as one, as we helped to pay tribute to those who had lost their lives on that infamous day. From great tragedy came sincere compassion, patriotism and a genuine love of neighbor. In the end, the pageant was the only live telecast to go on, and it ultimately helped raise the country's morale, giving the nation something positive to get behind.

That night, I crowned a new winner, Miss Oregon, Katie Harman, and welcomed a beautiful new sister into the sorority. Katie, a twenty-one-year old classic vocalist, sang a Puccini aria, "O Mio Babbino Caro," and was ecstatic to win. But she was walking into something no other winner had to withstand. Without having to say a word, we both knew it was the end of an era in our country.

As my role as the current Miss America came to an end, my life changed in many ways, but being in that particular position during that historical moment, I knew *no* American would ever be the same.

Katie used the Miss America spotlight to serve those touched by breast cancer. As a clear-headed and extremely courageous representative for America, Katie started out her year visiting the wreckage at the Pentagon and Ground Zero.

During her year, she would see a side of our nation that was both heart-wrenching and heartwarming, and would have firsthand experience helping our nation heal. I knew in my heart, Katie was specifically chosen to be the winner for such a time as this, from September 2001 to 2002. Just as I had been the one to serve as America's ambassador the year before, God had chosen *her* for this time in our nation's recovery.

The live show ended around 10 p.m. I walked backstage, kicked off my heels, put on my slippers and exhaled, "I'm free . . . " I felt like I had just graduated and earned my stripes. It was a bittersweet moment.

Aside from my concerns for Katie, I was happy for her victory and prayed that she'd have the courage and strength to endure her year. I knew too much as a former. I just wanted her to enjoy her moment, even though I knew she'd be calling me when her year was over—and I would be there for her. For now, my year was completed and hers was just beginning.

Tini, my fiancé by then, met me afterward, and we tried to create a diversion for ourselves from the craziness surrounding us by singing karaoke next door at Tun Tavern with some friends. At the stroke of midnight, the spell was broken.

Sitting quietly that night in my hotel room, I tried to begin processing things when I got a phone call from some former Miss Americas, who were celebrating with Katie. They told me to come to the after party, but I was physically, mentally and spiritually spent. I wished her all the best, but I didn't want to be a downer. I wondered again, with national security changing overnight, how the twenty-thousand-mile-a-month travel schedule would play out for her in the year ahead. Katie turned out to be an extraordinary Miss America, courageously and compassionately serving in the wake of 9/11.

The next morning, a limo picked Tini and me up and drove us to the airport. We said goodbye to Atlantic City and flew back to Hawai'i to finally begin a new life chapter together. I believe everyone should always have something to look forward to, in order to keep hope alive.

Despite the long road ahead, I *was* hopeful about my future and eager to spend the rest of my life with the man of my "real" dreams. However, the thought kept lingering, *What a dreadful ending to such a magnificent year.* I remember thinking to myself, *With all the traveling I have done this year, why was I spared? Lord, help me find my purpose while I'm still here on earth.* We were a nation on high alert and the war on terrorism had just begun.

CHAPTER 12

THE AFTERMATH

Being Miss America during 9/11 filled me with confusion and cynicism. For a good length of time, I was jaded by what I had seen during my year, especially at the tail end. I used to believe I was born with the optimism gene and suddenly, I saw the dark side of humanity.

I had developed a bit of paranoia after the tragedy, and didn't feel safe anywhere. The calamity was stuck in my head and it was a scary place to be. Every so often, my mind would flash to the live news scenes I witnessed on September 11, 2001. Even three years later, I felt "survivor's guilt" for remaining alive while others died on that fateful day. Severe post-trauma reactions to September 11 began to resurface. There were times I felt intense fear, horror, or powerlessness, but I tried to shake those feelings whenever I sensed their onset.

As I prepared for my post-year transition, many of my solidified plans crumbled in the post 9/11 recession, and left me feeling directionless. I struggled to develop a true vision of the world and to find peace within myself. It was a long drop down from the heights I was soaring on the year before. I used to be filled with so much hope and love in my heart and now I was overcome with fear, anxiety, anger at injustice, and with that came a partial loss of faith.

That fateful day on September 11 redefined the course of my life including opportunities that were planned in detail, which were suddenly taken away. I had several appointments scheduled for September 12 with some TV executives in Los Angeles, but after the attacks, all meetings were canceled indefinitely. I felt I needed to move back home instead, to find stability close to family, marry Tini, and redefine what mattered most to me. Going home to Hawai'i felt like the right thing to do.

Even without 9/11, I would have had to face reality, but with this new era we were entering as a nation I felt like I had literally just experienced the highest of highs and the lowest of lows. The most difficult part was having to deal with all those raw emotions in the public eye.

This homecoming as a former Miss America was vastly different from my Homecoming as the reigning Miss America. Close friends said I changed . . . and I did, on so many levels. People I loved didn't know how to act around me anymore, and vice versa. Some expected me to act like a queen, others like the girl next door. I could only be me, whoever I was at the moment.

It was awkward at first, as if I were learning how to walk again. It reminded me of the times I'd see Tini again during our long distance courtship, after being apart for months. I likened the readjustment phase to my siblings' experiences of going away to college for a year and returning home. They had told me that people back home remained the same, but they were forever changed because of their individual experiences while away.

There were many post-year requests that came into the Miss America office and were forwarded to my new manager (and sister) Tess to handle. I had a very busy travel schedule immediately after my reign, but the volume of appearances and amount of travel was far less than what I had been accustomed to. It was fine with me because I wasn't eager to jump on another plane if I didn't have to.

I yearned to be home with my family, wanted to plan my wedding, earn my master's degree, and start a family with Tini. Honestly, I was burned out and would have slept for a year if I could. Instead, I did something I dreamt of while constantly traveling. I stayed home for a week "vegging out," doing absolutely nothing. It was my new condo, which ironically, in a creepy twist of fate was Unit 911 in the building, and I had begun my lease just days before the attacks.

Donny Osmond was right. When I became Miss America, my life *would* change forever. And when I crowned Katie Harman a year later, my life changed again in that moment. No one prepared me for the way I was going to feel when I came home after the whirlwind. Unprepared for the big drop, I started to feel lackluster about life.

As a former Miss America, I definitely felt that a lot of pressure came along with the title because I had to constantly strive to look and act my best in social situations.

There was a certain level of expectation that people had when they first met me. I thought, *Everyone has their own idea of what and who Miss America should be.* I had a lot of anxiety, and even felt a bit distrustful at times. It was tough living up to unrealistic expectations.

When I went to church one day, a woman at my parish in Waikiki said right to my face, "Angela, you gained weight." I was shocked at her comment. I was at my ideal weight and I thought, *I'm exactly where I need to be.* The expectation to be perfect and the constant scrutiny seemed magnified when I came home.

A man working at the mall saw me shopping in his store, dressed in casual attire and with a puzzled look he asked me, "Where's your gown and crown?" as if I wore it everywhere I went.

Another time I was having dinner with some friends in Honolulu, and a man interrupted our conversation mid-sentence. He said, "My friend said you're Miss America. Here, sign this." Then he plopped a coaster on our table." Trying to be gracious, I said, "Sure, do you have a pen?" He replied, "Nope." So I went to the waitress to ask for a pen and when I returned he dropped three more coasters and said, "Sign these, too. For my friends back home, I'm visiting."

I never thought it would ever come to this, but I was depressed. Looking back, it was clearly a combination of coming down from such a high from my year, AND feeling the shock and sadness from 9/11.

One book that was extremely helpful to me after my year was Dr. Barbara Sher's, *I Can Do Anything I Want, If I Only Knew What It Was.* After I returned home from Miss America, I felt like I could conquer anything, but I didn't know where to begin. This book helped me get back on track. I was able to do a powerful activity that aided the healing of my inner child.

In this book, I learned that it was extremely therapeutic to forgive anyone that had hurt me in the past, including myself, and let it go. I learned the valuable lesson that forgiveness was more for my own healing than anyone else's. And in order for me to be fully absolved from above, I had to ask forgiveness from those I had wronged and send love to those who had hurt me.

When it seemed all the magic dust had settled, I found myself spending more and more time alone in my apartment. I read multiple inspirational and self-help books simultaneously, trying to find new meaning in my life. Once again, I wondered, *Why was I spared, God? I could have been in one of those planes. I could have been in New York, or at the Pentagon, or in New Jersey. What do you want me to do with the rest of my life?*

My question to God changed from, *Of all people, why ME?* on the night I won to *Why NOT me?* after 9/11. I still believed that everything happens for a reason, and I had to find those reasons.

My priorities changed completely. Before, I had plans to move to Los Angeles or New York to start a career in TV hosting and continue my public speaking. Now I was back in the islands trying to pick up where I left off, but that was unrealistic.

With my five-year goals in hand, I planned to tackle my to-do list immediately. In spite of my good intentions, I had little motivation when I came home. My progress was halted and I started to feel like I "didn't fit" all over again. I was hearing those conflicting voices in my head.

One day in the early months of 2002, I experienced something I never had before in my entire life. Standing outside on my patio on the ninth floor of my condo in Honolulu, I looked down at the glistening pool and the street cars bustling below, when an eerie thought crept into my mind, "What would it be like if you weren't here anymore?" An opposing voice said, "Don't even go there. What's wrong with you?" The other voice interrupted, "Just do it. Jump and see what happens."

I think my subconscious was playing out in my waking hours, plagued with vivid memories of people jumping out of the World Trade Center's top floors. They must have been in such mental anguish. They would rather jump immediately to their certain death than be burned alive. It was the lesser of two evils. My heart broke at the thought of those who lost lives that day and the loved ones they left behind. I couldn't shake those thoughts. I didn't know what was happening, but it scared me.

The voices in my head were competing to the point where it was so deafening, I began to cry. "STOP IT!" I said out loud, and walked into my house, locking the sliding door behind me. *What was happening to me?* I didn't know this Angie. I needed to clear my head. I got in my car and met Tini at Kahala Beach.

Swimming in the ocean was always freeing for me, so instinctively I headed for a secluded area of the beach. Tini asked me what was going on and I broke down in uncontrollable tears. I told him I felt like the weight of the world was on my shoulders and I didn't know why. I shared with him about the voices that were taunting me and told him I had social anxiety being in public.

I had traveled more than 200,000 miles in a year, made five hundred public appearances, experienced a year of celebrity status, and yet, my friends and family back home wanted me to be the same local girl I was before I left, but I was no longer that girl. I was different in so many ways. I didn't know how to deal with the loss of who I once was to the people I cared so deeply about. I knew it would take some time to process it all.

In the one year of reigning, I had gone through extreme high and low points and my head was spinning. I could barely breathe telling him all that I felt. *Why couldn't anyone understand me?!*

Tini hugged me and said, "Shhh, I'm here now. You don't have to deal with anything alone. We're together and we're going to be married soon. I'll always be here for you to hold you up when you feel weak. Everything is going to be ok." I didn't want to be anywhere else but in his arms. His words and his touch never felt as comforting, or as sincere as they did in that moment. I let down all the walls and facades I had built up during my year and it was freeing. He held me for a very long time as I cried all of my tears.

Just like he'd always done when we were in high school and throughout college, he calmed me down in his gentle and loving way. Forget my childhood imaginary egg friend, I had Tini. Before him, I never felt like anyone really had my back. Now more than ever it was clear to me that marrying Tini meant my life was going taking a positive turn. It seemed that I had hit rock bottom so I knew there was nowhere to go but up.

~ Serving Others ~

A month after my reign, my Miss Hawai'i TC, Leilani, and I hit the road for all my post-year speeches and appearances in Hawai'i and throughout the U.S.

In October 2001, just a month after 9/11, I started the Angela Perez Baraquio Education Foundation (APBEF), a 501(c)(3) non-profit organization promoting character education and awarded scholarships and grants to teachers and students exemplifying good character. I wanted to continue the work I started as Miss America, and this was the best way I knew how to give back to my local community.

APBEF hosted the first-ever statewide character education training program for 114 private and public schools in Hawai'i. My foundation also partnered with the Character Education Partnership in Washington, DC to honor a school that had qualified for the Hawai'i School of Character (HSOC) Award.

And what an unforgettable moment when my foundation hosted a special event, honoring my former K-6 PE teacher at Maryknoll Grade School, Mrs. Pattie Heatherly! I got to present her with a Character award for being a living treasure and a beautiful example of what it means to be a quality teacher who makes a difference in others' lives. Her countless years of service to Catholic education and youth was truly inspirational.

In December 2001, my alma mater, the University of Hawai'i at Manoa, invited me to be the commencement speaker for both the Graduate and Undergraduate Ceremonies. It was an honor to return to the campus that gave me both my college degrees. I was deeply humbled to have such a warm welcome by all the students and professors there.

That same month, I was asked to be the godmother of the Norwegian Cruise Line's Norwegian Star. I flew to Miami to christen the ship before its maiden voyage into international waters, and I met Brooke Burke there, who was the godmother for the Norwegian Sun. Together, we did media tours and attended all the inaugural events. It was ironic that she would be the co-host for the Miss America live telecast on ABC almost a decade later.

From 2002 to 2005, I was the spokesperson for First Hawaiian Bank.

Following in the footsteps of former spokesperson, Pat Morita, (better known as Mr. Miyagi from *Karate Kid*), I had big shoes to fill. It was fun doing all the commercial print, TV, and radio ads for the financial institution in Hawai'i, Guam, and Saipan markets. Through the bank, I worked closely with its local community partners and filmed public service announcements for Catholic Charities and the Hawai'i Food Bank. The bank's motto was fitting, "The Power of Yes is the Power of Possibilities."

In the meantime, Tini and I were still youth ministers at our church leading the Tongan youth choir every Sunday. By serving others and being a presence in the community, I was able to feel a sense of belonging again.

Things were looking up and I had every reason to fight through the angst I was feeling in the days after September 11. I went to Mass every Sunday and read the Scriptures for comfort. The words, *Come to me, all who are heavy laden . . . I will give you rest,* made me breathe easier. Being able to let go and let God take over was the answer to all my questions.

I realized that during times when I felt unprepared, unfit, and unworthy—when doubts and fears crept into my psyche—that's when God cultivated me. Like gold tested in fire, only He could take my meager attempts and turn them into astonishing things. Rather than wallow in self-pity, I decided instead to be of service to others.

~ The Power of Positive Thinking ~

By late 2001, work with my non-profit foundation was in full swing, but every once in a while, I would have bouts of depression. On top of that, I had to deal with opposition from my mother. I went through a lot of stress the year Tini and I got engaged from June 2001 to June 2002. Ma and Pa both had their reservations about our engagement. It was evident to Tini that he had to work much harder to prove to them and the world that he was worthy of marrying their "Angie Bebe."

To my parents, I was at the pinnacle of my career, and Tini was a part-time musician studying architecture. They wondered if he could support me and be the ideal partner they would have hoped for me. And Tini had other things working against him.

Aside from Mama, my sisters and other relatives were skeptical. The world was at my fingertips, and so were other prospects for a husband, so they probably asked why I was in a rush to get married. I know the family was looking out for my best interests and they were being protective of me, but I was in love with my fiancé. Tini was up against a force to be reckoned with; we both were.

Still, there was another part of the story. . .

Ma and Pa were surprised at the proposal because they didn't realize we were even *exclusively dating*! From their perspective, how *could* they have known we were together? They were aware that he lived in California but never saw him. They knew we were friends, but they didn't realize how close we got after he left for college, or that we were in constant contact and were seriously dating over a long distance—for a long time. They strictly saw Tini as a family friend and Albert's fellow altar boy. The proposal was shocking to them, and understandably so. Tini did not ask them for their blessing because he wanted to surprise me and he knew they would say no.

I couldn't believe it when I found out he didn't get their blessing beforehand. In the Filipino and American tradition, the man is *supposed to* get the woman's parents' blessing. I loved Tini, but I was upset that things weren't done the right way. *What could I do?* We were already engaged. Of course I *wanted* this, but not *this* way.

When Ma, Pa, Tini, and I talked together in my hotel room the night after the proposal, they were not happy. Then Tini asked point blank if they would have given him their blessing beforehand, and they both indignantly said, no, they wouldn't have. He *knew* that full well, and that's why he proposed onstage.

My mom used to tell us in high school and college, "No dating until you're married." That made no sense to me whatsoever. It seemed there was never a perfect time to start courtship with a man. Tini felt bad for not asking their blessing, but he knew that my parents would be against it, and he wanted to prove his love to me in the most genuine way he knew how.

We were just starting out, so at the very least, he wanted to find a way to surprise me and give me a proposal I would never forget. (That, he did.) He also knew my heart and that I yearned to be married to him more than anything. Plus, we had already put off our engagement an extra year after I won the state title.

Tini apologized profusely to my parents, and although it didn't happen overnight, my parents have long since forgiven Tini. They have a very close relationship today, and my whole family just loves him. *What's not to love!?* Even my sisters recognize that he is an outstanding husband, father, and provider for our family. We just needed to go through those growing pains as a couple.

But before all was well in the world between Tini and my parents, a week before my wedding in June 2002, I woke up one morning and could hardly breathe. I went to the emergency room because of chest pains. I took an EKG and the doctor ran tests on me. I was cleared of any concerns and the doctor said it was just anxiety. *Oh great, just anxiety.* With one of the biggest decisions of my life on the line—about whom I was about to marry and spend my life with—I had much to consider. Friends and acquaintances were murmuring about us too, and I felt it.

There was a popular saying among my high school cross country team, which became our mantra during races: "Take your body where your mind wants to go." I didn't want to be jaded anymore, so just like when I was competing, I started to retrain my mind. It was much too easy to get caught up in all that was wrong in the world, so I drew from my belief in the power of positive thinking, just to get through the days.

~ Signed, Sealed, Delivered ~

After eight years of dating, the day had finally arrived for Tini and me to seal our vows. We had to overcome challenges that included living six years in different states and winning my parents' approval, we were still standing, stronger than ever. Like most couples, we had our moments of jealousy and insecurity.

Despite untrue rumors swirling around in the media that professional athletes were love interests of mine, we were able to rebuild our trust and remain faithful to each other. Tini always said he'd wait for me, and he did. Even after my win, he hung in there.

Like most famous people who travel as part of their job, we certainly had our issues whenever I would meet celebrities on the road. Through it all, Tini and I remained each other's one and only. Our bond was unbreakable. As high school sweethearts, we remembered how we started out as friends and were looking forward to entering into marriage with a whole new level of faith, trust, love, and commitment.

For our marriage preparation, we attended classes with our parish deacon and went through our church's Engaged Encounter weekend. The experience was unforgettable. It's a weekend for couples of all faiths, who are engaged to be married. Some couples are strengthened and affirmed. Others decide marriage is not for them. We were reminded that a wedding is only a day, but a marriage is a lifetime.

We talked about hopes, dreams, traditions, priorities, and dealt with big questions like how many kids we wanted and how we intended to raise them, where we wanted to live, and our thoughts on marriage. We laughed and cried that weekend. Tini and I wrote our betrothals to each other and read them under the full moon during the retreat. It solidified our commitment to each other and confirmed that indeed God handpicked us for each other. Now, the wait was over.

On June 15, 2002, Tini and I received the sacrament of Matrimony at our church in Waikiki, where we had met eleven years earlier. My six sisters were my bridesmaids, and my sister Tess was my maid of honor. Tini's closest friends, including my brother John were in his line, and his brother, Taumata, was his best man.

My six sisters all wore the same sky blue outfits and had the same hair and makeup (courtesy of my "Glam Team" Pattie and Dennis). No one could tell the sisters apart—it was a novelty! Even the kids called the wrong woman, "Mommy" and the husbands did double takes on their wives because each sister looked identical.

It was fun for me to see all my sisters dressed alike. It reminded me of how we all had rice bowl haircuts when we were small. Seeing all of us together highlighted our similarities rather than differences. *Hey, this was my wedding, and I was going to do what I wanted!* My wedding was the first in the family to have all six sisters together in the bridal party. No matter what we had gone through, it meant the world to me to have my sisters stand beside me on my special day. Family is everything to me.

Lisa Hutchinson, of Monalisa Designs, created two original gowns for me: one for the ceremony, and one for the reception. My pageant director, Todd, and his awesome gang at Always Flowers provided the gorgeous bouquets, roses, and both the church's and reception's floral arrangements and decorations.

So many people donated and provided things we needed to make it the most memorable day. A former driver of mine, during my visits home as Miss America, owned a limousine company and wanted to gift me with cars for my wedding day. He said he always remembered how down to earth I was when he offered me teas of the world and I simply asked for Lipton, which he went out and bought for me next time he picked me up.

For my wedding, he asked how many cars I wanted. I thought he was joking when he said, "What do you want two, five, ten? You got it!" He ended up giving us four total. Two beautiful stretch limos for my bridal party, one for my parents, and one for Tini and me after the reception. It was an extremely generous gift and the extra touch of elegance made it dreamy for my whole family!

The girls stayed overnight in our honeymoon suite at the Royal Hawaiian Hotel (also known as the Pink Palace), while the guys prepared for the big day at a hotel in Waikiki across the street from our church. The irony was that even though I was surrounded by my family, a part of me still felt alone.

The moment we arrived, my girlfriends Maxinne, Brenna, Valerie, and Julie met me at the front of the church. As I walked out in my gown and train, a passerby thoughtlessly sped by in a hurry, stepped on my train and ripped the tulle from the back of my dress. Clearly, I was flustered, but my friends quickly came to the rescue and calmed my anxiety.

In a flash, they whipped out a sewing kit and immediately repaired the train before I entered the church. Those girls were by my side through all the preparations and behind-the-scenes planning. And they worked hard that day at the reception, too, never asking for anything in return. I will always be grateful to them for their friendship.

We were running a few minutes late, but my wedding planner, Valerie, signaled that it was go time. Groom, groomsmen, parents, choir, priests were all in place and then it got real. My parents met me at the entrance. Mama stood on one side, and Papa on the other. The music started. This was it. I knew this day was a long time coming, but it was the moment we'd been waiting for—the most important day of our lives. My heart was racing. Then I saw him.

Dressed in an all-white tuxedo, Tini began to serenade me with the same song he sang when he proposed to me exactly a year earlier. "You and I" by Stevie Wonder: *Here we are, on earth together just you and I . . . God has made us fall in love it's true. I've finally found someone like you.* He was so nervous his voice quivered, but he kept on. Tears of joy and longing flowed down my face, as I approached him. Walking arm in arm with my parents down the aisle was a physical metaphor for me leaving the life I once knew to enter into a new one. The second I saw Tini and heard his voice it was like coming home. At that point, with laser focus, I made a beeline toward the altar and could only think about being close to my future husband. Nothing else mattered.

The months of preparation with our deacon, boiled down to this moment, professing our love for each other publicly before God, our family, and friends and promising we would be there for each other for better or for worse, until death do us part.

The Mass, concelebrated by our priests, Father Choo and Father Mac, progressed beautifully and we incorporated Filipino and Samoan traditions into the celebration. During Meditation, Tini's dad, Jerome Grey, sang and played guitar to "We've Only Just Begun" by the Carpenters, and there wasn't a dry eye in the church.

After the dismissal, Tini and I walked happily, hand in hand back up the aisle toward the entrance. The most elated we'd ever been before, we kissed as a new married couple and were so excited to be the newlyweds we had instantly become.

It meant a great deal to us to see our family and friends greet us afterward before heading to the reception. My former eighth grade students, Rachael and Emerisa were there, along with relatives and friends from both sides who traveled far and wide. Some came from the East and West Coasts, and some as far as Samoa.

When the crowds left, our parents met us for family photos in front of the church. The poses were awkward at first. I knew my mom and dad still had mixed feelings about our marriage, and our union would take some getting used to, but in the end, they were happy for us, and that's all that mattered. It was time to move forward.

My mom said that she felt better when Tini's parents came over to our house just before the wedding, to apologize on Tini's behalf, to smooth things over and officially ask for their blessing. They wanted to make things right. That dinner at my house was a time to make peace. It wasn't until then that my parents were cool with us being together because they realized how much we loved each other.

Today, Mama says that Tini is a good husband and because he is such a good man, whenever she sees Samoans she "views them all as friendly, and assumes they are all kindhearted, just like Tini and his family." *So sweet!*

Our wedding reception was held at Kualoa Ranch at Paliku Gardens, nestled in front of the Ko'olau Mountain Range, overlooking Chinaman's Hat. It was a gorgeous sunny day in paradise, and in the outdoor tents were hanging lights that twinkled when evening fell. The day was just perfect. We had catered food stations and live entertainment, with Tini's friends from Reign and Jook Joint, graciously providing music for our guests. Everyone danced, drank, ate, and had a blast. Tini and I made our grand entrance to music from the CD, *Cinderella*. It was magical—a dream come true.

When it was time to show our slide show, (which had an SNL feel to it with spoof scenes from Superstar and Superman, featuring our Tongan Youth choir) the guests roared with laughter. Then it got sweet when the videographer inserted scenes from our vows into the edited video. Tini and I were both emotional from the footage. Tini wiped my tears, and the partying continued.

Before night's end, our choir members performed a Tongan dance, and I performed a hula while Tini played guitar and sang. Tini and I had also prepared a Filipino and Samoan dance together to honor our combined heritage. We had the touching father-daughter and the mother-son dance with our parents. Our first dance was to our favorite song, "Spend My Life With You," by Eric Benet and Tamiya, followed by the traditional money dance. Toward the end, after all the gifts were presented from the families who were representing villages from Samoa, there was a *taualuga,* the traditional Samoan ceremonial dance, performed by me (with the support of my Samoan sisters), where more money was collected and gifted to us. The outpouring of love and generosity filled my heart.

Seeing all the smiling faces around me, I was overjoyed, and couldn't have been more content. Everything I ever wanted, and everyone I loved was encapsulated in that moment in time. Afterward, Tini and I hopped into our long white stretch limousine to signal the end of our very long and delicious day. All our family and friends waved goodbye to us, as we drove off into the sunset, destined for the Royal Hawaiian Hotel.

~ Newlywed Game ~

A few days later, Tini and I left on our honeymoon cruise, on board the Norwegian Star, the same ship I had christened six months earlier. The boat took us around the Hawaiian Islands and to the Republic of Kiribati, our only international stop. The trip was playful and romantic filled with lots of love, laughter, and beautiful memories made along the way. From our spa treatments (mani-pedis and couples massages) to the indoor and outdoor pools onboard the ship, singing to "Reunited" in the private karaoke rooms, playing Bingo, watching Broadway shows, and dressing up for formal nights—it was absolutely decadent.

Roaming the deck on late nights, we found chocolate fountains and dessert tables in the wee hours of the morning, endless buffets, and restaurants boasting a wide variety of international cuisine. We ventured out to field excursions where we swam in the neighbor islands' waterfalls, went hiking, climbed vine ladders, jumped off cliffs, and acted like Tarzan and Jane on rope swings.

On Kiribati we saw pristine beaches, palm trees, and handmade fishnets, then got bike rentals and rode around what seemed like Gilligan's Island, buying crafts from the natives and playing with the kids running along the rocky paths. We attended a luau on Mau'i, on the lawn of a hotel and received lei from the dancers. They announced us as newlyweds and called us up to dance onstage. It was hilarious! So far it was a perfect start to a beautiful life ahead.

Tini and I have been happily married for twelve years now and my parents absolutely love Tini. He has proven time and again what a standup husband and father he truly is.

Whenever I ask my parents what the secret to their marriage is, Papa says, "Marriage is not 50/50, it's 100/100!" Mama says, "Love is a decision." While not exactly the most romantic answer, it's true. Tini and I agree that love freely given should be freely be received and that kindness is the key, but it truly stems from a conscious choice to love the other person daily, flaws and all.

Every year, when we watch our wedding video and slideshow we are reminded of that lifelong commitment we made to each other in front of God and our loved ones. As our children grow older, they watch the slideshow with us on our anniversaries and it shows them how much their parents love each other, which is really one of the best gifts we can give them.

On our ten-year anniversary, we renewed our vows in an intimate ceremony presided by our high school friend, the altar boy-turned priest, Father Preston Passos. It was just us and the kids. I was pregnant with

Keilah, and our eldest son Isaiah did the reading. Since the kids saw how much their father and I loved one another, Micah asked, "How do I know who to marry when *I* grow up, Mom?" I tell them what my priest used to tell us. "Pray to God for guidance about your vocation, whatever it may be. If you want to get married someday, start praying for your future spouse now. When you meet that person, you'll *know*." I wish the same type of pure love for them.

My parents' marriage has always played a crucial role in our upbringing. Tini's parents have also been married for more than forty years. And that's why it was difficult for my family to have seen some of my sisters go through rough patches in their marriages, which eventually led to divorce. They were losses that we collectively mourned as a family.

Marriage is hard work, but divorce is a painful experience for all parties involved, especially the children. It was tough on all of us, particularly for the youngest kids in our nuclear family: Gloria, Albert, and me. Like little deaths, we suffered the loss of our sisters' married lives. It took a long time to adjust to our new reality. Although the breakups didn't involve us directly, we were affected. After, it was necessary to cut ties with their former significant others out of respect for my sisters.

Experiencing divorce through my sisters' eyes has been a challenge, and I have compassion for everyone involved. But I know things happen for a reason, and I wish only happiness and peace in the future for all my siblings and their partners. I also pray that Tini and I are able to keep our own relationship strong. We both know it takes two to make it, one to break it. And like Mama says, "Love is a decision."

As heads of our family, Ma and Pa set the gold standard for marriage and continue to grow in love with one another. Each year on their wedding day, all of us kids would attend Mass with my parents and afterward we would sing them the "Anniversary Song" together, a tune memorized when we were very little, and one learned through our involvement with Marriage Encounter.

It became a tradition and once we hit the second line of the song, *all the joys, all the tears, all the memories through the years. What a perfect time to have an anniversary*, it was all waterworks. The song continued, *Who knows what lies ahead—what God has planned for us, what lies beyond the bend? My friend, there's one thing for sure, the good life will endure, while we're working hand in hand for Heaven's sake.* Mama automatically would start to cry and none of us girls could finish the song without getting choked up as well. We continued the tradition throughout adulthood.

With a bit of luck, my parents will celebrate their golden anniversary on June 6, 2015, a milestone for them and for us children. They are an inspiration and I thank them for the example they have given to Tini and me, as a couple that always puts their complete faith and trust in God.

CHAPTER 13

A MOTHER'S HEART

There's something special about the bond between a mother and daughter. My relationship with Mama may have been complicated through the years, but the love was always there. When I was a child, I saw Mama as the strict disciplinarian. Now, as a wife and mother, I see how everything Mama did for our family always came from a good place, even if it wasn't always evident growing up.

In the Philippines, Mama witnessed atrocities children should never have to see. As a little girl, she lived through the height of World War Two. I still get chills at the story she shares with us when she relives the moment she and her siblings were running away from the Japanese soldiers that had occupied Manila. The soldiers marched with guns in their hands and my mother recalls running for her life, with her siblings and her mom, my Grandma Teresita. They were exposed to the smell of death and dodged shrapnel while stepping over corpses.

Like a scene straight out of *The Joy Luck Club,* the 1993 film depicting life histories of four Asian women and their daughters, Mama talks about being five years old around 1944. All their food was confiscated by soldiers and she and her family were driven out of their home, forced to find a new place to live. The family would run wherever people told them to go.

Meanwhile, Japanese and American planes were dropping bombs above and she vividly remembers the sound of the aerial dogfights. "Run, run, run! Dapa! (Lie on your belly!)" When the bombing subsided, they'd stand up and run again. Later, during the day, they were told to go to Concordia College campus in Herran, where they could find safety there.

So they ran. They stood by the walls of the campus. Grandma shushed all the children, in hopes that their hiding place would not be discovered by the soldiers.

People brought any furniture they could carry from their homes to sit on. They all prayed silently. My mom was on her belly, hiding under a table. A bomb fell near her and all the shrapnel went flying. Just then, Mama's older sister, Charito, age seven, told Grandma, "I'm not feeling well, Mama. I'm thirsty." She sat on Grandma's lap and Grandma gave her a drink from the war canteen she had.

At that moment, a piece of shrapnel from the nearby bomb that had just exploded hit my Aunt (Tita) Charito. Because she was drinking water, the shrapnel hit the canteen before reaching her heart. There was no blood. Seconds earlier or later, it would have hit my Grandma, but instead the shrapnel hit young Charito, and she died instantly, in my Grandma's arms.

Mama was a wide-eyed witness to this devastating event, while my Grandma, upon realizing that her child was gone, began to hysterically wail in anguish. "My daughter! My daughter, my daughter is dead!" And yet, she and her kids had to keep moving to get to safety. Like faithful ducklings following their mother, the children all ran after Grandma, but my mom, fell down along the way.

My mother heard more bombs dropping all around her and thought she had been hit. Mama's sister, Tita Reby told my mom, "Get up! Follow me!" When she saw my mom on the ground, she screamed to Grandma, "Mama, Letty's hurt! Letty, stand up!" Thinking my mom was dead Grandma said coldly, "Leave her! Let's go!"

Frantically yelling to her kids to run for their lives as she was already carrying one daughter's corpse in her arms, Grandma must have felt helpless and in shock, but her instinct was to save herself so she could get her kids out of harm's way. My mom heard all this, including Grandma's words, but she herself thought she was halfway dead.

As she learned from the nuns that taught her in school, should she recite the Act of Contrition at the hour of death she would be forgiven of all her earthly sins and go to Heaven. So she began to do this, thinking these were her final moments. She covered her face and waited to be taken to Heaven.

Just then, she stood up and felt her arms and legs, and realized she was untouched by the shrapnel. She ran after her siblings and mother yelling, "Mama, Mama, I'm alive!" My other aunt, Tita Kelly was hit with a piece of shrapnel so she was bleeding. Grandma found a place to bury her daughter Charito while everyone witnessed, crying. The children were so young, all under twelve years old.

After that incident, Mama and her family settled down in their old house that was burned. They put some iron on the roof. Later they went to Laguna where Grandma had some relatives. The family rode and hitchhiked on American army trucks.

Mama recalls, "The Americans were so good to us. They always gave people rides when they asked. When everything was quiet the Americans started rebuilding the city. Those who submitted war claims got some money from the Americans to rebuild whatever was lost. Your grandma went back to dress making. I felt God had been watching us. It was so scary during those times."

Whenever I reflect on that story, I think of the strength of my Grandma Teresita and the courage of my mother in the midst of dire circumstances—even at five years old. Were it not for Mama's determination to stay alive, none of us, her children, would be here. Being a mother, I am inspired by Grandma Teresita's and Mama's unbreakable will.

Especially during wartime, Mama and her siblings were not sheltered from the realities of physical and sexual abuse, that occurred in their own neighborhood, if only from the soldiers . . . it's no wonder why my mom was so strict with her daughters. Many of her reasons for saying and doing things are deep-seated. It all makes sense now.

I still recall her Tagalog accent scolding us girls, "Knock your knees!" "Don't be indecent!" "You do not arrrrrrouse the passions of men!" In our youth, we'd shrug her off and wonder where her mind was, but she would respond vehemently, "I am your Mama, if I don't say it, no one will!"

When I was in high school, my classmates used to brag about how their moms were their best friends. Knowing it would never happen for me, I secretly wished I could have that kind of warm fuzzy relationship with my own mom. I didn't get why she had to be so strict with us. Once I asked her, "Why can't you be like my friends' moms? They do everything together." She snapped back, "I'm not your friend, I'm your mother!" That definitely brought me back to reality.

Mama may not have been our best friend, but she certainly valued our education and wanted to provide the best for us. When I was only five years old in 1981, my parents took all ten of us to Disneyland. Gloria, the youngest, was only one at the time. Albert was three. It was the best trip of my life.

The next time we would all return to Disneyland was when I was in sixth grade. My oldest sister was graduating from college and my parents thought it was necessary for all nine of us siblings to witness this milestone event. They bought all our tickets to go to Disneyland and Universal Studios, in addition to the plane tickets for all twelve of us. I can't even begin to imagine how much that trip must have cost, but I appreciated Ma and Pa for showing us the value of a college education.

During Ceci's graduation ceremony, we were all so excited that we brought a video tape recorder to commemorate the event. When Ceci's name was called, we all burst into applause and began whooping and howling in the auditorium. Afterward, a couple came up to us and said in all sincerity, "Welcome to America!" as if we had just gotten off the boat from the Philippines. We all started laughing, and the moment was all caught on tape for us to relive.

When Ceci graduated, we not only *believed* we could graduate from college, too, but we also knew that it was *expected* in our family.

Thinking back on those days, I must say that I don't remember much about the gifts I ever received as a child, but I will *never* forget the moments we spent together as a family. My mom and dad created lifelong memories for us when they saved up and made it a point to bring our entire family to Disneyland. Perhaps that's why I love the place so much. Those times together were priceless.

Not too long ago, I was cleaning out my closet looking through old journals, and found a letter Mama wrote me when I was fourteen. It was dated April 27, 1991. Apparently, she gave it to me during my Confirmation retreat weekend when all the parents wrote notes to their children. It was the only letter I have from her that was written just for me. I kept it after all these years. Even now, as I reread it, I start to cry. She wrote:

"Dear Angie, On this your Confirmation retreat, I'd like you to listen and observe the people, the things, and the place around you, and then feel the power of God's loving and tender care for you. And so this letter is being sent to you to let you know how very special you are to me, and not just my #8 child. Your most endearing quality is that of giving service with love." She went on, "You were always thoughtful and tried to anticipate what I needed . . . your quality of being loving when you serve will remain a very important resource in your life. Much more so as you receive the important sacrament of Confirmation, when you are made the defender of our faith, a soldier of Christ."

Then she recalled a vivid memory of me when I was *two years old*. At first, I didn't know where she was going with it . . . She said that whenever she would ask my siblings to get something for her, they would listen. I, on the other hand, would run quickly to get her bra without her even asking for it! Then I'd smell it and kiss it, and *then* hand it to her. I remember how Mama used to tell everyone that she nursed me the longest. She said I stopped at two years old and that's why I was the "healthiest." Other siblings only wanted the bottle after the few months they spent nursing. Mama tells me that was a memory that reminded her of feeling bonded with me. She wanted me to know that she saw qualities in me that were different from the rest and reassured me that I wasn't just a number, although many times that's how I felt.

At that point in my life as a teen, her words meant so much to me. *They still do.* It was just what I needed to hear on that retreat. I remember the music playing softly in the background while I read her letter for the first time. Everyone was in tears, reading their parents' heartfelt words to them.

My little daughter Keilah is almost two as I write this and the other day, she went to my dresser and pulled out my bra. She kissed it and handed it to me and smiled. I couldn't believe my eyes! None of the other three boys *ever* did that. But I also nursed Keilah the longest of all my children—thirteen months, as opposed to ten months for all three boys. It was history repeating itself, and I thought, *We all have a connection.*

When Keilah did what I used to do with my mom, I saw myself in her. Mama must feel the same way about all my sisters and me. I wondered how she felt when I won. I'm sure it was a proud moment for her because like me, she admitted that she never felt she was the pretty one among her sisters. When I look at pictures of my mom in her youth, I marvel at her beauty. She's *still* beautiful today.

When she was a teacher in Manila, some of Mama's friends told her that she looked like Gemma Cruz, the Miss Philippines who was the first Philippine delegate to win the Miss International title in 1964. When I returned to O'ahu for my Homecoming just weeks after being named the first Asian Miss America, Mama joked with me, "You know I was supposed to be Miss America, right? But God gave it to you instead. It's ok." We laughed about it. I guess Mama and I both were trying to find our place in our families and make a mark on the world. Ultimately, we both had our own unique paths to forge.

The week I came home to Hawai'i as the new Miss America, TV anchors Leslie Wilcox and Kirk Matthews interviewed Mama, Papa, and me on the *FOX2* morning news. They asked Ma to talk about all her children and what each one does. She went down the list. "Well, Cecilia is the oldest. She has a business degree and is a counselor . . . Jerome is Number Two. He is a pharmaceutical representative . . . " She named every child and their accomplishments. I sat there on the edge of my seat waiting patiently for her to get to Number Eight. It seemed like forever. Finally, she continued with the twins, then she was on Rose. *I was next!*

Suddenly, she paused after Rose, and turned to my dad, tapped him, and in her Tagalog accent said, "Claude, who is next?" *Silence.* I thought she was joking. But she was really stumped. I interjected, "Uhhh, it's me, Angie! I'm next!" "Geez," I said half-jokingly, "What does a girl have to do to get some attention around here?" The hosts fell to pieces in laughter. I thought to myself, *Not funny.*

But the viewers loved it. All people could talk about that morning was how hilarious and cute they thought Ma and Pa were. I wished she was joking, but she wasn't. Yet her forgetting my name on TV was no different from how I had felt my whole life, struggling to be noticed.

I remembered the time I began to emerge as a top contender in

Atlantic City, when all my state judges got excited to see me win a preliminary award. With the tough competition that year, I had to do something to stand out from the rest of the state winners. After I was crowned Miss America, my out-of-state judges reunited on O'ahu to celebrate my Homecoming. They made signs that said "SHE WAS NOTICED." They felt honored to have had a hand in choosing a Miss America, and I was honored to serve. In all honesty, I was also glad that I *was* noticed. I didn't feel invisible anymore, and it was something I longed for my entire life.

When my sisters and I were teenagers we were like any other adolescents. One by one, we went through our rebellious phase. One day in 1994 when I was eighteen, in the heat of the moment, I refused to follow Mama's rules and she yelled at me, so I threatened to leave the house. Calling my bluff instead, she kicked me out, like she had done several times before with my three older sisters. I was both devastated and liberated, following suit behind them.

Soon I was living with my sisters in their apartment in Kalihi, preparing for my first semester at UH. I was grateful that they took me in as a roommate. That was the summer I happened to start competing in pageants. By then I wasn't just doing it for fun, but by *necessity*. The winnings helped a lot with my college expenses, especially since I was now "independent." Still in disbelief that Mama let me walk out, I understood she wanted to teach me a lesson.

That summer, I saw her at Mass, where my siblings and I gathered each week as the church choir. During the Communion hymn we sang the song, "Isaiah 49." The first verse says, *I will never forget you, my people, I have carved you on the palm of my hand. I will never forget you, I will not leave you orphaned, I will never forget my own.* The second verse continued, *Does a mother forget her baby? Or a woman, the child within her womb? Yet even if these forget, yes even if these forget, I will never forget my own.*

As I sang the verses I got choked up, to the point where I couldn't finish the song. My sisters took over to lead the congregation and asked if I was ok. Not understanding the disconnect between Mama and me, I felt like I had been abandoned again, but found solace in knowing that God would never leave me alone and that He loved me unconditionally. After Mass, I hugged my mom and it was unspoken, but we had forgiven each other. I didn't see Mama much that summer, but I knew she still loved me from afar.

Mama pushed us beyond our limits in life, much like Coach Dana pushed me in basketball. Because she had such high expectations for us, we were able to surpass the competition in many areas of our lives. Now I am thankful she didn't treat me like a friend. She used to say, "You only have one mother. Who else, except your mom, will tell you the truth?" and she was right. Today, I use that line with my kids. It's all coming full circle.

My mother didn't believe she had ultimate control, she had a strong faith in God. And she truly wanted what was best for us in the long run, even if it hurt our feelings in the short term. Although she did not say it out loud often, we knew she loved us. She urged us to cultivate our God-given talents while leaving room for a bit of grace. Though I couldn't articulate this as a girl, I think I knew deep down that grace worked.

My parents have been married for forty-nine years, an accomplishment that any married couple can acknowledge and admire. As the years quickly pass, they know that they are in their twilight years and it's evident they are making the best of it.

Recently, my sisters, parents, and I drove together to wine country and had the most beautiful time together reminiscing and making new memories. It's nice to be adults and truly appreciate all that our parents did for us as children and to be able to enjoy them as individuals now that we are all at different stages in our lives.

I was in Hawai'i not too long ago speaking at a pro-life event and my parents wanted to be in the audience, so they had front row seats to my presentation. My parents had heard me speak before, but that was during press conferences when I was Miss America and on our TV show, but they had not seen me speak live on the particular topic on which I was addressing. I acknowledged them in the audience. They were surrounded by many people they knew.

Throughout my speech, I took the listeners on an emotional roller coaster ride with me and afterwards, people told me they laughed, cried, and were so happy to see me. They congratulated my parents and me and told them they must be so proud.

However, as I returned to my seat after my speech, my parents didn't say a word to me. I stayed afterward for a meet and greet with guests and took a slew of photos, but my parents stood quietly on the side waiting. I wasn't sure what was happening. This wasn't like them. They came to every high school basketball game and cross country meet and always beamed with pride whenever I was in a pageant or onstage. This reaction was new to me. All Papa said was, "Here's your plate so you can eat later. Let's go."

We got in the car and the ride back to their home was silent. I was leaving on a plane from Hawai'i to California the next day with my family, and I knew I didn't have much more quality time with them.

Finally, I broke the silence and said, "So, did you have a good time?" "Oh, it was lovely," Mama replied. "Yes, it was nice." Papa said. Then Mama went on, "I am so glad we got to see you and your beautiful family this trip, Angie. And your speech was so nice. Do you do it often? I have not seen you speak in a long time." That was the extent of her comments.

My interpretation of her behavior was that seeing her daughter become an open book and speak candidly onstage about her accomplishments, travels, trials, and personal and spiritual beliefs, in the context of the family she and my dad raised together was incredibly impactful. So much so, that they were both speechless. I knew my presentation meant so much to her and Papa, that even words could not express or encapsulate their emotions.

We got to their house, hugged, laughed, and took pictures. It was a moment I will not soon forget. I had a strong feeling that, just like that day after Mass the summer I moved out of the house, in those unspoken words there was a lot of love between us. We were never the "express your feelings" type of family, but there is certainly no shortage of affection in our household. Nothing else needed to be said.

Deep down, I wished for them to say how proud they were of me at the time, but those words never came. Soon, I was back on a plane to the mainland. Later, my dad told my younger sister Gloria that my talk was very moving, touching, and emotional. Mama told her she felt good about my pro-life stance and liked when I spoke about her giving life to ten children.

These stories highlight how many of us will always seek approval from our parents, American or Asian . . . even a Miss America in her late thirties is still needing recognition from her mother and father. And ultimately, all children become reflections of their parents.

Today, I appreciate that my parents knew the crucial role they played and how they drew the line between parent and friend. They were right. We could have many friends, but we would only have one mother and father. My parents weren't the type to be openly affectionate or say, "I love you" every day, but I knew they loved all of us immensely. This played out differently with all my siblings, but for me, that had to be good enough, even though I would do everything with the intent to please them or make them proud.

I asked my parents what they will do to celebrate their milestone 50th wedding anniversary next year. Mama replied half jokingly, "We'll see if I'm alive." She says that much more often now, as if she knows something we don't know. Or it could be her fears that she has already outlived her own mother by several years so she feels that she is living on bonus time. What we do know is that her health is not one hundred percent, and she's aging. We all are. In any case, I witness my beautiful mother living life more fully these days and with much more love and compassion for her family than I have ever seen before, and that inspires me.

My parents come from the Old World, the mother country. They were raised in the traditional Filipino way and we were raised the American way, with Filipino traditions in our background perspective. On one hand, we were taught to live in community and serve others. On the other hand, we learned to be competitive and individualistic in America, two very competing paradigms. In America, it's all about getting ahead and looking out for Number One. I had to find the balance between the two cultures that were equal parts of me.

When I watched Amy Tan's movie *The Joy Luck Club* for the first time, I could relate to the stories all too well. I thought of my mom, and her mom, and her mother's mother, down the line through our ancestry. Amy Tan was right, "All of us are like stairs, one step after another, going up and down, but all going the same way."

Grandma Teresita died when I was five. Mama said Grandma sewed five dresses for me, just because I asked. I wish I had gotten to know her better. I know she was a very prayerful woman. She had a fighting spirit, a will of steel, courage, determination, and an immense capacity to love. She passed down those qualities to all the women in our family. My Grandma Severina on my Papa's side died before I ever met her. Papa said she was always up before sunrise to take care of her eight kids' clothes and breakfast, and she was also a woman of strong faith. Tini's mom is the same way. And so am I.

Today I realize the great importance of the role of a mother, and I honor the women who came before me in my family tree—on both sides— for their faith, fortitude, and strength.

There truly is something special about a bond between mother and daughter. My mom was my first teacher and coach in many things. I am not much different from her in many ways, and for that I feel blessed. She is an incredible woman who has influenced me to become the woman I am today, and I am lucky to call her Mama. She and I have shared the same body, she nursed me when I was a baby, completely dependent on her loving care and protection. A part of me will always be a part of her, just as a piece of me will always be a piece of *all* my children, especially my daughter, Keilah.

~ Modesty and Authentic Femininity ~

As I grow in my Catholic faith, I continue to have a greater appreciation for my mother's concern for all her daughters' appearance in public, and how important it is for all women to be careful in regards to modesty. Looking back on the moment I competed in a swimsuit and heels on worldwide television over a decade ago, and all the moments I wore tight fitting or revealing clothes as a young teenager, I now see the situations more clearly and with very different eyes. I have gained additional perspective from being married to a wonderful husband and a mother to four beautiful children.

During and after my year of service as Miss America, I was very blessed to use that opportunity to spread the important message of self-esteem and authentic beauty to young women and people of all circumstances across the United States and beyond. Although I made the choice to wear a two-piece swimsuit on national television back then in order to win the award, I also made the choice to never do it again.

My husband was very proud of me at that moment, and he's still proud of me. And while it was an accomplishment that I will always celebrate, I am more conscious and respectful of my role as his wife and now as the mother of his children.

After I won Miss America, I went to New York and was a guest on *Late Night with David Letterman*. The host David Letterman introduced me to America as "the new leader of the free world." While on commercial break, he was peeking at a picture mounted on piece of cardboard. He kept looking at the photo, then at me. Curious at what he had on his desk I asked, "What's that?" He then revealed an eight-by-ten photo of me walking onstage in my swimsuit. I was shocked. I believe he wanted to show it to the audience and they would do a close-up of it on camera.

"You're not going to show that on TV, are you?" I asked. "I'm a teacher. My students are watching," I whispered. He didn't respond. Seconds later we were back on the air and I was on edge the whole segment.

He never showed the picture. Instead, he asked me to dance hula while his band accompanied me. Then he gave me a dozen roses. I appreciated Letterman for respecting my wishes. When I stated my boundaries I learned that other people had to adjust. I was beginning to feel stronger as a woman and it felt good.

In my youth, I was unaware of how my dress affected others. Now as a wife, I see the importance of my role to my husband, who loves and respects me for me. Especially in today's society, I have to be careful to dress and act appropriately in various situations, because in addition to being a wife, I'm also a mother, teacher, school administrator, and activist and everything I do affects my family and friends. It's a responsibility I take seriously. You and I are beautiful and wonderful in God's eyes, and we do not need revealing or tight fitting clothing to prove it. There is a time and a place for everything, so that's something to keep in mind when choosing appropriate attire for any given occasion.

I'm much more aware now that we are all human with natural frailties. Women can still be fashionable, while practicing modesty. I believe that we show our true strength when we celebrate our beauty, femininity, and uniqueness in healthy ways. I'd encourage young women today (including my own daughter) to make more conscious decisions now regarding dress, in general, for the sake of others they might encounter.

Having three boys of my own, living in the world that we do, I want to protect them from temptations, but I know that's not always possible. In that spirit, I try to teach them how to discern what's right and wrong, and make good choices for their future. My husband and I want to be good role models for them as well because ultimately, we are all responsible for leading the souls of our children and others back to God.

CHAPTER 14

LIFE AFTER THE CROWN

After eight years of dating (six years of it long distance), Tini and I would finally become husband and wife. We had overcome so many challenges, between living separate lives, swirling rumors in the media about my supposed love interests, and us fighting for approval from our in-laws.

We knew that only true love could have gotten us this far. Tini always said he'd wait for me, and he did. Even after my win, he hung in there. Someone once told him while I was on tour, "When all the dust has settled, and this year is over for Angie, the only real thing you will both have is each other." Those words got us through some difficult times, and they couldn't have been truer.

During my travels, I've met so many different people. Several handsome, intelligent, wealthy, and famous men have shown interest in me. But I always knew that Tini was the one for me. And he has always told me that I was the only one for him. Our bond was unbreakable. He and I remained true to each other all those years.

As high school sweethearts, we remembered how we started out as friends, and now we were entering into marriage with a whole new level of faith, trust, love, and commitment. For all my children, I wish this type of pure love, and hope to always be able to role model it for them with their dad.

For our marriage preparation, we attended classes with our parish deacon and went through our church's Engaged Encounter weekend. We talked about our hopes, dreams, and traditions and dealt with big questions like how many kids we wanted, how we intended to raise them, where we wanted to live, and what marriage meant to us. We laughed and cried, and it solidified that indeed, God had handpicked us for each other.

~ Proclamations ~

In my travels, I'd been given Senate Proclamations, legislative citations, and keys to the cities in various states. When I was in San Francisco for the Philippine Independence Day Parade, Mayor Willie Brown presented me with a plaque declaring August 12, 2001 "Angela Perez Baraquio Day in San Francisco."

When I returned home after winning Miss America, I received one of the greatest surprises of my life. The governor at the time, Ben Cayetano, also the first Filipino-American to serve as governor in the U.S., had issued a proclamation that October 14, 2000 to October 14, 2001 was "Angela Perez Baraquio Year in Hawai'i" in honor of my win as the First Asian Miss America! The distinction was extremely humbling and because this was from my home, it was that much more meaningful to me.

~ State Dinner Invitation ~

In 2003, another unexpected distinction came my way. I learned on the news that U.S. Olympic team light flyweight boxer, Brian Viloria, a Filipino from Hawai'i, was specially invited to attend a White House state dinner honoring the sitting Philippine President, Gloria Macapagal-Arroyo and her husband. I thought how I would have loved to be a guest as well! Since my time as the reigning Miss America had passed, chances were slim that I'd be getting an invite.

A few days after wishful thinking, I received a call from The White House. My presence was being requested at that very state dinner! I couldn't believe it. I put a thought out there, and BOOM, there it was!

When I received my official invitation, I knew another magical adventure was about to begin. The attention to detail for state dinners was evident, beginning with the elegant invitation.

Mine arrived beautifully scribed by the White House calligrapher addressed to "Ms. Angela Perez Baraquio and Guest." The return address consisted of three words engraved in gold lettering: THE WHITE HOUSE.

Inside was the official invitation with the gold presidential seal at the top, followed by the words, "The President and Mrs. Bush request the pleasure of the company of Ms. Baraquio at a dinner to be held at The White House on Monday, May 19, 2003 at seven-thirty o'clock," and the bottom left-hand corner bore the words "Black Tie."

A second ivory card read, "In honor of Her Excellency Gloria Macapagal-Arroyo President of the Republic of the Philippines and Attorney Jose Miguel T. Arroyo."

While I was ready to send my RSVP then and there, I realized I was in a predicament. As the new First Hawaiian Bank spokesperson I had already committed to attend a special event, which landed on the *exact same day* as the White House dinner. Of course, I wanted to go to Washington, but how could I cancel on my commitment? I contacted the head of Marketing, and ever so slightly mentioned my invitation to the White House. Reiterating my commitment to the bank, I told him that I would regretfully decline the President's invitation.

Initially, he was blown away that I had been asked to attend a state dinner. "Well, that's a good dilemma to have: either attend a bank event with its president and CEO or go to the White House to meet the President of the United States and First Lady for a state dinner. That's incredible! Although we would really love to have you there, this is a once-in-a-lifetime opportunity. You should go. We'll figure something out." *OK, thanks!!*

I was so grateful for his understanding and that he recognized the enormous honor of that invitation. In place of my presence at the banquet, I was allowed to pre-record a video presentation for the guests, and their event would be fine without me.

Immediately, we began making plans for our trip. The invitation allowed me to bring one guest, so of course, it was Tini, my new husband!

At that point, I had already visited our nation's capital at least five times, but this would be my *first* time at the White House with my honey as a married woman. For Tini, it was his first trip to Washington, and what a fantastic reason to go!

As the days drew near, I couldn't contain my eagerness. In contrast, Tini seemed cool and collected. My husband can be taciturn and unassuming, so his reactions can be confusing—sometimes when he's in a good mood, he looks expressionless. When I asked him how he felt about the trip to the White House, he shrugged it off. The "Samoa" in Tini projects a very simple island man, who doesn't need much or get impressed easily. It wasn't until the dinner date neared when he began to sense how monumental this event would be.

It was fascinating to learn that the first ruling monarch to attend a state dinner at the White House was Hawai'i's own King David Kalakaua in 1874, hosted by President and Mrs. Ulysses S. Grant! Kalakaua was nicknamed "The Merrie Monarch" because under his rule, hula and chants, once banned in public in the Hawaiian kingdom—were revived.

Never could King Kalakaua have envisioned that in a future era, a twenty-four-year-old young lady and hula dancer named Angie would represent his beloved Hawai'i as Miss America at a White House state dinner. The thought reminds me of what a privilege and responsibility I was given to uphold all that represents Hawai'i and its traditions, culture, and legacy.

With all the pomp and circumstance people associate with a state dinner, many fail to remember that behind the impressiveness of the social scene, the important business of politics and diplomacy takes place before it. Information between heads of state is shared, opinions are exchanged, powerful connections are made, and appearances are upheld. From a U.S. president's perspective, it is the highest form of honor that can be extended by our country to another, signifying the importance of the personal ties and the connection that our countries share.

~ Arrival Ceremony ~

This next part of my life story is a cherished memory that I hold very close to my heart. After everything I had been through during my life: my childhood, drawn out years of a long distance relationship, my time as Miss Hawai'i and as Miss America, my experiences with family and friends, 9/11, my struggle for acceptance, attention, with identity, everything—Tini and I finally got a chance to breathe and enjoy the fruits that came from being Miss America. Finally, we had a special date, a getaway, and he got to see a snapshot of what I did as Miss America.

While on the road, I always wished I could share my Miss America experience with him, and this was my first chance to do that. He had never been to Washington before and here he was, my tall, handsome Samoan husband, traveling in style, meeting the most influential people in the free world. I was so happy to share this moment with him.

Tini and I stayed at the Capitol Hilton and were prepared for a day that would be one of the greatest highpoints for us as a married couple. At the State Arrival Ceremony honoring the Philippine President and her husband, we were guided to the VIP area of the South Lawn of the White House to view the ceremony.

I was tickled to meet famous boxer Brian "The Hawaiian Punch" Viloria, and his manager, Gary Gittelsohn. The four of us were peas in a pod throughout the day, and it was a proud moment for Brian and me, both Hawaiian-born Filipinos.

Key administration officials stood across from Tini and me on the lawn. I whispered to Tini, "There's Alma Powell. I met her at the Kennedy Center when she gave me an award." I saw her wave at someone in my direction, but didn't presume it was me, so I looked away quickly. I didn't want her to catch me staring. Then the heads of state and their spouses appeared on the lawn. A voice broke through, "THE PRESIDENT OF THE UNITED STATES OF AMERICA," and everyone stood at attention. The President and First Lady greeted the President of the Republic of the Philippines and her husband. Then the official parties were introduced from Vice President Dick Cheney and Mrs. Cheney to the Chairman of the Joint Chiefs of Staff Gen. Richard B. Myers and Mrs.

Myers, followed by the introduction of their official Philippine counterparts.

Tini and I noticed dozens of men positioned with rifles, ready to shoot if any threat were to occur. There was a sense of reverence, protocol, and traditions that had been followed here on these grounds for more than two hundred years, and I was deeply moved by all of it. All political views aside, I had tremendous respect for the offices that each president held as the heads of states for the two countries that my family consider home.

At the conclusion of the Arrival Ceremony, Tini and I made our way back to the hotel to have lunch, check out the museums, and do some sightseeing before our special evening.

As we prepped, Tini put on his tuxedo, and I slipped on an a glamorous, floor-sweeping Carmen Marc Valvo sequin halter gown with glistening bodice beading and an open-back design. It was a sponsored gift I received during a wardrobe fitting in New York, and this would be the first time I'd wear it. (The next morning, that dress would be mentioned in the *Washington Times* article next to a description of First Lady Laura Bush's Oscar de la Renta gown.)

Finally, Tini began to get nervous, "Do I look OK?" My man looked tall, dark, and handsome. "You look great," I said, and kissed him. I was giddy about our romantic night out with the Presidents! He must have sprayed his hair at least five more times because he wanted to look just perfect. He said, "I want to look dignified. We are going to meet the President . . . at the White House!" Seeing his unemotional side give way to an excited inner child, I laughed and told him, "This is the reaction I've been waiting for! Let's have fun tonight!"

~ Security Clearance ~

We drove up to the property, and we had to stop at about five different security checkpoints. This was after 9/11, so Washington was on guard, more than ever before. We finally got through all the gates and pulled up to the North Portico entrance, staring in utter amazement. The White House looked like a palace twinkling with lights, glittering on the horizon. Thinking of all the history that took place at this residence, I felt like we were in a Hollywood movie.

Each guest received a small envelope containing a name card with the guest's hand-lettered name. Mine read, *Ms. Angela Perez Baraquio* and the other *Mr. Tinifuloa Grey*. The name card we were given was to be handed to a White House official to publicly announce us at each entrance, once inside the foyer. In the envelope was a card with our table assignment.

Upon arrival at the East Wing of the White House, we were met by the press. Reporters from *The Washington Times*, *The Washington Post*, and

People asked Tini and me how we felt about being guests at the White House, and what we were looking forward to that evening. Then we walked through double doors into the East Room where finely dressed hosts took our handwritten calligraphy cards and announced our names. We felt like royalty as we made our red carpet entrance into the reception area. A socialite escorted us to a cocktail reception on the State Floor, where we were offered glasses of delicious champagne. Tini and I nudged each other. *We were really here. Together. How cool was this!?*

While mingling at the reception, our new friends, Brian and Gary, found us. We four stuck together most of the evening. The East Room was crowded with high-profile guests from all over the nation. The state dinner not only showcased America from a diplomatic viewpoint, but also brought together and put a spotlight on people in America that all have a part in the country.

Gary looked around in amazement and said, "I work with celebrities in Hollywood all the time, but these are the most powerful people in the world! My friends PORTRAY these folks!" He interrupted himself to say, "There's Justice Sandra Day O'Connor at two o'clock." We slyly turned our heads. We all couldn't believe we were rubbing shoulders with these elite, and we were having a blast!

Then I spotted *NBC Nightly News* anchor, Tom Brokaw. I walked over to him and introduced myself and everyone in the group. Next, we saw Donald Rumsfeld, and I walked over to say hello and thank him for his courage in saving all those lives at the Pentagon on 9/11. I introduced him to the gang. We moved throughout the room and caught sight of Dick Cheney. Brian went over to say hi first, and we joined him after. Conversation was lighthearted and amusing.

Soon, all the guests lined up in the East Room to enter the Blue Room. As each couple entered, their names were announced. There was one couple ahead of us, and I was just beaming. Here was our grand entrance: "Mr. Tinifuloa Grey and Ms. Angela Perez Baraquio." I walked in first and shook President Bush's hand. He was a gentleman and was very much at ease. He said it was nice to see me again and introduced me to the entire room as "one of the most beautiful women in the nation."

I can't express how amazing it felt to have the President acknowledge me like that to some of the most important people in the world. Tini looked proud of me. President Bush, his wife Laura, and President Arroyo recalled meeting me during my year of service, which surprised me. They must meet so many people daily. I introduced Tini to everyone as my husband before we took our official photo. It was a thrilling moment, to say the least.

After moving through the receiving line, we made our way into the State Dining Room. On the way there, I saw Alma Powell and decided to say hello. "Hi Mrs. Powell, I don't know if you remember me . . ." She stopped and smiled. "Angela! It's so nice to see you. I waved at you this morning, but you didn't see me. I was trying to get your attention." Tini and I laughed, and I told her we thought she was waving to someone else. I introduced Tini to her, and we exchanged more pleasantries.

Then we greeted her husband. I said, "General Powell, do you remember me?" He seemed delighted and remembered our very first meeting in Washington, when we took a photo together holding my Miss America crown, just days after winning. The first thing he said jokingly was, "You tried to put the crown on me!" We all shared a laugh. It was exciting for Tini to meet all these people for the first time and for me to see many of them again. Gary took our photos with each official, and we all hurried to find our seats, which were all at separate tables, even Tini's.

I gave my husband a kiss and walked toward my table. As he passed by, I overheard some ladies comment, "Did you see that young man? He's so handsome!" I felt so proud and giggled to myself thinking about all the hairspray he put on his hair at the hotel to look presentable. He was making a splash among the elite, and I was having the time of my life watching it all.

~ Musical Chairs ~

At state dinners, they seat spouses at different tables, even the President and First Lady, so that people have a chance to create new connections. Every effort is made to include one member of the President's staff who becomes the host of their table. The table hosts become familiar with the guests' names and each individual's background so that they can initiate interesting conversations for the group.

I was seated at the First Lady's table in the front near the fireplace, next to the podium with the gilded eagle where presidents propose their toasts. To my left was Mr. Leslie Wexner, CEO of Limited Brands and Susan Graham, the musical entertainer for the evening. To my right, John Degioia, president of Georgetown University; the First Lady Laura Bush; and Attorney Arroyo. Also at our table was Tom Brokaw, anchor of *NBC Nightly News* and Mitch Daniels, director of the Office of Management and Budget. The table next to us was hosted by President Bush who was seated beside the Philippine President.

During dessert and coffee, we were treated to a surprise. The Strolling Strings played "Some Enchanted Evening" and I thought it captured the essence of that night perfectly. I already missed Tini at Table Four near the back of the dining room. We made eye contact, blew flirty kisses and mouthed, "I love you" to each other from across the crowded room. A moment later, I saw Tom Brokaw do the exact same thing to his wife, who was seated across the room from us. It was very sweet.

~ Toasts ~

As dinner was winding down, the toasts began. President Bush toasted his guest from the gold eagle podium. He spoke about how our countries were connected by an ocean, united by a shared history, and sustained by bonds of family and culture. President Arroyo went on next and said that the bonds between U.S. and the Philippines run deep. She pointed out that our countries have stood side by side at every crucial point in modern history including WWII, the Cold War, Korea, Vietnam, and the war on terror.

While the two presidents spoke just feet away from me, my mind quickly raced back to Mama's stories of how grateful she and all Filipinos were when the American General Douglas MacArthur famously returned to liberate the Philippines from 1944 to 1945 from the Japanese occupation in Manila. Mama was five years old at the time and vividly remembers the impact that Americans made in her young life. After seeing her older sister die in the war in her mother's arms, American soldiers liberating the Philippines and throwing Milky Way chocolate bars to the children was etched into her memory. So much has changed since 1945.

~ After Dinner ~

The Cross Hall connects the State Dining Room with the East Room. As the crowd made their way through the hall toward the evening entertainment in the East Room, Tini and I met up outside the dining room where we swapped table stories.

Just then we realized we were walking right behind the President and Mrs. Bush! At every turn, it seemed like we were next to them in line. Cameras were everywhere, and we didn't want to seem like we were following them in every shot. We were laughing because we felt like Tom Hanks in *Forrest Gump* attending a historical event happening in real life!

All of a sudden, First Lady Laura Bush turned around, tapped me and said, "Angela, you know what we forgot to do?" she said wistfully. "We forgot to have everyone at our table sign our programs." I sighed regretfully, and we continued to move forward in the hallway. Apparently, there's a White House tradition that after dinner, guests take their menu card and each person at the table signs the back of it so you can remember exactly who was seated with you. It *was* too bad I didn't get everyone's autographs before they left!

Once we were inside the East Room where it was open seating, we could have sat near the President and First Lady. However, following protocol, it was expected that we'd only interact with them once during the entire evening. I had definitely exceeded my quota and wanted to give other people a chance to sit next to our esteemed party hosts.

We turned around and let people behind us go ahead of us. Tini and I moved to the opposite side of the room to steer clear from the cameras. Even with that, my friends in Hawai'i called me to say they saw me on *C-SPAN's* two-hour coverage of the day's events. For two twenty-seven-year-olds, Tini and I felt like we got more than on our fair share on that evening.

~ The Entertainers ~

Every administration is different. President Obama once asked Beyonce Knowles to perform at the White House. At this state dinner, however, President Bush and the First Lady invited Mezzo-Soprano Susan Graham to provide the evening entertainment. Susan sat at our table hosted by the First Lady. She was accompanied Brian Zeger, her piano player.

Entertainment was presented in the East Room where additional guests were invited after dinner. Tini and I felt honored to be VIP guests throughout the entire day at all the events. The highlights for me were Susan's renditions of Gershwin's "Someone to Watch Over Me" and "Summertime." She ended the set with "Bless This House," a beautiful tribute to the White House. Tini and I held hands as we listened, and I thought about all the history that took place in that room. If those walls could talk, I wondered what they'd say. I was reveling in the moment and I didn't want the night to end.

~ So This is Love ~

After the evening entertainment, President Bush thanked everyone and informed the guests that though his administration tends to go to bed early, those of us who wanted to dance could do so. He added, "We can strike up the band for you."

He and Mrs. Bush retired for the evening with the expectation that we would continue to enjoy ourselves. The Marine Band played in Entrance Hall, but we didn't see the presidents dance at all. As Gary, Brian, and I chatted, Gary asked Tini if he could dance with me since no one was on the dance floor. I was happy to oblige. Most people were mingling and having coffee.

Then Brian and I shared a dance, while Tini and Gary were looking at the famous portrait of JFK in the foyer. Tini wandered up a few steps to see where the Grand Staircase led. He didn't realize that it was the chief stairway connecting the State Floor and the Second Floor of the White House, the official home and private living quarters of the President of the

United States!

Just then, a Secret Service agent pounced. He told Tini with a straight face, "Sir, if you take one more step, I'll have to shoot you." He was just doing his job. My big Samoan husband sheepishly walked back down the stairs. We were cracking up about the mishap, unsure if the agent was joking or not. *Either way, it was hilarious!*

The remaining guests gathered around the Hall, and finally my husband asked me to dance. Tini and I were the only ones on the dance floor. I had to catch my breath as I gazed into the eyes of my tall, handsome date with girlish admiration. He took my hand and swept me off in a waltz. Soon, everyone noticed. I truly felt like Cinderella at the ball dancing with my Prince Charming. It was a dream moment come true. We relished the experience and were in no mood to leave.

Tini and I had such a strong romantic connection that night, and I was so proud to be his wife. He held my hand tightly as we danced and told me he loved me. He never realized the scope of my work as Miss America and thanked me for giving us this unbelievable opportunity. I thought about all we had been through as a couple.

Sometimes I felt like it was us against the world and my mind wandered back to the words of the Stevie Wonder song he sang to me at our proposal and wedding. *We can conquer the world, in love you and I . . .* Tini was right next to me through it all, and this evening was a gift that God gave both of us to enjoy together.

We didn't want the night to end, but it was already ten p.m.! After the party, our driver was waiting for us outside of the East Portico, where he dropped us off *before* we were transformed by the magical evening. Tini and I danced out of the grand foyer through the formal entrance of the White House as if we were on a cloud.

What we took away from this occasion was the symbolic value of the White House. The landmark stands for something bigger than the President's address; it stands for the home of the American people. That evening, it was *our* home.

CHAPTER 15

MAKING MY WAY

When we returned to Honolulu from Washington, it was as if Tini and I were thrown back from another dimension. Tini was taking a break from Architecture and exploring career opportunities in his true passion: Music. Meanwhile, he worked in the tourist industry at Kualoa Ranch and was out in nature every day, where he felt right at home. It was a welcome change from the stifling physical space he was in months before.

I found that when he was happy, so was I. He was having a good time, and his friends certainly didn't believe him when he said he had to take a few days off to attend a State Dinner at the White House! Over time, I would I encourage him to stop everything else, pursue his persistent dreams of writing and performing music, and never look back.

Life didn't slow down for me either. I was back on the road traveling to the east coast with my TC, Leilani, on a four-city tour. We had such a great time together and reminisced about when we were together at Walt Disney World and Atlantic City when I was Miss Hawai'i.

When we returned to Honolulu, I wasn't multitasking anywhere near as much as I did during my year, but I had become accustomed to an intense schedule.

My scholarship winnings paid off my bachelor's degree in Elementary Education and in August 2002, they funded my master's program in Educational Administration at the University of Hawai'i at Manoa. Becoming a school administrator would mean greater responsibility, but with it, the opportunity to shape policy *and* affect many lives. I needed formal training in effective leadership.

I was reminded why I went into teaching in the first place. It was not just a job or career—it was my vocation. I was passionate about making a difference in the lives of young people, but I didn't need to limit myself to four walls. As a national speaker and author, I found that the world became my classroom and I would *always* be a teacher, but more importantly, a lifelong learner.

While in the master's program some classmates recognized me from the newspapers and television. "Aren't you on TV?" and those in the industry would ask, "Aren't you a teacher?" Both questions in those instances made me feel as if I neither belonged here nor there. With so many competing labels stamped on me, and I had to reconcile all the different sides of me as a Catholic school teacher, TV host, Miss Hawai'i, Miss America, local girl, and grad student. The Miss America crown was a prestigious symbol, but the title alone didn't define me; winning the title was *just one* facet of me.

I also heard comments that I wasn't Filipino enough because I didn't speak the language fluently or reside in our mother country, or I was too Filipino for others. People assumed I must be half white because I won Miss America, and were surprised to learn about my Filipina, Spanish, and Chinese heritage.

Some comments were hurtful. The struggle to fit in continued. I felt out of place in my own home town. It was hard to explain to someone who had not walked in my shoes, but then again, no one *had* been in my shoes before.

I was navigating through my conflicting sides of me and quite possibly having an identity crisis. It was a confusing and lonely time. My friend and Miss America historian, Ric Ferentz, was a compassionate friend and sounding board for me. He helped me transition back to *normalcy* after my year—whatever that meant. As if my life could ever go back to being normal after all I'd been through.

One thing Ric did that *really* helped me was validate my feelings. I just needed someone to tell me it was OK to go through what I was experiencing. I tried sharing my thoughts with Tini and other friends, but they didn't really get it because they had never been through the pageant system or experienced what I had. It was *new* territory.

Ric told me that it takes at least ten years for past titleholders to process the whirlwind. Now that I've been there, I have to agree. I won almost fourteen years ago and I'm only now realizing what it's like to be outside the eye of the storm. It was not an easy thing to navigate through, but I had no choice.

Being around pageants most of his life, Ric knew how I felt and didn't try to solve my problems. He just listened. Talking with him was a turning point for me in my own healing process. It was just what I needed. Tini and I were grateful to Ric for helping me through that difficult time. His love and support were instrumental to me at that time. In 2011, my dear friend

Ric passed away. I will always remember his kindness, and he will be sorely missed.

My life as a "former" was just beginning. It was a title I would need to learn to live with for the rest of my life, for better or worse. While it was certainly an honor to have the title, it wasn't always easy to carry the torch of an American ideal.

One Miss America jokingly shared, "The funny thing is, no matter how old you get, even when you're a grandmother like me, people still call me *'Miss' America.* At this stage in my life, it's rather odd." Another one lightheartedly added, "Having the title of Miss America is like having gum on your shoe. No matter how hard you try, it sticks with you!" *That was funny!*

Phyllis George, Miss America of 1971, once told me, "We take our legacy very seriously. You could land on the moon, you could be President of the United States, or you could win an Academy Award, but people will always say 'former Miss America'. It's just so much a part of American culture, and we've survived wars, scandals, and we're still here." I was humbled to join the ranks of such distinguished women, but just as they realized in their own time, my new status would take some getting used to.

~ Living Local ~

In 2004, my sister, Berna, a former *FOX2 News* anchor, decided to start her own TV show. She was already well known in the community and established herself as a TV personality long before I ever came onto the scene as Miss Hawai'i. Berna had a show idea for wholesome family entertainment that would highlight the good news of Hawai'i hosted by her and her sisters. The "Baraquio" name was already recognized throughout the state, so Tess, Rose, and me—the three sisters who all played basketball, performed in High Tide, and attended college together—agreed to start our own TV show as the main hosts, writers, and producers.

The four of us had many ups and downs together in our formative years and we had a lot of issues to sort out. We had to learn how to respect one another not only as sisters, but as adults, colleagues, and business partners. Together, we decided to embark on this new venture, and our first episode of *Living Local with the Baraquios* premiered in April 2004 at the Hilton Hawaiian Village (where I was crowned Miss Hawai'i just four years earlier). We were slowly growing out of our childhood patterns as sisters and were moving into adulthood together.

I enjoyed working alongside my sisters. During my year, I did many television appearances, but none was more rewarding than the time I spent on set with my own family working and producing good family-friendly television together for our home state.

By 2014, our show celebrated a milestone: ten years of being on the air in Hawai'i! The show features the best our state has to offer in terms of people, places, food, and music. When I became Miss Hawai'i I said that no matter where I go, I am Hawai'i, and I learned that I can take aloha spirit that I grew up with and share it with the world.

Since 2004, our parents and every sibling had been featured on the show. I have been blessed to work alongside my sisters on something that has been a positive staple in Hawaiian television for a decade.

The segment I produced on our *Living Local* TV show was called "Angie's Album" where I interviewed celebrities and influential business and community members. One of the guests on *Living Local* was Jason Scott Lee, an actor from Hawai'i who played Bruce Lee, *Dragon: The Bruce Lee Story* and the young boy Mowgli in *The Jungle Book*.

One day Jason and I met up for lunch and a young Asian guy at valet got all excited to meet us, "Oh my gosh, Brandon Lee! Can I get a picture?" Jason responded calmly, "Brandon Lee died in an accident while filming 'The Crow.'" I added, "This is Jason Scott Lee." The valet gasped and apologized for the mistake. Then he turned to me and said in awe, "And you . . . Kelly Hu!" Jason replied, "This is Angela Baraquio, Miss America." The valet was just giddy to see people he thought he recognized, "I love you guys! Can I get a picture?" Jason and I were cracking up after we did our photo-op. To be mistaken for two big celebrities was not a bad thing.

Several years later I met up with Kelly Hu, actress and former Miss Teen USA 1985/Miss Hawai'i USA 1993, and over lunch we shared another good laugh about that incident.

~ Baby Carriage ~

Tini and I enjoyed two years of "couple time" before we got bit by the baby bug. We tried for seven months to get pregnant and finally, it happened. We were ecstatic!

Five months into my first pregnancy, I was asked to host an in-room video for the Four Seasons Resort Hulalalai on the Big Island. The client was looking to cast a male for my husband in the video, and they wanted someone with an international look and a pleasant speaking voice.

My sister Tess recommended my husband, Tini, to the casting agency, and when he went in to audition they gave him the role on the spot! Tini and I were elated to film for five days at this five-star resort. It was work, but definitely served as a second honeymoon. The producers hid my growing tummy as much as possible so the video would seem timeless.

I graduated with my master's degree in December 2004, two weeks before I gave birth to my first child, Isaiah, born that New Year's Eve. Seeing my baby for the first time brought an overflow of love into my heart. Isaiah was a physical manifestation of mine and Tini's love for one another. My gratitude for this precious life erased any animosity or anger I had toward anyone. It was healing to let go of all that negativity and feel complete and utter forgiveness toward anyone who had ever hurt me in my life. This child was pure love, and that's all my heart could feel.

We had waited for so long to have him—literally, I was in labor for forty hours! For my first child, I thought I'd have a natural pregnancy just as my mom did for all ten of her children, but that didn't happen.

Instead, because of complications, I gave birth by emergency C-section. Quickly I accepted this fact, as I was being wheeled into the operating room, shaking while signing papers on the operating table. It was a scary experience, and Tini held my hand the whole time, while his parents and family in California offered Masses, said rosaries, and lit candles for us.

To prevent future complications, my subsequent pregnancies were all destined to be scheduled C-sections. None of us in the family, however, could have ever fathomed the circumstances under which my second child would enter this world.

~ The Big Move ~

Being born and raised on O'ahu, I told Tini when we first met in high school that I would never leave or move to the mainland. I was determined to live and die in Hawai'i and there was no way around it. Tini's parents and siblings lived in Southern California, and we enjoyed visiting them and going to Disneyland at every opportunity! My sister Ceci lived close by in Orange County, and my younger brother Albert lived in Newport Beach. My younger sister Gloria had just graduated from college in California, so at least three siblings of mine were already living there.

I loved visiting the mainland, but knew that Hawai'i would always be my home. Then one day in March 2005, I told Tini I was ready for a big change. I was beginning to feel claustrophobic living on the island—that seemed so huge to me as a little girl—after having traveled to more than three hundred cities in America in one year.

On a familial level, I also felt like I reverted back to the same old patterns from my childhood like being left out, misunderstood, and feeling lonely. It was a stark difference from the confidence I felt as Miss America traveling around the country speaking passionately about character education in our nation's capital and meeting presidents.

Life in Honolulu felt stagnant and I needed to shake things up. I could easily rely on my parents or siblings if I needed anything, and I got a ton of perks from the TV show and from folks who recognized me as a former Miss Hawai'i or Miss America. But these weren't the things I wanted. I didn't want to raise my children to think that things came so easily. I was shifting, and I needed space to do it. I was ready to create a life of my own without dependence on my family or anyone else. It was scary, but necessary for my growth.

I finally told Tini we should move to California. We both were nearing thirty, and our son was fifteen months old. I told him that it would be a great place to raise our family, near his relatives and some of my siblings. We'd also be near more career opportunities for me in film and television.

He was shocked. In fact, he didn't take me seriously until I told him that we needed to start planning our move right away if we wanted to be in California this time the following year. But I showed him I meant business, and in March 2006, we arrived in Orange County with our son and a container full of our belongings.

While we continued to rent our home in Hawai'i, we bought a second home in Anaheim—the home of Disneyland! I knew in my heart God wanted me in California, but I wasn't sure why. We had enough savings to sustain us until Tini could find solid work in the real estate industry, and I could focus on my career as an entertainment personality and/or speaker. It was a new life, and the sky was the limit.

~ A New Life ~

In February 2006, a month before we left Hawai'i for the big move, I suspected that I might be pregnant with Baby Number Two. We landed in California and Tini had to travel right away to New York on a business trip. He was working as a musician with a production company in Hawai'i, and had booked the trip before we planned our move.

While he was away, I took a pregnancy test and it was positive! I called Tini to let him know that we were expecting. Of course he was happy, but also surprised. We both needed to change gears. We had a new house, a new life, and now a new baby on the way. That little plastic stick with the two lines on it changed everything. We knew we wanted to have at least two kids, two years apart, and although Baby was right on schedule, we weren't expecting the time to arrive so soon.

I learned once again that when I try to make plans and map out my life just as I want it, God intervenes. Jeremiah 29:11 reminds me of this truth, *For I know the plans I have for you,* declares the Lord, *plans to prosper you and not to harm you, plans to give you hope and a future.* Ultimately, His Will is better than ours. With my new baby Micah in utero, I focused on motherhood for a second time and my career plans to speak, travel, and be a TV host in L.A. would just have to wait.

At first it was hard being away from my family and closest friends in Hawai'i—everything I had ever known. Then finding out I was pregnant after I just left my home of thirty years made me even more homesick. I sat in our four-bedroom house on a cul-de-sac, wondering what to do next so I started unpacking and moving in.

Tini's parents were living with us at the time. They helped us in our transition to California by offering to help us take care of our fifteen-month-old, Isaiah. I was glad to have Tini's parents nearby as mother and father figures for me. Their presence eased my loneliness when I missed my family.

With all the stress and newness mounting, the shadows began to lurk again, and every so often, the thought of all my plans unraveling crept into my mind. Every morning for a month, I woke up and lay in bed wondering what I had just gotten myself into. *Did we make the right decision to move?* There were so many changes happening so fast, and suddenly, I felt out of control. I was out of my comfort zone, and I wondered if I was even in my right mind.

As much as I tried to keep them at bay, I had a resurgence of the depression and dark thoughts I had in 2002. I *never* thought of actually hurting myself physically, but I *did* have dreams of going to sleep and never waking up again.

The weight of all I had experienced in the past six years since winning Miss America was finally taking its toll on me. There were times I wanted to walk away from everything. I was exhausted and tired of worrying about how we would provide for our growing family with the sudden change of plans.

Then I wondered if I was doing *enough* with my life. After my incredible high as Miss America, and the big drop after 9/11, I never really had time to process what I had just been through. All the high expectations others and I had for myself crept in again. I wanted the anxiety and all the unrealistic expectations to stop. *I had hit rock bottom.*

After Isaiah's birth in 2004, I saw life with new eyes, but there was always a question lingering in the back of my mind, *Was God still there watching over me as He always had before?* Maybe it was the uncertainty of my career path, or perhaps it was my hormones acting up. I started to have doubts about my faith. This was unlike me and I couldn't understand it. Every day I felt like I was dangerously close to the edge. I had gone to a place I told myself I'd never go again. I prayed fervently to get out of my rut.

Up until the time we moved to California in 2006, I never really had a chance to be alone with my thoughts. Now it was quiet with no distractions. I was a new mother with a toddler, and had another infant on the way. I wasn't teaching anymore, I left my family and the TV show we built together back in Hawai'i, I had none of my closest friends surrounding me, and I wasn't exactly sure of my place in the world. All my plans for television hosting were put on hold indefinitely and that was hard to handle.

Even with all the resources I needed at my fingertips, I was beginning to allow myself not to care anymore.

That kind of thinking was unhealthy because I was pregnant with my second child and I knew that I had to be healthy and strong for him. Something had to pull me out of the depths of my own thoughts that were sinking me with each passing day. I didn't want to go back to that mental prison. I prayed harder than ever, asking God to take away any counterproductive thoughts. It was a time of redefining myself. I needed to use my time differently, and I felt the necessity to work again.

When I was in Hawai'i hosting *Living Local* I interviewed celebrities and influential business and community members who lived in the state. The late Al Masini was one of my featured guests. He was the creator and producer of many TV shows like *Entertainment Tonight, Lifestyles of the Rich and Famous,* and *Star Search.* Al was kind enough to introduce me to a hosting agent in Los Angeles, who signed me as talent. I was prepared to work hard and break into mainstream television.

I was hoping to find a hosting gig like Oprah Winfrey's, where I could have a TV show with wide reach and positive influence. I strove to find meaningful work that inspired people, especially women, and celebrated those who made a difference. But most of the auditions I went on were for gossip magazine type shows and home shopping channels. Not exactly what I was going for.

It was six years since I had won Miss America, and I knew pageant girls, in general, had certain stigmas and stereotypes attached to them. Some people made me feel like it was too late, that I should have struck while the iron was hot, right after my year, because timing is everything. The 9/11 tragedy and trauma prevented me from doing so and I wasn't about to defend why I decided to move home to Hawai'i after my year.

I immediately booked a gig in Cincinnati. It was a TV series called, *Facing Life Head On.* In it, I spoke about the value of life at all stages, and how important it was to defend the most vulnerable in society, specifically unborn babies. What I got out of that experience was that ultimately, when we fight for what we believe and face life with courage and faith, even when it feels unbearable, we embrace our crosses willingly, like Jesus did and there will be a reward. As devout Catholics, my parents always taught us to defend life and that was something I took very seriously.

I left that trip renewed and hopeful. Being away from the situation gave me clarity and I was more resolute about what I needed to do. Finding full-time TV work in L.A. would just have to wait. My babies meant everything to me. I resolved to face *my own life,* head on.

On the flight home, I thought about something my mom shared with me only a few years earlier, about when she gave birth to her fifth and sixth children, the twins, Tess and Berna. Her doctor asked her if she wanted permanent sterilization because she had so many kids already. Mama was slightly offended and responded that she and my Dad would accept any children God gave them. After changing doctors she eventually had Rose, then me, followed by Albert, and Gloria. She and my dad believed that all of us were miracles and have a purpose to serve no matter how long we are destined to be on this earth.

Before I moved to California in 2006, my eldest brother Jerome shared with me that he had run into my mom's former doctor in the story I just mentioned. She congratulated him and my parents for the accomplishment and he graciously thanked her. But later he told me, "You know what I thought? If Mama had listened to her, you wouldn't have been born and never would have become Miss America."

My pro-life work reminded me how important life was. It was good for me to be around other Catholics, because I was returning to my roots. I was reignited and slowly got back on track. I reconstructed my career plan: teaching, motivational speaking, and TV. That also meant networking and meeting people.

When I came back to California from filming in Ohio, my brother Albert took me out to eat for my birthday. I told him all about my travels over local Hawaiian barbecue. It was just the soul food we needed to catch up. He told me how happy he was that I moved to California and how we should hang out more often. I was so happy to have family close by. He was one of the reasons I moved to California.

I had been attending events in L.A. and decided to bring Albert with me. I introduced him to my friends who loved his sparkling personality. He was the life of the party and made me, the rambunctious sister, seem quiet in comparison. My female friends couldn't stop talking about him, and some people said he reminded them of the singer, Pharrell Williams. He was apparently mistaken for Kobe Bryant as well. Some of my friends nicknamed him "Hollywood" because when he walked into a room, he was like a superstar that got all the attention.

Things looked promising as I was active again, attending red carpet events and even an event for the Filipino American Library. There, I met many fellow Filipino successes like Gina Alexander, a former guest on *Living Local*, businessman/producer/director Ted Benito, apl.de.ap, the Filipino-American rapper/record producer from the Black Eyed Peas, singer/actress Tia Carrere, and Camile Velasco who represented Hawai'i on *American Idol*. It was nice to start meeting people within the Filipino community in L.A., and it helped take my mind off being homesick.

Meanwhile, the anticipation was growing for the arrival of my second child. As my pregnancy progressed, I became preoccupied with the baby's health rather than my own feelings of panic and anxiety. The meetings with my doctor were getting more frequent, and every time I saw an ultrasound of the miracle growing inside me, I forgot about myself. Every Sunday, we attended Mass as a family and meditated on what God wanted for our family.

Thankfully, the self-coaching mechanism I had always been able to count on, made an appearance again, and I started to think positively and became proactive about having a career backup plan. Instead of wallowing in what could have been, I began to creatively imagine different ways to move forward as a growing family.

With conscious prayer and positive thinking, I was in a better place, ready to welcome my new child into the world. I was more hopeful about life. After all, the weekly ultrasounds showed me how precious my child, and any child, really is and what miracle the gift of life can be.

Isaiah, our first child, arrived by emergency C-section, after forty hours of labor. He was born on New Year's Eve 2004, perfect and healthy. For safety reasons, we decided to schedule a C-section for the second child's birth for November 17, 2006.

~ Keeping It Real ~

Tini and I had a great summer before our family would become a party of four. Opportunities still arose: A Los Angeles producer casted me as one of the panel of coaches for the TV show *Pageant School: Becoming Miss America* scheduled to be aired on *VH-1* and *MTV*. In October 2006 I was honored to work alongside former Miss America Phyllis George and former Miss Louisiana, Erika Schwarz. After we wrapped the shoot, Erika called me to see if I wanted to attend Justin Timberlake's *Sexyback* CD release party a few days later. *Uh, totally!* Tini and I were stoked to be invited, and of course, we found a babysitter.

There I was, eight months pregnant and going clubbing. *Oh yeah!* So we pulled up to the very chic and cool warehouse in L.A. with a valet parking guests' cars. We showed up in our simple SUV followed by a Rolls Royce behind us. Nick Cannon stepped out of the shiny Rolls, followed by his Samoan bodyguard who Tini happened to know.

We were in a star-studded party of celebrities. When we arrived, we saw Hugh Hefner and the Girls Next Door. Then Tini said he saw Hillary Duff. I was going to say hi because Hillary and I were members on the President's Council together and I hadn't met her yet, but when I looked closely, it wasn't Hillary Duff, it was Lindsey Lohan! *Oh, Tini . . .*

As we excitedly walked inside, eager to share a not-so-typical date night together, the valet came running up to us and said, "Excuse me, Sir. Your car won't start." I thought he meant that he didn't have the key, so I told Tini to hand it to him, but the valet reiterated, "No, I *have* the key, but your *car* won't start. We'll have to jump it." I was mortified! Tini was so embarrassed, and apologized profusely to the man, but the valet said, "It's ok, we'll jump it for you. Go ahead and have fun inside." They were really gracious and tried to make us feel comfortable, even though they were pushing our car to the side of the road. *Unbelievable!* I was shaking my head, but soon we started cracking up and went in the party.

The interior resembled a Vegas nightclub where drinks, appetizers, music, and celebrities were everywhere. I was leaving the ladies' room as actress Krista Allen walked by. I was a huge fan of *Days of Our Lives* throughout college and I said to myself, *That's Billie from Days!* It was a trip seeing her in person.

Later that evening, Justin Timberlake arrived from his Jay Leno appearance, and my friend Erika introduced us to him and his girlfriend, Cameron Diaz. They were both really sweet. Justin congratulated us on our pregnancy. Later that night, we went home with our "celebrity swag bags" feeling like rock stars—except for the fact that we were worried that our little SUV might not make it home! *Oh well, back to reality!*

Everyone needs moments of humility. No one is exempt from embarrassing moments. Driving home, we definitely got back down to earth. Our heads were still in the clouds, but our feet were on the ground. And Tini made sure to change the car battery first thing in the morning. Every time we retell that story we say, "Hey man, we were just keepin' it real!"

~ Stand for Something or Fall for Anything ~

Whenever I feel as if the world is too vast to make a difference, I remember that in order to change the world, I need to change myself first. Growing up, I often found myself saying, *If you want something done, do it yourself.* I learned not to wait for anyone to make things happen. I can take baby steps and achieve great things. Some people watch things happen, others make things happen. I like to be the latter.

Gandhi said one of my favorite quotes, "Be the change you wish to see in the world." I try to live by that motto whenever I feel like complaining about what's wrong with the world. It takes great courage for anyone to take action to make social change. Part of being authentic is to be proud of who you are and what you stand for.

After my year, I became more involved in the political scene. As Miss America, I was encouraged to not take sides in order to be a representative of all people. However, I considered myself an Independent, and voted by conscience, not by party.

As I mature, so has my worldview and my ability to form values and opinions, contribute to society and my community, and to make a positive difference. My innate desire to promote a culture that affirms life is something that has become increasingly important to me over time.

In 2007, Tini's dad, Jerome Grey, a singing legend in Polynesia, was playing music at the Mai Tai Bar in Long Beach. He started slurring his words and suddenly, in the middle of his set, he collapsed. My brother-in-law J.T. was working there and immediately called 911. Dad was rushed to the hospital just in time. Miraculously, he survived his stroke. At first, he reverted back to speaking only Samoan, but through music, he was able to regain his speech in English as well. In 2008, he even recorded a new CD called, *Remember Samoa* with his sons Tini and Taumata to perpetuate the Samoan culture and pass on his legacy of music to his sons.

For the first time, Tini sensed his father's mortality and decided then and there to pursue music full-time. In tribute to his father, he decided to learn all he could from him and continue his legacy. Tini's dad is famous for writing the unofficial national anthem of their country, "We are Samoa." He has performed worldwide and is well-known all across Polynesia. Tini realized that it was his duty and his deepest desire to continue the family music legacy. I supported him wholeheartedly, just as he supported me for so many years.

Around this time, a pro-life activist with a movement called "I Am Whole Life," approached me to see if I might get involved. The mission is to promote the dignity of the human person from the moment of our beginning to our natural death, regardless of ability, age, status, ethnicity, or sex, which aligned with my Catholic values and upbringing. I began to do more speaking engagements and appearances in honor of this organization and their mission that every life is precious.

People sometimes ask me why am I Pro-Life? And I reply, "What's the alternative, Pro-Death? If that's the case, I am For Life." All any of us can do is speak our truth. Being a mother, a daughter, a sister, a wife, and a teacher, I see how miraculous and fragile life is at every stage.

I understand that there are extreme circumstances in which people feel the need to inflict harm to self or others. But I personally take the stance of non-violence, non-destruction, and proliferation of life. I feel that we can always find a way to honor life through faith, forgiveness, and temperance. But I don't judge anyone for the decisions they make; only God can. But this is my personal truth, and I feel the need to share it in a world that has become numb to violence and destruction and has favored personal desires over family and community.

Tini and I have lost two babies since we were married in 2002. Losing our children was devastating. Out of six pregnancies four babies made it, and two are in Heaven. Not a day goes by without us praying for them. We have named our little angels and know that we will see them again someday. Our faith tells us that, and we believe it. After all, you can't belong to something in which you don't believe.

From 2006 to 2008, I was appointed by President George W. Bush to be a part of the President's Council on Service and Civic Participation. Service was a component of character education, and I was glad to be a part of a council that was basically an extension of my platform. It was quite an honor to be contacted by the White House once again, this time to be a Presidential appointee. The Council brought together twenty-five high-profile leaders from business, entertainment, sports, education, government, nonprofits, and the media.

The President's Volunteer Service Award program was created as a way to thank and honor Americans, who inspired others to engage in volunteer service, by their demonstrated commitment. Recognizing and honoring volunteers sets a standard for service to others.

It encourages a sustained commitment to civic participation and inspires others to make volunteering a central part of their lives. Our mission was to increase the number of volunteers in America during our tenure and find ways to recognize the valuable contributions volunteers are making in our nation. I was proud to be able to be a part of something that recognized Americans for doing good in the community.

By 2008, the country was in a recession, but now that Tini was in the entertainment business, our company was thriving because people still needed to book parties and entertain their guests. In the meantime, I returned to my first love: teaching. Even though I taught full-time, I still traveled as a motivational speaker and went home periodically to be a guest host on *Living Local*. It was my first year returning to the classroom, and after seven years of traveling as a professional speaker, the transition back to Catholic education took some getting used to—after all I had been through as Miss America.

I was a first-grade teacher at a Catholic school in Anaheim. Barely two months into the school year, we found out that our school was in danger of being closed down, due to low student enrollment. The parents, faculty, and staff fought to keep it open, but after fifty-one years, the school closed down indefinitely in July 2009. It was a tough blow to all the stakeholders. Only a handful of teachers got placed in new schools. I was one of the few to be hired within a month by another Catholic school in Newport Beach. There, I taught third-grade for three years, before taking maternity leave, when I was pregnant with my fourth child.

In the meantime, I continued to travel as a speaker and was invited to Kansas to help raise money for Catholic schools there, so that all children who wanted a Catholic education could have access to it, regardless of their financial situation. This cause was very close to my heart because I know how hard my parents worked to give us a quality Catholic education, but also, in light of my school shutting down due to the economy, it was a way I could help in some small way.

In 2010, while my new school was out on vacation for spring break, I was invited to New York to be on the *Hannity* show. Just because I was a guest on Sean Hannity's Great American Panel, I got a phone message from someone who resorted to name-calling, not for anything I said, but *just* because I *appeared* on the show, which was the first time I had ever received any negative responses directly aimed toward me since I won Miss America. It was hurtful and disheartening, but as with any adversity, it made me stronger, confirming my stance on moral issues and the importance of speaking up about it.

Knowing that I can't please everybody, I continue to speak my truth in all things. Because if you don't stand for something, you'll fall for anything.

CHAPTER 16

MY AMAZING LOSS

The chronology of upcoming events in this chapter is twofold. On one hand, there was my perspective, and on the other hand, I discovered there was another reality going on simultaneously.

It was October 2006 when my whole family decided to meet in Southern California for a reunion celebrating two of our sisters' birthdays. My younger brother Albert joined us after quitting his cruise ship job at the last minute. He showed up on my sister Ceci's doorstep with all his belongings in a garbage bag. As happy as she was to see him, she was surprised at the news that he was moving in. We had a wonderful time at the reunion, and it felt like old times. All of us gathered around eating homemade food like Papa's sinigang and adobo and Mama's garlic fried rice and pancit. We challenged each other singing karaoke and played our favorite card game, Trumps. Those were the typical activities at Baraquio gatherings.

My parents flew back to Hawai'i, and later that weekend, my mom told me that Albert called her in Hawai'i, saying he was having girl problems and asking her to pray for him. She wanted to make sure that I talked to him about what was going on. I thought that was strange. It was unlike Albert to call Ma out of the blue. On top of that, he asked her to send him a rosary. I reassured Ma I'd make it a point to call him that week.

Other siblings called me, telling me Albert was having a hard time. They seemed so worried about him, and I thought, *Why is everyone so worried? He's fine. It's just a tough time in his life. If I know Albert, there's nothing wrong. Just relax everyone, and give him some space. Albert has always been resilient, he'll bounce back.*

209

~ Circle of Life ~

November 2006 rolled around as I waited for my second child to arrive. We had already decided to name him Micah. My due date was November 26. Since I had complications with my first birth, doctors highly suggested another C-section with my second. We decided to schedule it for November 17. I also knew we had to plan a birthday gathering for Albert on November 15. He was turning twenty-eight years old, and birthdays are always a big deal for us to celebrate life.

On November 9, I called Albert like I said I would, and asked him what was going on. We had a good heart-to-heart, and he told me that he was having girl problems and was questioning life. I sensed he was down, so I invited him to stay over at my house on Saturday and come to Mass with our family on Sunday. I told him we also needed to plan something for his birthday on the fifteenth, so whatever he wanted to do, we'd do it. I had suggested Shabu Shabu restaurant, and he was fine with it.

~ Saturday, November 11, 2006 ~

That Saturday, November 11, I had not heard from Albert all day and it was getting close to five p.m. I called him asking where he was and he answered, "Oh yeah, sorry Ang, I'm really busy. I got some business to take care of. I'll talk to you later. I love you. Bye." He sounded tired and preoccupied. I was so upset at my little brother, but it was typical of him. He frequently made plans and then flaked if something else came up.

I didn't have time for his games. I wanted to be a good big sister and have a nice weekend bonding together, and he totally blew me off. Tini was gone that weekend at a conference an hour away. Because I was six days from delivery, his sister Ana stayed with me in case my water broke.

That night, around ten p.m., I got a call from Albert's landlord. When she called the house, I assumed it was for Ana, since they were close family friends. I immediately passed the phone to Ana when I saw his landlord's name on caller ID. Ana took the phone to the other room. When Ana emerged, she told me that our family friend needed her help with something. I thought it was rather late for her to be going out, but she said she needed to go and she'd be fine. So Ana left and Tini's brother Taumata came over to take her place in case I needed anything.

The rest of the night was uneventful. I had no contractions, and I was thankful that Micah decided to wait for his daddy to come home the next day. I called my brother Albert on Monday, November 13 and asked him what he wanted to do for his birthday. He told me I should talk to Ceci and handed over the phone to her. Ceci got on the phone and told me that my two brothers John and Jerome were coming into town for Albert's birthday on November 15. I was so excited my brothers could be here for Micah's birth as well! Ceci told me they were only coming for a day or so, and then the brothers had to go back home for work. I figured I'd persuade them to stay at least one more day. After all, my surgery was scheduled for November 17. What was one more day?

~ Wednesday, November 15, 2006 ~

On the evening of November 15, we all met at Shabu Shabu restaurant on Albert's birthday, and everyone seemed grim. The ambience was quieter than usual, and I said sarcastically, "What's wrong with everyone? Nice party . . ." It was abnormally silent. We ordered food, and I asked, "Who has a card for Albert?" No one had one. "Ok, I guess I'll go first then." So I read my traditional birthday card to Albert because no one else brought a card for him. Or presents. That was odd. I pulled Albert aside and asked if he was ok. He told me he was thinking of moving back home to Hawai'i, but he wasn't sure.

For his birthday, my brothers bought him a ticket home so he could spend some time with the family. I read him my card, telling him how much I loved him and that he was not alone. God was always with him, and we would always be here for him, too. I also gave him a bag full of spiritual books, the ones that helped me through *my* roughest times. I told him to be sure to read those books on the plane home to Hawai'i. He promised he would. Then he thanked and hugged me. I thought, *See, Albert's fine.*

After dinner, Albert and his girlfriend rode with me to Ceci's for birthday cake. He sat in the front with me, and we reminisced about all our hilarious moments together as siblings. We laughed so hard that we were both in tears! Remembering how he used to scare me in the stairwell and how we played all those pranks on each other, we also quoted old movies, sang songs, and relived childhood memories till we could barely breathe. By the time we regained our composure, we had arrived at Ceci's house, where the family karaoke competition was already underway.

Once inside, and still giddy from our car ride, Albert rubbed my big belly, kissed it, and said how happy he was that I was bringing a baby into the world. I told him the baby's name was Micah. He asked, "Angie, how do you do it? How do you stay in the public eye and still have such a strong faith in God?" I told him it wasn't easy, but it was a conscious decision I had to work on every day. I said I wasn't perfect, but our goal should be to be perfect like Jesus was even if it's humanly unattainable. Perfection is still something to strive toward. He told me that his girlfriend was in a depressed state, and he was trying to save her. He said, "Maybe I can be her angel," and added that he felt like he was going through a mid-life crisis. I told him to pray for things to get better because everything is temporary.

Meanwhile, the other brothers were relentlessly nagging us, trying to interrupt our conversation. John yelled, "Hey! What's going on over there? Hurry up!" They wanted us to sing—now. So we obliged, thumbed through the karaoke song book, and the first duet we could find was "Tonight I Celebrate My Love for You." As the song progressed, we tried to stifle our giggles when we realized the lyrics were certainly not meant for a brother-sister duo. Our older brothers had a field day teasing us and trying to throw us off. But we held our competitive composure for a bit.

By the time we were harmonizing on the chorus, we fell apart and our score plummeted. Through laughter, the brothers mocked and teased us so we would fail miserably. Eventually, we couldn't finish the song because we were cracking up so hard. I hadn't laughed that much in years! I was so happy. Being around family was just what I needed. I had been alone in my own head for so long that I forgot what was important.

Later that night, I asked Albert to be the godfather of Micah. Albert's mouth dropped, and he said, "Angie, I don't know what to say. That's such an honor. Thank you. Yes!" and he hugged me. I said, "When will you be back?" Albert said, "In about two weeks." "Perfect, I'll plan the baptism for then."

My sister Ceci told me she had to bring Albert to his house to get his clothes for his big trip back to Hawai'i with the brothers on November 16. He was sleeping over her house that night. I said, "Wait a minute, you are all going back to Hawai'i tomorrow? I give birth in two days, just postpone your flight for *one day* so you can at least meet your nephew." My brothers were insistent. They had to be home the next day. I was so upset and confused as to why they would come for such a short trip.

Before they left, John said, "Angie, try to come home for Christmas. You never know if it's the last time we'll all be together." I hugged him and said, "No, I won't be home for a while. I'll be here recovering from surgery. I really wish you guys could stay." They apologized, and I left the house in a salty mood. I was being a brat, but it was always hard to say goodbye.

~ Friday, November 17, 2006 ~

The day of my scheduled C-section on November 17, I got up at 4:45 a.m. and went to the shower, when suddenly, my water broke! The timing was perfect. Micah was meant to come that day. I got excited to meet my bundle of joy in just a few, short hours. I told Tini it was go-time and we were already packed to go, right on schedule. Everything went exactly as planned. Micah was born at 8:03 a.m. I spent the day nursing him and changing diapers. I was in Heaven, loving my flawless, brand new miracle. Now that my baby was here, my mind had no room for negative thoughts. I thanked God for Micah and for the grace of being in a better place.

~ Saturday, November 18, 2006 ~

The first twenty-four hours after Micah's birth flew by. On November 18, family and friends visited, and I was in good spirits. When they left, the nurse took Micah for a bit, and I was alone with Tini in the hospital room.

Tini sat down next to me and said, "Honey, I have to talk to you about something." He looked very serious. I thought, *He's going to tell me what a miracle this is and how much he loves me, etc.* I was ready to take it all in.

He said, "It's about Albert."

"What?" I thought, *This is weird. SO not what I was expecting.*

He continued, "Albert tried to take his own life."

"WHAT!" I got angry, "What are you talking about? Why would you say that? When? You're lying."

Tini went on, "Last Saturday, November 11. We didn't want to tell you because of the safety of you and Baby." My mind raced back to the late phone call that night from Albert's landlord when Ana left abruptly.

I held my newly sewn stitches and tried to keep it together. I went into complete shock, heaving, and could barely breathe. "He's still alive. He went home with your brothers. He's OK now." Tini said calmly.

Crying uncontrollably, I thought, *This isn't happening.* My worst nightmare was coming true. And it wasn't happening to me, but to my little brother. I felt helpless being far away from him. I wanted to call him, *talk* to him. Events from the past week were reeling in my head, trying to piece it all together. *What happened when? Who knew what, and how could they all keep this from me? Tini, Ana, Taumata, Ceci, John, Jerome . . . Albert!* So many emotions flooded me: rage, sorrow, betrayal, gratitude, shock. Just then, Micah was brought back into my room, and it was time for him to nurse again. I fed him every hour-and-a-half through tears, as I continued to sob relentlessly in distress and confusion.

~ Monday, November 20, 2006 ~

On November 20, I was in my hospital bed, and the news came on. There was a report on suicide rates, and it said that the highest rate of suicide happens in males in their late twenties. Albert was twenty-eight. I still couldn't wrap my head around what just happened. I wanted to call my brother, but I wasn't ready to deal with it.

~ Back to November 11, 2006 ~

I found out later that my brother-in-law Mike found Albert in his car unconscious on 11/11, and they rushed him to the hospital with just enough time. Any longer, he probably would not have survived. A friend of

213

mine told me that the time 11:11 is the hour of the angels. Albert had planned to die that day, but God had other plans. Before he was brought back to consciousness that night in the hospital, doctors and nurses said it was slim chance that he would make it, let alone be healthy. He was in a coma, and doctors said that if he came out, he might be a vegetable.

When my sister Ceci was in the hospital with Albert on November 11, he was completely unconscious. When Ceci prodded him with two fingers at his chest, he instantly sat up with eyes wide open. Ceci said, "Albert! What happened?" Albert said, "Where am I?" "Where do you think you're supposed to be?" "With God in Heaven." He proceeded to tell her that he was going toward a light, when all of a sudden, he started rolling back down this tube and he was back on earth. Ceci believes that despite *Albert's* will, he was brought back to our family, by the grace of God. She believes we all have an ordained time to leave this earth, and it wasn't his time to go.

Later, my brother-in-law Mike said about finding Albert, "There were many angels present that day, with one of them apparently getting inside my head."

~ Back to November 20, 2006 ~

On November 20, Albert called from Hawai'i and left me a message on my cell phone apologizing for what he did. I called him back and asked him if he was really sorry, if he really wanted to die. He said he did, but couldn't explain it. What could be so bad that he could go to those lengths to think about taking his life? Then I remembered my own bouts with depression and stopped myself in my tracks. Who was I to judge? I realized it's not beyond any of us to think such dark thoughts. I was there once, at the tipping point, but the trick is not to go there at all.

My brother John, in Hawai'i, was fielding Albert's calls and making sure that he had someone with him at all times. Albert stayed in John's house, with John, his wife, and two young children under age six. Albert told me he felt embarrassed and like a prisoner, with everyone watching over him. He wanted to come back to Orange County so that he didn't have to explain anything to anyone. "Angie, everyone I know has heard about what I did. I don't want to be here." I didn't know what to tell him anymore. The charade was over for him, too. Before, when he knew I didn't know about his attempt, he was fine around me, but awkward and ashamed with everyone else. And others treated him differently, too.

~ Thanksgiving ~
Thursday, November 23, 2006

Albert wrote journals on his computer every day. He started going to group therapy sessions in the islands and was seeing a doctor in Hawai'i. They all said he was fine. Others in the group talked about their horrible childhoods, and Albert only spoke highly of his family and his upbringing. The medical staff was confused as to why he was there. He seemed so well-adjusted.

I was still in California trying to make sense of what had just happened. I felt disoriented, not quite sure where I was. My day-to-day routine included changing diapers, nursing Micah, and recovering from surgery. That in itself was a lot to deal with, but to have to process everything that Albert was going through was too much. Seeing him on his birthday when he didn't even want to be there, attempting to take his own life; trying to figure out what pushed him so far over the edge . . . I needed to focus on the tasks at hand: the needs of my newborn and my two-year old.

Meanwhile, my family was celebrating Thanksgiving in Hawai'i. Ma and Pa had bought Albert a workout bench and he vowed to get healthier. One day his spirits were up, then they'd be back down again. Upon my dad's request, Albert sang "He Ain't Heavy, He's My Brother," on the karaoke mic that night, just he had done many times before when he was in elementary school, prior to his voice changing.

It was hard to see my brother slipping away from us mentally. He didn't want to eat, he was already so thin, and losing weight every day. Nothing interested him anymore. I prayed that Albert would get better and get past whatever he was going through in his mind. I had to *let go, and let God* take over.

My baby boys needed me now more than ever, and I was busy being a mother of two. That Thanksgiving, I gave thanks for my entire family and the gift of life.

~ Wednesday, November 29, 2006 ~

A week passed by, and Micah was eleven days old. On the morning of November 29, 2006, we got a phone call from my sister Ceci.

Healing from my surgery, I was sleeping on the ground in the kids' room, feeding my baby. The phone rang in the living room, and I heard Tini get up from our room to answer it. I heard him talking and then hang up. He walked into the kids' room.

I asked him, "Who was it?"

"Ceci."

"What?" No reply. "What?!" I was upset now.

Tini paused and looked down. He took a deep breath and said, "Albert did it."

"When?"

"Last night," Tini replied.

At first I was numb, then I became furious. My immediate reaction was, "SO SELFISH!"

I was seething, and then I broke into tears. We knew it was a possibility, but now it was a reality. I could not believe my ears. NO, my brother was not dead. *NO. NO. NO! It can't be! It's not true.*

Words cannot even *begin* to express the emotions I felt all at once—anger, helplessness, sadness, torment, sympathy, loss, frustration, regret. This was the first death in our immediate family, and Albert was the youngest boy, *my baby brother!* I thought, *This was not a natural death, this is not what God wanted.* He had gone where none of us ever dared to go. Tini just held me as I sunk into his chest. I heaved and tried to gasp for air.

~ Back to Tuesday, November 28, 2006 ~

On the evening of November 28, 2006 the police found Albert lying in the dark on a patch of grass outside a Honolulu credit union. He had taken the bus there to die, and he was carrying the Sacred Heart prayer books and the card I had given him on his birthday in his backpack. My brother, Albert—we were so close, and now he was gone. The party boy with the goofy laugh, the charming grin, and the dark side he never revealed until his last days, had crossed over.

I couldn't believe my little brother actually did that to himself. The scary thing was that I myself had those *fleeting* thoughts, but my first instinct as a human was self-preservation. I never got to the point where I deliberately planned to hurt myself or end my life. I had to wrap my head around this.

Suddenly, I wondered if I ever really knew my brother. All night I tossed and turned. His decision was so permanent. Albert was dead. I would never see him again, never feel his hugs, hear his laugh, grow old together with him, have him see my kids grow up, see him on birthdays. I had grand thoughts of sharing holidays and going on trips together, and now I would never be able to just call him to say hi. In fact, even after his death, I couldn't bring myself to erase his number from my phone for years. All those hopes and dreams were shattered the day he died.

~ Wednesday, November 29, 2006 ~

The day I found out about his passing, I saw something I had never seen before nor ever saw again, while living in our house. There were about thirty black crows walking around on the ground in our cul-de-sac. I quickly remembered my Angel Inspirations book saying that birds are messengers from Heaven. *If you see birds, they may be trying to tell you something.* Just like the night I had seen the three white birds hovering outside my window before I won Swimsuit in Atlantic City, I wondered if this was a horrible message about Albert's torment and consequences for his actions. I was stricken with doubt and fear.

The shocking loss of our beloved Albert shook our family to the core. His death tested our faith and family bond. Up to that point, my life seemed to have all the makings of a fairy tale. The plot not only twisted unexpectedly but took a turn for the worst. I stayed up all night in my living room lying on my couch with Micah on my chest, crying and asking aloud, "Where are you, Albert? Why did you do this?"

I started to examine my own faith and questioned my beliefs I had professed all those years in Catholic school. The hurt, the questions about the afterlife, consequences of his actions, the taboo it put on our family and all the generations to come, the guilt that accompanied the questions. Is there anything I could have done to have saved him or prevented this? Why didn't I see the signs? I was frustrated about not being able to say goodbye knowing his condition. He said he'd be back in two weeks for Micah's baptism. The world stopped for me, and I resented the fact that life appeared to go on as usual for everyone else. Even in my anger, I could not stop crying for days on end.

I could not have gotten through Albert's death without Tini and the kids. My baby Micah loved me unconditionally, and my husband showed a compassion and understanding beyond anything I could have hoped for from a partner. He was my stronghold. My little two-year-old Isaiah would say, "Mama, you ok? Why you crying?" and he'd hug me and try to comfort me.

One day Ceci came over to the house to check on me and see how I was healing from my delivery. My stitches were coming apart at the seams because of all the crying I was doing, also an indication of how my life was unfolding. She and Tini asked me if I planned to go to Albert's funeral in Hawai'i. I thought, *Why should I leave everything to go? He had no problem leaving us and we were supposed to celebrate a life he didn't want to live?*

Initially, I had a lot of anger to work through. Of course, much of it was a reflection of my own feelings that I dealt with just a few months prior. I told Ceci and Tini every excuse in the book and was adamant about staying put in California. The truth was, I didn't know how I would deal with the reality of seeing my brother's limp body, and I wasn't ready to face the finality of his decision and how it would affect my family and the generations to come.

On December 1, at my two-week postpartum appointment, I met with my doctor and told her about my brother. She told me I should definitely go to the funeral. With her clearance to travel, my excuses were running out. So after hours of contemplation, I booked our tickets and confirmed with the family that I would be there for the funeral. But I wasn't going happily.

I had told my sister Berna that I was so upset at him for doing a selfish act and not thinking about us. She said, "Angie, he was in so much pain. He was a tormented soul. How could he think about *our* feelings when he couldn't understand his own?" I had no intention of seeing his side of things at the time. It was hard to admit that Albert's pain mirrored my own.

Berna described what the family was experiencing back home. The medical examiner called Ma and Pa to identify his body and the rest of the family in Hawai'i met them there. When they got to the mortuary and viewed Albert's dead body for the first time as a family, it wasn't Mama but Papa who was in denial.

At first, he said it wasn't Albert lying there, but when the family assured him that it was, he kept saying that his son was only sleeping. With faith and a wavering voice, Papa commanded, "Albert, get up! Jesus raised Lazarus from the dead. Get up, Albert!" When Albert did not move, Papa prayed as he had done so many times before, but this time more fervently, "Eternal God, in whom mercy is endless and the treasury of compassion— inexhaustible, look kindly upon us and increase Your Mercy in us, that in difficult moments we might not despair nor become despondent, but with great confidence submit ourselves to Your Holy Will, which is Love and Mercy itself."

My sisters began weeping profusely at the sight of our parents crying at the feet of their youngest boy. No parent should ever have to outlive their child. My mother, typically the more outspoken one, didn't say anything except prayers for his soul. With every litany she could muster up from her arsenal, the countless words all jumbled together in a desperate and incomprehensible manner. And she didn't stop praying. I cried on the other side of the phone, just listening.

Berna continued to share how the family went to dinner together and caravanned to St. Theresa Church to light candles and be on constant vigil, saying novenas and praying for Albert's soul. My heart broke listening to the rippling effects of Albert's decision.

Albert left final thoughts in letters and journals on his laptop clearly stating that there was nothing we could have done to save him. Mama's thoughts on this subject helped me to cope as his sister. She was his mother who loved and raised him. These are her words as she prayed to God:

"You had given him to us, now please take good care of him. Every day as we pray for him we ask, 'God please help Albert and help him help us.' We have to live and take care of what is now. We have to do whatever is needed right now. We think we have no time because we have so much to do. We offer it all to you."

On December 7, Tini, Isaiah, Micah and I arrived in Honolulu. The whole family met with a therapist, who was also a Catholic priest. He told us that Albert was safe now, and that we had to focus on taking care of ourselves because we were still here in the land of the living.

On this dark day, we stayed at my sister Berna's house in Nu'uanu. Nu'uanu is said to have many ancient Hawaiian spirits lingering in the area. Micah and Isaiah were crying all night, and Micah's umbilical cord fell out, bleeding. All the toys in the room were going off by themselves. The wind was howling, and there were strange noises all night. It was unsettling, and none of us would sleep. Tini sat up and held my hand while we placed our other hands on the children and led us in The Lord's Prayer. Midway through our prayer, everything silenced. When calm settled in, we retired to bed.

The funeral in Hawai'i on December 8 was on the Feast of the Immaculate Conception. It turned out to be a beautiful tribute to Albert. Hundreds of loved ones from our past and present came to pay their respects. The outpouring of everyone's love and support lifted our broken spirits while a ray of sunlight coming through a window lit up a picture of Albert's big smiling face on the poster near his coffin—the way I'll always remember him.

To celebrate his life, the family arrived in all white clothing at St. Philomena's Church, the parish where Albert served as an altar boy, and where we sang in the choir as kids. At the service, my sister Lucy played the piano like old times, and as people entered, our family sang worship songs as we had so many times before. This time, we were all choked up and helped finish each other's verses while physically holding each other up during the songs. I have never seen my big brother John so somber, wearing dark shades as he played guitar. When the service began, Tini sang for the family because we all knew we could not. I was thankful that my husband was my rock, once again.

Later at the burial grounds, we watched them lower his casket and cover up the grave with dirt. Five white birds flew over his grave and landed right on top of the place where Albert lay. His casket was decorated with images of the Pieta (Mother Mary carrying Jesus' body after he was crucified), and when we laid Albert to his final rest, we had the feeling he would also be in the comforting arms of Our Blessed Mother's eternal embrace. I had to also envision that reassurance for myself in times of deep sadness over Albert.

After lunch, the sisters got together for coffee to commiserate. We bonded while sharing stories of our childhood and laughed at fond memories and happy times. We talked about how we missed Albert and how hard it would be to go on. Even though I resisted the trip, I was glad I came. I told them one song came to my mind as I sat there with them.

It was Gloria Estefan's song, "Always Tomorrow." The sisters all sang with me and we were swaying to the music, holding each other, half-crying, half-smiling. *I've been alone inside my head for far too long. Never really wanted it that way, but I let it happen. If I could do it all again my life would be infinitely better than before. I wouldn't waste a moment. Make time for laughing with my friends. Make love, make music, make amends. Try to make a difference, try to love, try to understand. Instead of just giving up I'd use the power at my command. 'Cause there's always tomorrow to start over again.* I was singing that for Albert *and* me.

I thought how much I love my family. Albert was gone, but we were still alive. I had gone through extreme highs and lows in one month's time: Albert's twenty-eighth birthday, Micah's birth, Thanksgiving, Albert's death, Micah's baptism, Albert's funeral, Christmas, Isaiah's second birthday, New Year's Day. And just a few weeks later, Tini's dad would suffer from a stroke. Mine and Tini's faith would continue to be tested like never before. We had no idea what God had in store for us next. We could only live in the present and be grateful for each moment.

Today, I try to cherish every moment, be present in all I am doing. In my life, I have seen multiple births and deaths, but each one has forever imprinted a trace of their souls on my heart. I hope you stay open to God's Will for your life and no matter how difficult things are: have faith that it always works out somehow. You are exactly where you need to be right now.

It's hard to think about the depth of pain Albert was going through on the two nights he tried to take his life. I have to believe that God is a merciful God and that He loves us unconditionally. My anguished brother had a rosary and holy objects in his possessions both times as if he were a warrior going to spiritual battle and asking for protection from the demons that he said were trying to overcome him. In the notes he left behind, he wrote, "The devil is trying to take me. God forgive me for this sin I am about to commit." Those words still give me chills.

After Albert's death I learned that not all, but most people, are walking that delicate line between sanity and insanity. I will say that I now have compassion for those who have so much as flirted with the notion of ending their life. With constant prayer and awareness, we can all stay on the healthy side. If you are having suicidal thoughts or are close to the edge, or maybe someone you know is showing signs of apathy and listlessness, please get help or at the very least, enlist in a spiritual director's guidance. I am sending you immense love and am praying for you right now.

~ From Doubt to Faith ~

After my brother died, I had so many questions. I wondered, *Where was his soul? Is anyone there helping or meeting him on the other side?* I felt responsible in some way, and still felt helpless. Then I asked myself, *Do I really believe in what I say I believe?* To those who have experienced a crisis of faith, I've been there. And now, I am certain that God is real. He is merciful and compassionate. Love exists, and love conquers all.

In regards to death by suicide, the Vatican states, "We should not despair of the eternal salvation of persons who have taken their own lives. By ways known to him alone, God can provide the opportunity for salutary repentance. The Church prays for persons who have taken their own lives. Grave psychological disturbances, anguish, or grave fear of hardship, suffering, or torture can diminish the responsibility of the one committing suicide." So while I believe suicide is not what God intends for any of us, I surrender to the fact that in Albert's mental suffering, God will have mercy on his soul.

I also believe in Jesus' promise of eternal life for all who believe in Him. John 11:25 quotes Jesus, *I am the resurrection, and the life: he that believeth in me, though he were dead, yet shall he live.* I believe with our prayers, we will see Albert again in the afterlife.

The ordeal and shocking heartbreak of losing Albert eventually strengthened our faith. We drew on our beliefs from childhood and our experience solidified what we were taught. As my sister Ceci put it, "It was possibly the best scenario that could have happened in the worst situation." So from initial doubt, came great faith. My whole family had to practice the art of "losing with grace." And this was my biggest loss, especially being played out in the public eye.

~ Healing ~

I realize now that when I was secretly in that deep dark hole in 2006, Albert was going through *his own* mental anguish at the same time, also in secrecy. Since his passing, I have given him hugs in my dreams, in my mind. Albert tells me, "Angie, you're not me. You can do what I could never do. You need to be strong because you are continuing what I wasn't able to do." My work with the pro-life movement and bringing issues to the forefront about mental health is mainly driven by my experience with Albert and my hope is that this story, as hard as it is to relive all over again, will somehow positively change lives and save a few along the way. It's why I wrote the song, "Living For You."

Albert's dying changed me forever. In 2006 I had hit rock bottom emotionally and spiritually. Feeling completely depressed, I struggled with anxiety and even daydreamed about going to sleep and never waking up. Then with the baby, a new life growing in me, I realized it was no way to think. I made a decision to end those self-defeating thoughts. But truly, it wasn't until my brother took his own life that I became resolute to stop thinking that way and start finding God's purpose for me in this life. I realized the true sanctity of my existence, and saw the precious, miraculous, and fragile gift that our time on earth is.

I decided to stop *enduring* life and start *living* it to the fullest.

Tini and his brother, Taumata co-wrote the song with me. I penned the lyrics to "Living For You" because I wanted to live the life that my brother wasn't able to, a life that I was afraid to embrace, until he died. The process was cathartic, and the jolt I needed to rise above my own feelings of loss. The song begins with, *The memory's so clear of your last days here. I wanna hear your voice, wanna touch your face, I wanna see you breathe. It's hard to say goodbye.*

There was a lot of doubt that accompanied the initial loss. The chorus rings in my head, *I miss you so, I should let go. You're looking down, wish I could see you again. I need to know there's something after this life. This is not the end, Oh I'll be living for you for the rest of my life.* Simple words to encapsulate a lot of hidden meaning. That doubt eventually led me to a stronger faith.

There had always been music between us whether it was at church, during car rides, while trying hard to ignore each other at a dance club, or belting out karaoke, side by side laughing. I always felt that he was sending me messages through songs, packed with shared meaning and memories.

One of his favorites was Coldplay's "Speed of Sound." He also was a fan of Sugar Ray. The last day we spent at Downtown Disney together the song playing overhead was Sugar Ray's "Someday." After he died, I'd turn on the radio when I thought of him and I'd hear these songs as if he were reaching out to me from beyond. Once I even turned on the radio and serendipitously heard the entire version of The Hollies' "He Ain't Heavy, He's My Brother" and The Krush's "Waialua Sky." I could feel his presence as if he were physically right next to me. Music and my faith have helped me through the toughest times.

Weeks after the funeral, my older brother John was the one, in the midst of all our grief, who called the family together for a meeting. He was entrusted with Albert in his last days and while he did his best to keep him alive, Albert exercised his own free will. John felt that it was imperative that we all did something in tribute to our brother.

Since we had always had music in our lives, he suggested that we record a family album not just to aid in our own healing, but in the healing of others who had lost loved ones in the same manner. In order to recover from our loss, he said we needed to help others.

I thought, *My brother John is so different now. He's all grown up, so full of love.* The relationship between my John and me has changed drastically since we bht5432qdswere kids, especially since Albert's death. He is much more loving toward everyone, including me. It's a welcome change. When Albert was alive, he told us to love each other and stop fighting. Our family has gotten so much closer since Albert's passing. When we listen to that simple but profound advice we see huge shifts in the way we as a family treat each other.

~ Lost + Found ~

With each year, the month of November marks another year of my beautiful son's gift of life, and another year of my little brother's untimely passing. That month we witnessed a life for a life. One entered the world, and one exited. That month reminds us that life is precious at *all* stages.

Another track on the album was written by my sister, Tess, called "Just Another Day." She sums up well how important the month of November will always be to us. She starts with November 15, 1978. *I can still recall, that November morn that you were born, All we wanted was to hold you, kiss and play and laugh, with you. And as you grew somehow we knew that the angels would never leave from your side. Those close calls and second chances, kept your smile with us for another day.*

She continues to November 11, 2006. *I can still recall, that November morn when you were torn. Between the life that lay ahead and the life that you once led. Maybe time will never tell us just what was happening in your heart. All the love poured out from us. Was it just not enough?*

And finally, she remembers November 28, 2006. *I can still recall that November morn when we let go. Though we made a promise to never leave your side. And we were flying, like a family to our dreams, lifting higher and higher it seems. To the promise of today, to the promise that you'd stay, for just another day.*

Albert is in our nightly prayers and every year during this month we remember to celebrate his birthday and death anniversary.

In his final days, Albert had two conflicting voices in his head: one to stay, one to go. We each have our breaking point, but the big difference is the fight inside of us. Albert's "I want to die" voice was overpowering. It was much more powerful than his will to live. Learning from him, I am more certain than ever that my "I want to live" voice is stronger, and I want to share with others that life truly is sacred. And I know now it's a waste of precious time to even think or live as if it were not.

Albert was the youngest boy, and he was childlike in many ways. He was surrounded by outspoken people, including his seven sisters. He had financial problems, his living situation was in flux, and he had girl problems. I think he was still experiencing culture shock moving to Orange County, attempting to be on his own, away from his normal support system in Hawai'i, where he lived for twenty-five years of his life—similar to how I

223

felt when I first moved to Orange County. Doctors said he was suffering from a major depressive episode. Under all that pressure, he collapsed under his own despair.

Albert reached rock bottom in his mind, and saw death as his only way out. I have faith that God held him carefully in His hands, even in his moments of weakness. As the title track on our family CD goes, *only when we're lost can we be found.*

~ Breaking the Silence ~

In the second half of 2007, my husband decided he wanted to start a family business that allowed him to play music, perform live, create a Polynesian floor show and do what he enjoyed most: sharing his love for authentic Polynesian entertainment with others. On August 2, 2007, our company, Isle Entertainment, was born. Based in Southern California, our business provided luau entertainment for private events and parties across the state. Tini's dad was one of our top musicians, and Tini's whole family got involved: his brother, Taumata was a musician, his sisters, Sisa and Ana, helped with bookings and Tini's mom helped with the costumes.

We hired professional musicians and dancers to be a part of our troupe. While sending out media press releases to promote our new company, *Orange County Register* called me to set up an interview for the front page story in the "Morning Read" section.

That's when news of my brother's death became public. What started out as an interview about Isle Entertainment, quickly turned into a story about me and my brother's relationship and his death. Next, the *700 Club* called, and I was interviewed by my friend and former Miss America, Terry Meeuwsen. It was difficult to go public about something so private, something considered taboo in society. Yet, I was compelled to talk about it and I see now why it was necessary to share our family's story.

I have personally been told by people who were considering suicide that after they heard my story and the way Albert's death affected me and my family, they gave up on the idea of ever committing the act. They said my story had saved their lives. I began to see how crucial it was to talk about a subject that's so often ignored or misunderstood.

After that, I continued to share my experiences with Albert's death in my speeches and I have witnessed the saving power that has been working through me to help others. It was my Catholic faith that kept me grounded throughout the most turbulent time of my life. Unlike other suicide survivors, we were given a second chance. At his first suicide attempt he was going toward the light, but God sent him back down the tunnel to his body, likely for *our* benefit. I see that as a special grace, which helps me to focus on the positive. I feel it was by God's grace that we were given bonus time with him. That second chance we got is something I will hold on to forever.

Famed author Dr. Seuss summed up my feelings about my time with Albert, "Don't cry because it's over, smile because it happened." Each member of my family has dealt with my brother's death in their own unique way. For me, talking about it helped in my healing process. For other siblings, it was better to tuck it away and not think about the vivid details or repercussions of this act of suicide.

The fact that Albert had his rosary, scapular, and sacred objects like novena cards and books with him at his death makes me believe that he intended to have these holy objects on his person as he transitioned to the next life. I look to Psalm 86:5-7 and can't help but think Albert was feeling these sentiments: *You, Lord, are forgiving and good, abounding in love to all who call to you. Hear my prayer, Lord; listen to my cry for mercy. When I am in distress, I call to you, because you answer me.*

Albert's faith was unwavering to the very end, but sadly he couldn't overcome his weaknesses and inner demons. He didn't have enough fight in him to live and acted against his human instinct of self-preservation.

I write this book channeling all the love I have in my heart for my brother, my family, and all those who have lost a loved one to suicide, and for those who struggle with depression and anxiety.

~ Life is Life ~

In Hawai'i, I worked on a campaign against assisted suicide, fighting for people's rights to live and die with dignity. Whether you lose a baby to miscarriage as I did twice, or a loved one to abortion or suicide, the loss of life still occurs. Life is life at any stage, and to me, it's worth defending. Had my parents not believed in life, my nine siblings and I would not be here sharing the beautiful life we do as a family.

It was an honor for me to host a TV special about two of Hawai'i's saints, Mother Marianne Cope and Father Damien de Veuster, who moved to the island of Moloka'i in the 1800s to care for patients suffering from Hansen's disease, also known as leprosy. They taught me what it is to be selfless. Both saints are beautiful role models for all of us in caring for those who are rejected by society. When King Kalakaua sent a decree across the country to ask for people to help those with leprosy in the islands, only one responded. Fifty letters were sent out, and only Mother Marianne from Syracuse, New York, responded to the king's decree. She said, "I'm hungry for the work." Saint Marianne saw the dignity of the human person at all stages of life, regardless of the crippling Hansen's disease/leprosy, which surrounded her.

When I give pro-life talks I remember the place where I was born and raised, the culture that helped shape me. The Hawaiian culture is one that is Life affirming, rooted in aloha: we love and take care of the land ('aina) and everyone in it, especially our keiki (children) and kupuna (elderly). This is who we are as a people of Hawai'i and we must not forget that important ideal. If we claim that life is a gift given by God, then we must try to make the most to aim high and be all God has called us to be for His purpose.

I am a mother who has had four babies and two miscarriages. There is no doubt in my mind that Life is a miracle. Like Mama says, "Our children are only 'on loan' to us from God." At one point we all return the source of oceanic love. You win some, and you lose some. I suppose this is the game of life.

Isn't it true that the closer we get to the end of our lives, the faster time goes by? As I approach my fourth decade of life, I notice how time is moving faster than a freight train. Everything changed for me after Albert died. Even now, I see people differently. They are beautiful, eternal spirits walking around in physical, temporary bodies. Each person is special, unique, and miraculous. But I believe we will all return to our source some day. While the Church and I believe that suicide is never a good thing, the hope lies in the fact that **God's Mercy is endless and his Love is unconditional.**

For me and my family, the healing process of losing a loved one to suicide is ongoing. No matter how many death anniversaries we have for Albert, each year we will honor and remember his life. We have learned to accept what we cannot change and move on the best way we can.

Our family is stronger today than we've ever been. Albert's death confirmed my beliefs about Life. Every breath we take for granted is a miracle, and yet I have compassion for those who are weak or ill, just as our Albert was.

~ You'll Be In My Heart ~

While I am adamantly against the act of suicide, I cannot help but accept what my brother did. I am finding that the best way to heal is to celebrate the joy-filled life he lived and all the happy memories we shared together as siblings. I strongly believe that with all of our prayers, Albert truly is in a better place. Learning from his letters, his irreversible action, and my own experiences with depression, I want to help others who are still living and willing to be truly alive.

Suicide is a rising epidemic that needs to be addressed. As a society, we have shown little regard for the sanctity of life in general. Teens, middle-aged folks, and the elderly take medications too easily. We pop pills to sleep, to stay awake, to take the edge off, to focus. We struggle to keep up with our neighbors. We begin to live in an urban matrix of media, bank accounts, and fancy houses. Often so much that we forget about community, connection, nature, and simplicity. Life, for someone who gets entangled in this matrix, becomes unlivable. To maintain the facade of things, some isolate themselves mentally, not authentically expressing what they are experiencing on the inside.

Now I see that all we really need is love and connection, not isolation, fame, or fortune. **This is the life that's better than a fairy tale.**

Mark Twain once said, "Courage is not the absence of fear. It is acting in spite of it." May we all have the courage to be strong, the compassion to embrace the weak, and the wisdom to reach out to those who are suffering in silence.

In his final goodbye letter before his second attempt, Albert basically "absolved" all of us by telling us that there was nothing we could do to save him. He knew we loved him and he chose this path, despite our urging not to. We all have free will. And we have to accept when our loved ones exercise that will.

If I could talk to Albert now, I would say, "I'm sorry, Albie, for being so mad at you when you died. I understand now that you were in so much pain. But you were a spiritual warrior and you fought hard at the end, it just wasn't enough for you to live. I forgive you for leaving us too soon. I hope you can forgive yourself."

My song, "Living For You," on the Baraquio Family *Lost + Found* tribute CD to our brother, Albert, sums up how I feel even today. *Days and years gone by emblazon my mind, and as the years unwind you are by my side. When you left this world a part of me just died.*

The song ends, *You're in my prayers every night and every day. I love you . . .*

227

CHAPTER 17

LIVING HAPPILY, EVEN AFTER

"Someone's life is about to change forever . . ."

Those prophetic words spoken by Donny Osmond on the night I was crowned Miss America 2001 had more meaning packed into them than I could have ever imagined. I had no idea how much my life and the lives of my loved ones would change from that point on.

I always tell my students and my own children to dream big—*anything* is possible. And I truly believe it because I'm living proof of it. Don't let anyone stop you from dreaming. And forget about the naysayers. If your mind can conceive it and your heart can believe it, you can achieve it. I never thought my dreams would take me all over the country as Miss America and that the blessings would continue well past my year of service. The crosses I had to bear made me stronger, and yours will make you stronger, too. Embrace them, and see what God has in store for you.

There were so many times in my life when I found myself at a crossroads, not knowing where to go. In those times, I turned to God and asked Him for His protection and guidance to choose the right path. I could have gone in *so many* other different directions, but the compilation of all my choices led me to where I've been and where I am now. Good character is knowing, caring, and doing what's right. As I review the life I've lived, I see clearly how the Hand of God was always there protecting me, whether I knew it or not.

More than a decade after my win, I have processed the whirlwind and I'm finally settling into my role as a "Forever Miss America." I am honored to hold this esteemed title and hope to continue to strive toward the ideal in all areas of life. Even though we are born with sin and shortcomings, we are given this life to progress spiritually. Perfection, although elusive, is something worth striving for.

While writing this book, I see how much I've matured and realize that I'm much more comfortable in my role in the family, and fully embrace the unique woman God created me to be. My hope is that you have been inspired, even if it is just by ONE chapter, experience, or story that touched you.

When I go to Heaven and meet Jesus face to face, I hope to be able to say I ran the good race and fought the good fight. I want my life to have been a blessing to others, and I do not intend to return to my Maker empty-handed.

~ Being Filipina-American ~

I'm so grateful to be a Filipino-American and I enjoy the fruits of both cultures. I reflect on how my family almost remained in the Philippines. Had we not left in that window of time, we might still be in the Philippines, and my life would be completely different. As a child, I have fond memories of our family visiting Uncle Normand's grave every year at Punchbowl Cemetery in Honolulu, honoring him for his service to our country. It wasn't until I became an adult that I learned the story about how he aided us in our immigration to this great country, even in death.

This is why, every year on Memorial Day, Veterans' Day, and on our country's Independence Day I think of my Uncle Normand, our angel, and I pray for him and all the men and women who gave and currently give their life to live as we do in America.

Just recently, I realized that my Uncle Normand was born on November 11 (the day of Albert's first attempt) and died on June 7, which happens to be my brother-in-law Mike's birthday (the one who found Albert on November 11 in his car and basically saved his life). These dates are hardly coincidences. Mike said that apparently an angel entered his mind. I believe my Uncle Normand is one of the many angels in Heaven watching over our family to this day.

~ The Role of Parent, Wife and Mother ~

As a wife and mother, my priorities continue to evolve, and I keep envisioning new dreams. Aside from my advances in my entertainment career, I continue motivational speaking, working in elementary schools, balancing work and family, and finding new ways to be a servant of Christ. When things get rough, I fall back on one of my favorite quotes from Scripture. Philippians 4:13 was a prayer I said often to remind me of my human frailty and God's power. *Without Him I am nothing, but with Him, I can do all things in Christ who strengthens me.*

Our family didn't have much growing up, but we learned how to live simply and be resourceful. It's hard to believe, but we were once the grateful recipients of Thanksgiving food drives and donations. And sadly, we didn't attend many birthday parties because there wasn't extra money to buy gifts for our friends. However, these life lessons taught us discipline, efficiency, gratitude, humility, frugality, and the ability to live within our means. And when we were given a private school education, we were appreciative for our schooling and, in turn, gave back and served our communities.

My parents don't have a lot of material wealth because they sacrificed everything for us to have a better life. However, they have abundant spiritual wealth and passed that on to us when they made sure to do whatever it took for us to have attend Catholic schools. Mama and Papa taught us how to live in abundance and in lack, and still be happy because the light of Christ burned within our hearts. When I became Miss America, I appreciated everything I had and worked twice as hard for what I wanted to achieve. My parents' bootstrap mentality and strong work ethic thrived in me. I soaked up their teachings and admonitions like a sponge. Beyond our basic needs, Ma and Pa's most important gift to me and my siblings was the cultivation and practice of our faith.

While writing this memoir, I see the thread of constant longing for my parents' approval—especially Mama's. I tried my whole life to please her and make her proud, many times without success, at least in my eyes. Yet, I know now just how proud she is of me and I think it goes without saying how much we love each other.

~ They'll Know We are Christians By Our Love ~

Sometimes people wonder how a Christian person can be happy amidst tragedy, or how believers can have faith in something or someone we can't "see." For me, I am a follower of Jesus by my genuine concern and love for others. I can only do this with laser point focus on Jesus. I heard a quote once, attributed to Saint Francis of Assisi. "Preach the gospel at all times. Use words if necessary." We have to be a living example for others because we may be the only Bible some people may ever read.

How do we react and live in times of trouble? Are we humbling ourselves to listen to His Will? According to the Franciscan order, Jesus came to earth not just for our salvation, but he gave up his life as an act of love for us. Jesus, the son of God, loves us more than we love ourselves. My brother Albert, with his childlike innocence and faith believed in God. How can a merciful God forsake his children?

What I love about being a Catholic is the tradition of our faith and that it traces back all the way to Jesus Himself. The word "catholic" actually is defined as universal, all-embracing, all-inclusive, useful to all. Our current Pope Francis is a beautiful example and the epitome of what Christians are called to be. On December 11, 2013, *The Washington Post* headline read,

"Love Pope Francis? You'll love Jesus." With mercy and humility, our pontiff leads Catholics all over the world. He conveys a genuine Christianity that traces back to Jesus' own example. That's something I can rally behind. Jesus healed people, body and soul, throughout his ministry and he worked miracles. He can do the same in your life, no matter what you are experiencing.

My maternal and paternal grandmothers were very prayerful women. My mom was raised in a convent for years taught by the nuns, who gave her spiritual guidance and formation in her early years. She absorbed the teachings at a young age and took it to her heart. A mother's prayers are so powerful and Mama's prayers have led to many seen and unseen miracles in our lives, one of them being the grace to have Albert with us for a few more weeks, against his will, before he did the inevitable.

As part of a community of faith, I know it's hard to follow God in times of trouble, but what counts is how we live and how we model to others the way we follow Jesus. The prophet Isaiah reminds us to be a people who produce fruit. He says, *For just as the rain and the snow come down from Heaven, and do not return there until they have watered the earth, making it bring forth and sprout . . . so shall my word be that goes out from my mouth: it shall not return to me empty, but it shall accomplish that which I purpose, and succeed in the thing for which I sent it.* When we receive God's word on good soil, we do bear abundant fruit. In hearing His Word to love others as he loves us, we sacrifice like Christ in our own homes, neighborhoods, and schools.

What are we doing with the advice that God gives us? Are we ignoring it, or are we listening to His call? Do we go on with life in selfishness, or can we be of service to others in love and prayer? Life is a gift given by God, and I, for one, will try to make the most of it. I challenge you, as I challenge myself, to aim high, not just for worldly things, but for all things eternal. I resolve to stop living in a place of fear, which can only come from the Evil One.

We all experience extreme highs and lows, but what matters most is what we do in our lowest moments to help us get through the next day because we never know what lies around the corner. Be patient and have faith that whatever you are going through it will pass. God will lead you if you let him. If you try to lead and think God will follow you, you'll set yourself up for disappointment. Trust in God. If we want to be like Him, we need to have love and compassion for everyone.

~ Better Than a Fairy Tale ~

I'm an ordinary person who has lived an extraordinary life with God's guiding hand leading the way. Just as a driver in a new town is dependent on his navigation device to get him to his final destination, I also defer to

God to take the lead so my life will run smoothly. Life is just better than I could have ever imagined when I let God do the driving. Mama was right, **"If you obey God and do His will, your life will be better than a fairy tale."**

My life continues to be a fairy tale because I am married to my real-life Prince Charming, and we have our little princes and princess. Tini performs at the Disneyland Resort and when we have our date nights at the park, we reminisce about times we would go there together before we were married. To share our lives with our children is priceless. While we are not perfect, our imperfect lives are all I could ever ask for, just as long as we're together.

In high school, I took a class about Peer Education and one activity my teacher did involved a rose. She told us our purity was like a beautiful rose in bloom. She had us pass it around the class and each person was to take a petal from the rose. As it got to the last person, there were no more petals, just a stem with thorns. She likened it to people who give themselves away to countless partners without commitment. Each person takes a piece of you and soon, there's nothing and the love is no longer sacred. All that is left is emptiness. Falling in love is only special when you give your heart to someone who is worthy of you. Someone who protects your security and safety, listens to you, loves you for who you are. Take your time and pray that God guides you to the one who is intended for you.

Tini and I have been through the fire together, and we are still standing. My husband has given me as an adult what I enjoyed so much as a child . . . a loving family. Our four children are the fruits of our union, and all my most defining moments have been family moments. I've been incredibly blessed with a family that is full of love, and I pray the same for you. With Faith, Family, and Friends, your life can turn around and change for the better starting today. I'm looking forward to the beginning of the rest of my life and that starts *now*.

~ My Message to the World ~

My second grade teacher told me so many years ago that my name means "messenger." While my public speeches have emphasized different things like character education, forgiveness, reconciliation, and the importance of life, my overall message is to live with faith, hope, and love. Becoming a teacher, then Miss Hawai'i, and then Miss America has helped me share my messages with the world.

God is love. He is merciful and constant, and He loves us unconditionally. Even when we walk away, He never leaves our side. Today, I'm in a better place from where I was on September 22, 2001, just eleven days after 9/11. I've done the work I needed to do on myself, and that difficult process of soul-searching and finding meaning in life has been healing. No matter what you are going through, you never have to go through it alone.

~ The Sun Will Rise Again ~

The road of life has taken me on many twists and turns. It took some time for me to see why I was born into this world, and with each day my purpose gets clearer. My family and I have been through much together and we are better off because of our struggles. I've learned to live in the moment, see people for the miracles they truly are, love my neighbor and help others in need, especially through prayer. I'm grateful to know there's hope for a brighter day and that there is always tomorrow to begin anew. The sun WILL rise again.

In the Bible, Martha, the sister of Lazarus, believed the resurrection was an event. Jesus showed her *and us* that the resurrection is a person. He proved that knowledge of eternal life is a personal relationship, and victory over death is not a future expectation but a present reality. Because of this truth I know I will see my brother Albert again in Heaven someday. With prayers, we continuously remember him and lead him to the light. I believe he is now an angel looking down upon us, guiding us through the rest of our lives.

~ Moving Forward ~

Today, I am proud to say that I have returned to my roots as an elementary school teacher and administrator, while still traveling as a national speaker, TV host, and now, author. I am also a first-year vice principal and junior high language arts teacher at a Catholic school in Southern California. It was always a dream of mine to teach in a Catholic institution and have my children attend the same school, and now that dream is a reality.

Even in fairy tales the plot sometimes twists unexpectedly, but I am living proof that you can still end up living happily, even after great tragedy and loss, after demons have threatened to take your spirit. I have had wonderful parents, siblings, friends, and my own family by my side at every turn with a strong faith that brought me back from the depths of my despair. I am indebted to all those who have helped me along the way.

Looking ahead, remember that your life can change for the better when you change your attitude and decide to love and be happy. In my crown, every individual jewel contributes to its beauty. Like each jewel in the crown, every one of us contributes to the beauty in this world. I believe that with a daily positive mindset and a conscious decision to be your best self and to be of loving service to others, you can get what you always wanted out of this life and the next.

Now, go out and do something positive for yourself and others. Someone's life IS about to change forever—Yours. Who's life will YOU change? As you mentally pen your own memoir, know that you have the power to own your future and create a life you love. May the next chapter be the good parts of your tale . . .

so you, too, can live **happily, EVEN after.**

ACKNOWLEDGMENTS

Heavenly Father, thank you for loving me, guiding me, and holding me in Your Hands. I am grateful for all the victories and the struggles.

Mama, you chose life for all your children. Then you selflessly and lovingly bore us, and cared for us. I marvel at the woman you are and I hope to have the same strength and faith that you have modeled your whole life. I love you very much.

Papa, you have always been my hero, our family's provider, protector, and role model for all the men in our lives. Thank you for your quiet strength and for your beautiful smile and words of wisdom when we need it. You always knew how to make me feel better when I was sad as a child and today, just seeing you makes me happy.

To all my siblings and your children for being my support system. Ceci Addams, Joshua Bolan, Jerome, Nikko, and Sterling Baraquio, Anthony Ater, Lucy Baraquio, Catherine Messina, Lorenzo, Cosmo, and Alessio Rossi, John, Mel, Blaze, and Echo Baraquio, Tess Baraquio, Berna, Rick Zack and Zoe Hamada, Rose, John, Luke, and Seth Harman, Albert, and Gloria, thank you for making my life beautiful!

To my Grey Family: Emily and Jerome Grey, Julie, Peter, Ben, and Iulieta Figarski, Sisavai'i, Tyman, Ta'iuta, Ta'ita'i, Matamatagi, and Manatua Uiagalelei, , Anamativa, J.T. and Oriana Niumata, and Taumata and Silulu Grey, thank you for welcoming me into your family. I am so blessed to be a part of your aiga. Alofa tele atu ia outou.

Tini, the love of my life, my best friend my soul mate. Life wouldn't be as beautiful without you in it. I will love you for eternity. Thank you for giving me the greatest years of my life and for blessing me with our incredible children. There's no one else I would rather want to walk with on this journey. Thank you for holding down the fort! You and the kids have been so patient as I finished writing this memoir. You complete me.

Thanks to my four children, my biggest accomplishments:

To Isaiah, you are so responsible, faith-filled, kind-hearted, intelligent, and talented! You never cease to amaze me. I am so proud of you for the young man you are becoming. Always keep your inner light burning strong.

To Micah, I wish I could create and build like you! Your imagination is full of wonder and excitement and you help me to see life through your eyes. Your name Lotoalofa means "loving spirit," and you have always shown me that you are just that. Thank you for all the thoughtful kisses, the "I love yous" and handmade gifts. Always remember you were my *best* surprise!

To Jonah, your smile lights up a room and you have such a passion for life. Thank you for bringing me so much joy. Your big hugs and kisses always melt my heart. You have no fear and I love your bravery. Remember your "Monster Mama loves you so!" Never stop taking chances.

To Keilah, my little girl. When I see you smile it makes my heart sing. Your spirit shines through in your eyes and your laughter. You have a way of making everyone around you feel special. I pray you grow up to be as loving and faith-filled as all the women who came before you.

Abella Carroll, you are such a talented editor. Thank you for helping me articulate my feelings in this book. You gave me a priceless gift of helping me find my voice and letting it flow. I am so grateful to you for bringing my story to life.

Gloria Baraquio, my little sister and my heart. Thank you for helping me share our story. There are no words . . . give me my independence! Love you, Baby Cindy! Thank you for always being there for me.

Maxinne Pacheco, my BFF. You're top tier and you know it! We have been friends since we were on the verge of adulthood and now look at us, married with children. Thank you for being the best friend a girl could ever wish for. Love you and Abby Rei so much!

Howard Pacheco, thank you for sharing your gifts with me. Your cover art and formatting work are beautiful! Everything you touch turns to gold because you do it with such precision and love. I appreciate you and all you do.

Tino Montero, *maraming salamat po* for introducing me to the Miss America Organization! Had it not been for your support and guidance, I would never have gotten onstage for any pageant, nor would I have mastered my competition walk. You taught me how to have the poise and grace necessary onstage!

To my former boss, pastor and spiritual director, Father Maurice "Mac" McNeely, thank you for encouraging me to follow my dreams and for being one of the most inspiring, supportive, and loving spiritual directors I've ever met.

Father Preston Passos, you were always a thoughtful family friend and like a godfather to both Tini and me in high school. Your generosity was and still is overwhelming. Thank you for renewing our vows for our tenth anniversary and baptizing our fourth child.

Uncle Gordon Mark, you may seem tough on the outside, but you have a heart of gold on the inside. Without your belief in me, I can't say where I'd be today. You gave selflessly of your time, talents, and treasures at all times and treated me like a daughter.

Todd Oshiro, my former pageant director, *therapist/coach,* and friend. You helped me with many emotional breakthroughs along my (sometimes painful) journey. You were there for me in the exciting moments and helped me through my toughest times. It was so comforting to know I had you, Tom Tom, and the gang, loving and supporting me in everything I did.

Special Thanks

The Perez Family, the Baraquio Family, The Frears, The Deschaines, The Laolagis, all my nieces and nephews and godchildren, Valerie and Flora Elefante, Brenna and Keahi Kahana, Julie Ledgerwood, Juliet Lighter, Jana and Bobby Focht, Bill Carroll, Duane Family, Carolyn Sapp Daniels, Brook Lee, Candes Gentry, Tricia Fujikawa Lee, Jennifer Hera Pimentel, Billie Takaki Lueder, Trini Ka'opuiki, Renee Belanger, Sonia Amir Bowie, Lauren Meehan-Machos, Pattie Heatherly, Dana Takahara-Dias, The Codas, Dick and Martha Lyles, Christina Capecchi, Lisa Wilmore, Leslie Green, Tui and Maile Letuli, Daniel Pouesi, Naomi Masina, John and Judith Loyola, Glenn and Cristie Clancy, Just a Girl Productions, Karen Nakamura Photography, Nate's Photography, The Miss Hawai'i Sorority, The Miss America Sorority, Living Local Family, FHB Family, Miss Hawai'i 2000 Executive Committee and Volunteers: The late Thom. McGarvey, Raymond Abregano, Jr., Muriel Anderson, Larry Nakano, Dennis Momyer, Tim Los Banos, Warren Wong, Titilia Barbour, Suzy Mahelona, Fred Mateo, Marcelo Pacleb and 24-7, Jon Paul Akeo, Tom Tom Kaeka, Always Flowers 'Ohana, Neva Rego, Bonnie Parsons, Leatrice Moniz, Davey Ann Basque, Randy Hongo, Kala Gongob, Michael Casupang, Steven Soong, Adam and Nina Duncan, Ryan and Mandy Brown, Ed and Leilani Keough, Pattie Kuamo'o, Dennis Guillermo, Lisa Hutchinson, Natalie Brown-Aiwohi, Aunty Nettie, Teresa Bringas, Brenda Reichel, Steven Lee, Paul Legg, Peter Nenezich, APBEF board members Tini, Tess, Billie, Harry Alonso, Bryan Andaya, Judy Nagasako, John Zak, Arnold Wong, Harvey Lee, The Miss America Organization: Sam Haskell, Art McMaster, Sharon Pearce, PJ Santos, Laura Gallagher, Doreen Gordon and entire MAO Staff, Bob Renneisen, George Bauer, Mary Blackburn, Susan Schneider, Bonnie Sirgany, Joann Silver, the late Ric Ferentz, MAO Volunteers, Fr. Choo, St. Augustine Parish and Tongan Youth Choir, HFCA Faculty, Staff, and Students, Carolyn Kuahulu, Rachael and Emerisa, St. Anthony Claret Family, OLQA Family, Sharon and Wayne, Albert Ainu'u and Hit-TV Crew, Carolyn Berry and Dave Wilson, Jimmy and Vicki Borges, The Thompsons, Reign, Tihati Family, Isle Family, Tupua Family, Maugas, Timos, Tagaloas, Riveras, Jimenezes, Adas, Korionoffs, Maligas, Marie Edwards, Dennis Massey, Common Kings, Anselmos, Woodbury Family, Ted Benito, Rex Sampaga, Alexanders, Helen Curtin, Sandy Nelson and Robert Hirahara, Babette Perry, Jason and Alex Jones, Dyogis, Joey Galon, Lisa Lew and Peter Brennan, Mike B., Micah and Celina Sumner, St. Anthony of Padua Parish and School and everyone who's touched my life.

Made in the USA
Lexington, KY
09 October 2014